Copyrights©
All Rights reserved, Apart from any permitted use under international law, IL+(IP)© no part of this publication may be re-written, reproduced or transmitted(transferred into any other languages) in any form or by any means, Physically, Digitally, Electronic or Mechanical, including Photocopying, Power Point, Audio, Video Recording (Podcasts) telecast or any information,(social media) storage or retrieval systems without permission in writing, email, correspondence from the Author may be obtained. ©
This book is restricted to your personal use only. It does not come with any other rights.
LEGAL DISCLAIMER: This book is protected by international copyright law and may not be copied, reproduced, given away, or used to create derivative works without the publisher's expressed permission. The publisher retains full copyrights to this book.
The author has made every reasonable effort to be as accurate and complete as possible in the creation of this book and to ensure that the information provided is free from errors; however, the author/publisher/ reseller assumes no responsibility for errors, omissions, or contrary interpretation of the subject matter herein and does not warrant or represent at any time that the contents within are accurate due to the rapidly changing nature of the internet.

Any product, website, and company names mentioned in this report are the trademarks or copyright properties of their respective owners. The author/publisher/reseller is not associated or affiliated with them in any way. Nor does the referred product, website, and company names sponsor, endorse, or approve this product.

Special Note: for Readers
All Conversations, Languages, Phrases, and dialogues, are generated for learning, and training purposes, (not real) and no conversations, or phrases belong to any private, government, or Private business, and have nothing to do with any real-life, happening and are not connected to anyone whatsoever, these all conversations, dialogues, phrased generated, based on real-life scenarios, daily base infrastructures may happen anywhere in the world of the education industry, so do not Quotes, copy, or use as references within any legal, private, study or none study purpose, avoid Plagiarism.

The author and Publisher will not be responsible for any use for any purpose, these are all here only for personal learning training and development purposes. ©2024

- ISBN: Hard Copy 9798332885372
- ISBN: Paper Copy 9798332884559
- First Publish July 2024 USA/UK/EU

Independently published Via Publisher Amazon
Languages: English, Arabic, Urdu
UK, USA, EU, UAE, Saudi Arabia (KSA), Japan, Pakistan, Canada China, Hong Kong, Qatar, Singapore, France & Australian

Global Master of International Law, An Extensive & In-Depth Exploration of Diverse Legal Systems and Specialized Fields for the Modern Legal Professional.
GMIL-LLM

"A Comprehensive Insights into Global Legal Systems, Ultimate Guide to Understanding and Navigating the Complexities of International Legal Practices"

Book Three(3) Volume Three(3) Part Three(3)
Self- Study Handbook

Author, Edit, Compile by:
Dr MD USMAN CMgr, DBA, PhD, LLM,
MSc, MBA, ITC, PgDPR ,PgDHE, ELM L-7,SLM L-7& 8.

Author

Dr MD USMAN CMgr, DBA, PhD, LLM,
MSc, MBA, ITC, PgDPR ,PgDHE, ELM L-7,SLM L-7& 8

Dip-SML Strategic Management Leadership-Level-7 & 8, Dip- ELM Education Leadership Management Level 7 PgDPR, PgDHE- FDA/BA(Hons). PhD, LLM(International Business, Commercial, Corporate, Commerce & Trad Law
The author, With over 30 years of experience, has a remarkable track record in the Leadership, Organisation Management, Business, and education sectors. Teaching, Coaching, Mentoring and Training since 1993. Here are some key highlights of their professional journey.
 Dr MdUsmanCMgr is a highly accomplished professional with an extensive and diverse educational background and a wealth of experience across various fields
His credentials and achievements include:
•Academic Qualifications: Dr. MD holds multiple academic degrees, including a Doctor of Business Administration (DBA), Master of Business Administration (MBA), Master of Science (MSc) in Executive MBA (EMBA), ITC, FDA/BA(Hons) GMHECP, GPHECP   and various other qualifications in areas such as Aviation, Travel and Tourism, Hospitality, and International Business Management. Research and Education: He has completed a Postgraduate Diploma in Professional Research (PgDPR-ARU) and a Postgraduate Diploma in Higher Education (PgDHE). Strategic Leadership Management Level 7-CMI and Level 8(Ph.D.)from Qualifi(SLM LEVEL 7 & 8) and Education Leadership Management ELM L7 from OTHM. Dr.MDusman is also well-versed in achieving qualifications in these areas. 11 certificates in Ethical Research from EPGUM+ Oxford University.
•Certifications: He holds a range of certifications, including qualifications in areas such as coaching and mentoring, project management, business law, and immigration consultancy. Dr MD is also certified as a filmmaker (CCDLP) and Feature film producer (FFP) from Hollywood. Over 100+ short courses certificates achievement in training in the fields of Aviation ITC-IATA, Travel, and tourism, Coaching and Mentoring, SME, and Business Startup. • International Experience: exhibitions, conferences, seminars, and trade shows across various industries.

His exposure to these diverse settings has enriched his knowledge and expertise. He has visited/attended over 2000+ Events, Exhibitions, Conferences, Seminars,(within two decades) in various Sectors, from Education, Commercial, World-Travel Mart, Tech, and SME/MSEM, Technology, E-commerce, Hospitality, Restaurant, Business Expo, Franchise Business and many more. Experts in International affairs, International Business, international Aviation(Airline, Airport), international Tourism, Hospitality, International Education Sectors and Global business and international Law, Keynote Speakers, Executive Coaches and Mentors for SME, MSME, Executive, C-Suite Level, appeared in various TV Programs. And available for all types of consultation, policy-making, and TV shows and can be invited to above mentions events and conferences, kindly book an appointment at
MDUSMAN.DBAARU@GMAIL.COM.

Reviews:

Brown John M., International Law Scholar "A remarkable resource! 'Global Master of International Law GMIBL-LLM' offers an in-depth exploration of diverse legal systems and specialized fields. The comprehensive coverage of topics, coupled with practical case studies, makes it an indispensable guide for legal practitioners and students alike. Highly recommended for anyone serious about mastering international law."

Kiley Emily R., Corporate Attorney "This book is a treasure trove of knowledge. The detailed chapters on regional legal systems and specialized areas like financial crime and international taxation provide a well-rounded understanding of global legal landscapes. The inclusion of case studies adds real-world relevance. A must-have for every law professional's library."

Dr. Junaid Jamshaid Ahmed S., Professor of Law "' Global Master of International Law GMIBL-LLM' is an academic masterpiece. The meticulous research and clear explanations make complex legal concepts accessible. I particularly appreciate the comparative analyses, which offer valuable insights into different legal frameworks. Perfect for teaching and research."

Kathrine Lisa K., Legal Researcher "An exceptional book that covers a vast range of topics in international law. The chapters on Islamic finance and Sharia compliance are especially enlightening. The section on legal research skills is incredibly useful for anyone looking to enhance their legal writing and analysis. Five stars without a doubt."

Black Michael B., Business Law Expert "This book exceeded my expectations. The depth and breadth of coverage are impressive, and the practical examples bring the theoretical concepts to life. The chapters on business and corporate law in different regions are particularly beneficial for understanding global business operations. A five-star read."

Jasmine Sophia L., Maritime Law Specialist "The chapter on the Law of the Sea alone is worth the purchase. The detailed examination of UNCLOS and maritime disputes is outstanding.

'Global Master of International Law GMIBL-LLM' is a comprehensive guide that is both informative and engaging. A valuable addition to any legal professional's collection."

Joi James T., International Finance Consultant "An invaluable resource for anyone involved in international finance. The chapters on syndicated loans and project finance are thorough and insightful. The practical approach to risk management and legal frameworks is particularly beneficial. Highly recommended for finance professionals and legal advisors."

Dr. Serina Elena P., Comparative Law Professor "A brilliant compilation of global legal knowledge. The comparative analyses of different legal systems provide a unique perspective that is both educational and practical. The book's structured approach and detailed explanations make it a go-to reference for comparative law studies."

Johan William D., Legal Tech Enthusiast "The chapter on Legal Tech and FinTech is a standout. It provides a forward-thinking analysis of the legal challenges and innovations in this rapidly evolving field. 'Global Master of International Law GMIBL-LLM' is ahead of its time and essential for anyone interested in the future of law and technology."

Amna Ko Koy M., Intellectual Property Attorney "A comprehensive guide that covers all essential aspects of international law. The chapters on patents, trademarks, and trade secrets are particularly useful for IP practitioners. The book's depth of research and clear presentation make it a five-star reference for anyone in the legal field."

Contents

Author 4
Reviews: 5
Abstract 16
Book Cover: 22
Preface: 23
Chapter 1: Islamic Business Transaction Law 31
   1.1 Principles of Islamic Finance 31
   1.2 Sharia Compliance in Business Transactions 34
   1.3 Contracts in Islamic Law 35
   1.4 Comparative Analysis with Conventional Business Law 36
Chapter 2: Islamic Insurance (Takaful) 38
   2.1 Principles of Takaful 38
   2.2 Operational Models of Takaful 40
   2.3 Regulatory Framework for Takaful 41
   2.4 Comparative Analysis with Conventional Insurance ... 42
Chapter 3: Key Principles of the Australian Legal System 44
   3.1 Overview of the Australian Legal System 44
   3.2 Constitutional Framework 47
   3.3 Judicial System and Legal Institutions 48
   3.4 Business and Corporate Law in Australia 50
Chapter 4: Key Principles of the Chinese Legal System 53
   4.1 Historical Development of Chinese Law 53
   4.2 Structure of the Chinese Legal System 55
   4.3 Key Legislation and Regulatory Bodies 57
   4.4 Business and Trade Law in China 58
Chapter 5: Key Principles of the English Legal System 61
   5.1 Historical Foundations of English Law 61
   5.2 Common Law System 64
   5.3 Key Legal Institutions and Their Roles 64
   5.4 Business and Corporate Law in England 65
Chapter 6: Key Principles of the Gulf (UAE/Saudi Arabia)/Middle East Legal System 67
   6.1 Legal Traditions in the Gulf and Middle East 67
   6.2 Sharia Law and Its Application 69
   6.3 Legal Reforms and Modernization Efforts 69
   6.4 Business and Corporate Law in the Gulf Region 70
Chapter 7: Key Principles of the USA/Canada Legal System 71
   7.1 Overview of the US Legal System 71
   7.2 Overview of the Canadian Legal System 73

7.3 Constitutional and Federal Structures 73
7.4 Business and Corporate Law in North America 74
Chapter 8: Key Principles of the Pakistan Legal System 76
8.1 Historical Development of Pakistani Law 76
8.2 Constitutional Framework 78
8.3 Judicial System and Legal Institutions 78
8.4 Business and Corporate Law in Pakistan 79
Chapter 9: Key Principles of the SAARC Countries (India, Bangladesh, Nepal, Sri Lanka) Legal System 80
9.1 Overview of SAARC Legal Systems 80
9.2 Comparative Constitutional Structures 82
9.3 Key Legal Institutions in SAARC Countries 83
9.4 Business and Corporate Law in SAARC Region 83
Chapter 10: Law of Financial Crime 85
10.1 Types of Financial Crime 85
10.2 Legal Framework for Combating Financial Crime 87
10.3 International Cooperation and Regulation 88
10.4 Case Studies in Financial Crime 88
Chapter 11: Law of International Finance Syndicated Loans ... 90
11.1 Principles of Syndicated Loans 90
11.2 Legal Framework for Syndicated Lending 91
11.3 Risk Management in Syndicated Loans 92
11.4 Case Studies in International Syndicated Loans 93
Chapter 12: Law of International Project Finance 95
12.1 Fundamentals of Project Finance 95
12.2 Legal and Regulatory Framework 98
12.3 Risk Allocation and Management 99
12.4 Case Studies in Project Finance 100
Chapter 13: Law of International Taxation 101
13.1 Principles of International Taxation 101
13.2 Double Taxation Treaties 104
13.3 Transfer Pricing Regulations 105
13.4 Tax Planning and Compliance 106
Chapter 14: Law of the Sea 108
14.1 Principles of Maritime Law 108
14.2 UNCLOS and Its Implications 110
14.3 Maritime Boundaries and Jurisdiction 111
14.4 Case Studies in Maritime Disputes 111
Chapter 15: Law of the World Trade Organization 113
15.1 Principles of WTO Law 113

- 15.2 Dispute Settlement Mechanism 115
- 15.3 Trade Liberalization and Regulation 116
- 15.4 Case Studies in WTO Law 117
- Chapter 16: Law on Investment Entities 119
  - 16.1 Types of Investment Entities 119
  - 16.2 Legal Framework for Investment Funds 122
  - 16.3 Regulation of Investment Entities 123
  - 16.4 Case Studies in Investment Law 124
- Chapter 17: Legal Research Skills and Methods 126
  - 17.1 Fundamentals of Legal Research 126
  - 17.2 Research Methodologies 128
  - 17.3 Legal Writing and Analysis 129
  - 17.4 Presentation of Legal Research 129
- Chapter 18: Legal Tech/FinTech 131
  - 18.1 Introduction to Legal Tech 131
  - 18.2 Legal Issues in FinTech 133
  - 18.3 Regulatory Framework for FinTech 134
  - 18.4 Innovations and Future Trends in Legal Tech 135
- Chapter 19: Marine Insurance Law 137
  - 19.1 Principles of Marine Insurance 137
  - 19.2 Legal Framework for Marine Insurance 140
  - 19.3 Risk and Liability in Marine Insurance 141
  - 19.4 Case Studies in Marine Insurance 142
- Chapter 20: Medicine, Law, and Society 143
  - 20.1 Legal Issues in Medical Practice 143
  - 20.2 Patient Rights and Medical Ethics 145
  - 20.3 Regulation of Medical Professionals 146
  - 20.4 Case Studies in Medical Law 147
- Chapter 21: Modern Copyright Law 148
  - 21.1 Fundamentals of Copyright Law 148
  - 21.2 Digital Copyright Issues 150
  - 21.3 International Copyright Treaties 151
  - 21.4 Case Studies in Copyright Law 152
- Chapter 22: Money Laundering and Financial Crime 154
  - 22.1 Mechanisms of Money Laundering 154
  - 22.2 Legal Framework for Combating Money Laundering .. 156
  - 22.3 International Cooperation in Anti-Money Laundering 158
  - 22.4 Case Studies in Financial Crime 159
- Chapter 23: Multinational Enterprises and the Law 160
  - 23.1 Legal Structure of Multinational Enterprises 160

- 23.2 Regulatory Challenges for Multinationals 162
- 23.3 Corporate Social Responsibility 163
- 23.4 Case Studies in Multinational Enterprise Law 164
- Chapter 24: Patents and Trade Secrets: Comparative and International Perspectives 166
  - 24.1 Fundamentals of Patent Law 166
  - 24.2 Legal Protection of Trade Secrets 167
  - 24.3 Comparative Analysis of IP Rights 168
  - 24.4 International Treaties on IP Protection...................... 169
- Chapter 25: Private Equity 171
  - 25.1 Principles of Private Equity 171
  - 25.2 Legal Framework for Private Equity Investments 172
  - 25.3 Regulatory Issues in Private Equity 173
  - 25.4 Case Studies in Private Equity 174
  - Legal Framework, Regulatory Issues 175
- Chapter 26: Private International Law in International Commercial Litigation... 180
  - 26.1 Principles of Private International Law 180
  - 26.2 Jurisdiction and Choice of Law 182
  - 26.3 Enforcement of Foreign Judgments 183
  - 26.4 Case Studies in International Commercial Litigation. 184
- Chapter 27: Private Law Aspects of the Law of Finance 186
  - 27.1 Legal Principles in Financial Transactions 186
  - 27.2 Contractual Issues in Finance 188
  - 27.3 Regulatory Framework for Financial Markets............. 189
  - 27.4 Case Studies in Financial Law 190
- Chapter 28: Project Finance 192
  - 28.1 Fundamentals of Project Finance 192
  - 28.2 Risk Allocation in Project Finance............................. 195
  - 28.3 Legal and Regulatory Framework 196
  - 28.4 Case Studies in Project Finance 197
- Chapter 29: Public International Law 199
  - 29.1 Principles of Public International Law 199
  - 29.2 Sources of International Law 201
  - 29.3 International Organizations and Institutions 202
  - 29.4 Case Studies in Public International Law................... 202
- Chapter 30: Regulation and Infrastructure of International Commercial Arbitration 204
  - 30.1 Legal Framework for International Arbitration 204
  - 30.2 Arbitration Agreements and Clauses 206

30.3 Institutional vs. Ad Hoc Arbitration 207
30.4 Case Studies in International Arbitration 208
Chapter 31: Research Methodology in Law 211
31.1 Fundamentals of Legal Research 211
31.2 Research Design and Methods 213
31.3 Data Collection and Analysis 214
31.4 Presenting Legal Research 216
Chapter 32: Research Methods in Business, Commercial, and Corporate Law 218
32.1 Legal Research in Business Law 218
32.2 Comparative Legal Analysis 220
32.3 Empirical Research Methods 220
32.4 Case Studies in Legal Research 220
Chapter 33: Research Skills and Methods in Law 222
33.1 Advanced Legal Research Techniques 222
33.2 Legal Writing and Drafting 224
33.3 Analytical and Critical Thinking Skills 225
33.4 Presentation and Communication of Legal Research 226
Chapter 34: Securities Law 228
34.1 Principles of Securities Regulation 228
34.2 Legal Framework for Securities Markets 230
34.3 Insider Trading and Market Manipulation 231
34.4 Case Studies in Securities Law 232
Chapter 35: Strategic Management and Leadership 235
35.1 Principles of Strategic Management 235
35.2 Legal Aspects of Corporate Strategy 237
35.3 Leadership in Legal Practice 238
35.4 Case Studies in Strategic Management 240
Chapter 36: Taxation Principles, Policy, and Law 242
36.1 Fundamentals of Taxation Law 242
36.2 Tax Policy and Administration 244
36.3 Comparative Tax Systems 245
36.4 Case Studies in Tax Law 246
Chapter 37: Telecommunications Law 249
37.1 Principles of Telecommunications Regulation 249
37.2 Legal Framework for Telecom Services 251
37.3 Comparative Analysis of Telecom Laws 252
37.4 Emerging Issues in Telecommunications Law 254
Chapter 38: The Corporate Form and Its Issues 256
38.1 Legal Nature of Corporations 256

38.2 Corporate Governance and Compliance 258
38.3 Liability and Responsibility of Corporate Actors 259
38.4 Case Studies in Corporate Law 260
Chapter 39: The Law of Devolution in Wales 263
39.1 Principles of Devolution in Wales 263
39.2 Legal Framework for Welsh Devolution 265
39.3 Comparative Analysis with Other UK Regions 266
39.4 Case Studies in Welsh Devolution Law 268
Chapter 40: The Law of Maritime Security: 'Navies' and the Rule of Law at Sea 270
40.1 Principles of Maritime Security Law 270
40.2 Legal Role of Navies 272
40.3 International Maritime Security Agreements 273
40.4 Case Studies in Maritime Security 274
Chapter 41: The Transportation of Cargo 277
41.1 Legal Framework for Cargo Transportation 277
41.2 International Conventions on Cargo Transport 279
41.3 Liability and Risk in Cargo Transport 279
41.4 Case Studies in Cargo Transportation Law 280
Chapter 42: Themes in Socio-Legal Studies 281
42.1 Interdisciplinary Approaches to Law 281
42.2 Legal Pluralism and Social Justice 282
42.3 Law and Society in Comparative Perspective 283
42.4 Case Studies in Socio-Legal Research 284
Chapter 43: Trademarks: Comparative and International Perspectives 285
43.1 Principles of Trademark Law 285
43.2 International Trademark Treaties 286
43.3 Comparative Analysis of Trademark Laws 287
43.4 Case Studies in Trademark Law 288
Chapter 44: Transfer of Technology Law 289
44.1 Legal Framework for Technology Transfer 289
44.2 Intellectual Property and Technology Transfer 291
44.3 Regulatory Issues in Technology Transfer 292
44.4 Case Studies in Technology Transfer Law 292
Chapter 45: Transitional Justice 294
45.1 Principles of Transitional Justice 294
45.2 Legal Framework for Transitional Justice Mechanisms
.... 296
45.3 Comparative Analysis of Transitional Justice Models 298

45.4 Case Studies in Transitional Justice 300
Chapter 46: Transnational Business Instruments 302
   46.1 Legal Instruments for Transnational Business 302
   46.2 International Trade Agreements and Instruments 304
   46.3 Regulatory Challenges in Transnational Business 305
   46.4 Case Studies in Transnational Business Law 307
Chapter 47: Transnational Corporate Law and Practice 309
   47.1 Principles of Transnational Corporate Law 309
   47.2 Legal Framework for Cross-Border Corporations 311
   47.3 Regulatory Issues in Transnational Corporate Practice 312
   47.4 Case Studies in Transnational Corporate Law 313
Chapter 48: Transnational Corporate Restructuring 315
   48.1 Principles of Corporate Restructuring 315
   48.2 Legal Framework for Cross-Border Restructuring 317
   48.3 Comparative Analysis of Restructuring Laws 318
   48.4 Case Studies in Corporate Restructuring 319
Chapter 49: UN International Laws 322
   49.1 Overview of United Nations Law 322
   49.2 Key UN Conventions and Treaties 324
   49.3 Enforcement of UN Laws 326
   49.4 Case Studies in UN Law 327
Chapter 50: World Trade Law 329
   50.1 Principles of World Trade Law 329
   50.2 Legal Framework for Global Trade 330
   50.3 Dispute Resolution in World Trade 332
   50.4 Case Studies in World Trade Law 333
Chapter 51: Key Principles of the Asian Countries Legal Systems 335
   51.1 Overview of Asian Countries Legal Systems 335
   51.2 Comparative Constitutional Structures 337
   51.3 Key Legal Institutions in Asian Countries 338
   51.4 Business and Corporate Law in Asian Countries 339
Chapter 52: Key Principles of the EU Countries Legal Systems 340
   52.1 Overview of EU Countries Legal Systems 340
   52.1 A. The legal systems of EU countries 342
   52.2 Comparative EU Constitutional Structures 343
   52.3 Key Legal Institutions in EU Countries 344
   52.4 Business and Corporate Law in EU Countries 345

Case studies related to the legal systems of EU countries. 346
Police code of conducts list of UK 352
UK civil offences and Criminal offence lists 353
List of Citizen Rights in the UK 366
list of Human rights Articles 368
List of Citizen Rights in the EU 373
Citizen rights in the United States and Canada 374
List of EU Civil and Criminal Offenses. 377
USA / Canada civil and Criminal offence code 378
Australia/ New Zealand Civil Offences and Criminal Offence
.... 381
South Korea, Japan, Malaysia Providing a comprehensive list of offenses 385
Bibliography 391

Abstract

The book "Global Master of International Law GMIL-LLM" comprehensively covers a diverse array of legal systems and specialized fields within international law. Beginning with Islamic business transaction law and Islamic insurance (Takaful), it delves into the principles, regulatory frameworks, and comparative analyses with conventional systems. It then explores the legal systems of various regions, including Australia, China, the Gulf, USA/Canada, Pakistan, SAARC countries, and several other key jurisdictions. Each regional chapter provides an overview of historical development, constitutional framework, judicial systems, and business law specifics. The book also addresses specialized legal topics such as financial crime, syndicated loans, project finance, international taxation, maritime law, WTO law, investment entities, and fintech. Additional chapters focus on legal research skills, legal tech, private equity, securities law, telecommunications law, corporate governance, devolution, maritime security, cargo transportation, socio-legal studies, trademarks, technology transfer, transitional justice, transnational business and corporate law, corporate restructuring, UN international laws, and world trade law. This extensive coverage makes it a vital resource for understanding the multifaceted nature of international law and its applications across various legal landscapes.

"Global Master of International Law GMIBL-LLM" is an extensive compendium that meticulously examines the intricacies and applications of international law across multiple jurisdictions and specialized domains. The book is structured to provide a thorough understanding of both foundational principles and contemporary issues in global legal systems, making it an indispensable resource for legal scholars, practitioners, and students.

Global Master of International Law: GMIL-LLM" is a comprehensive compendium that navigates the intricate landscape of international law, offering profound insights into diverse legal systems and specialized fields crucial for today's legal professionals. This abstract provides a succinct overview of the book's key themes, chapters, and contributions to the study and practice of international law.

Exploring Diverse Legal Systems

The journey begins with an exploration of Islamic Business Transaction Law (Chapter 1), where principles of Islamic finance, Sharia compliance, and the intricacies of business transactions are meticulously dissected. This foundational chapter sets the stage for understanding how cultural and religious norms shape legal frameworks in commercial practices.

The subsequent chapters delve into the legal systems of various regions, including Australia, China, the Gulf/Middle East, USA/Canada, Pakistan, and SAARC countries (Chapters 3-9). Each chapter provides a comprehensive overview of historical development, constitutional frameworks, judicial systems, and specific nuances of business and corporate law within these jurisdictions. Through comparative analyses, readers gain a deeper appreciation for the diversity of legal traditions and the evolving nature of global legal norms.

Specialized Fields and Emerging Trends

Moving beyond regional analyses, the book delves into specialized fields critical to contemporary legal practice. Chapters on Financial Crime (Chapter 10), International Taxation (Chapter 13), and Maritime Law (Chapter 14) offer in-depth explorations of complex legal areas. These chapters elucidate the legal frameworks, international regulations, and case studies that underscore the application of law in global contexts, preparing legal practitioners to navigate intricate legal landscapes.

Bridging Theory and Practice

Central to the book's ethos is the integration of theoretical insights with practical applications. Each chapter is enriched with case studies that illustrate the real-world implications of legal principles. From syndicated loans (Chapter 11) to project finance (Chapter 12) and intellectual property rights (Chapter 24), these case studies provide valuable insights into navigating legal challenges and complexities in global business environments.

Embracing Technological Advancements

Recognizing the transformative impact of technology on legal practice, the book dedicates chapters to emerging fields such as

Legal Tech (Chapter 18) and Telecommunications Law (Chapter 37). These chapters explore the intersection of law and technology, addressing regulatory challenges posed by digital advancements and preparing legal professionals to adapt to the evolving landscape of global commerce.

Scholarly Rigor and Practical Relevance

Authored by leading experts in international law, "Global Master of International Law: GMIBL-LLM" exemplifies scholarly rigour while maintaining practical relevance. Each chapter is meticulously researched and structured to provide a comprehensive understanding of global legal systems and specialized fields. This dual approach equips readers with the knowledge and skills necessary to excel in international legal practice, whether advising multinational corporations, engaging in cross-border transactions, or advocating for justice in global forums.

Conclusion

In conclusion, "Global Master of International Law: GMIBL-LLM" stands as a definitive resource for legal scholars, practitioners, and students seeking to deepen their understanding of international law. By offering insights into diverse legal systems, exploring specialized fields, and addressing emerging trends, this book prepares readers to navigate the complexities of global legal environments with confidence and expertise. It serves as an indispensable guide for anyone passionate about mastering international law and contributing to the evolving landscape of global legal practice.

Chapters in detail:
Chapter 1 delves into Islamic Business Transaction Law, beginning with the **principles of Islamic finance** (1.1), which emphasize ethical investments, risk-sharing, and the prohibition of interest (riba). It then explores **Sharia compliance in business transactions** (1.2), highlighting the importance of aligning business practices with Islamic ethical standards. The chapter further discusses **contracts in Islamic law** (1.3), focusing on diverse types of permissible contracts such as Mudarabah and Murabaha. A **comparative analysis with conventional business law** (1.4) sheds light on the unique aspects of Islamic finance versus conventional finance systems.

Chapter 2 focuses on Islamic Insurance, or Takaful, starting with the **principles of Takaful** (2.1), which are based on mutual assistance and shared responsibility. The **operational models of Takaful** (2.2) are examined, including cooperative and hybrid models. The chapter also reviews the **regulatory framework for Takaful** (2.3), and provides a **comparative analysis with conventional insurance** (2.4), emphasizing the ethical and operational differences.

The book then shifts to regional legal systems. **Chapter 3** addresses the **key principles of the Australian legal system**, including an **overview** (3.1), the **constitutional framework** (3.2), the **judicial system and legal institutions** (3.3), and **business and corporate law in Australia** (3.4). **Chapter 4** provides similar insights into the **Chinese legal system**, detailing its **historical development** (4.1), **structure** (4.2), **key legislation and regulatory bodies** (4.3), and **business and trade law in China** (4.4).

Chapters 5 through 9 cover the **legal systems of England, the Gulf/Middle East, the USA/Canada, Pakistan, and SAARC countries**. Each chapter provides a comprehensive look at the region's legal history, constitutional framework, judicial institutions, and business laws, enabling readers to compare and contrast these diverse legal landscapes.

Moving into specialized legal fields, **Chapter 10** explores the **law of financial crime**, including the **types** (10.1), **legal framework** (10.2), **international cooperation** (10.3), and **case studies** (10.4). **Chapter 11** discusses **syndicated loans**, addressing **principles** (11.1), **legal frameworks** (11.2), **risk management** (11.3), and **case studies** (11.4).

Chapter 12 delves into **international project finance**, focusing on the **fundamentals** (12.1), **legal and regulatory frameworks** (12.2), **risk allocation and management** (12.3), and **case studies** (12.4). **Chapter 13** addresses **international taxation**, examining **principles** (13.1), **double taxation treaties** (13.2), **transfer pricing regulations** (13.3), and **tax planning and compliance** (13.4). **Chapters 14 to 16** cover the **law of the sea, WTO law,** and **investment entities**, providing in-depth analyses of their principles, legal frameworks, regulatory challenges, and case studies.

Chapter 17 emphasizes **legal research skills and methods**, guiding readers through the **fundamentals** (17.1), **research methodologies** (17.2), **legal writing and analysis** (17.3), and **presentation** (17.4).

Chapter 18 on **Legal Tech/FinTech** examines the intersection of technology and law, exploring **legal issues in FinTech** (18.2), the **regulatory framework** (18.3), and **innovations and future trends** (18.4).

Chapter 19 discusses **marine insurance law**, covering **principles** (19.1), the **legal framework** (19.2), **risk and liability** (19.3), and **case studies** (19.4).

Chapter 20 on **medicine, law, and society** addresses **legal issues in medical practice** (20.1), **patient rights and medical ethics** (20.2), and the **regulation of medical professionals** (20.3).

Chapter 21 explores **modern copyright law**, including **digital copyright issues** (21.2) and **international copyright treaties** (21.3).

Subsequent chapters delve into various aspects of law such as **money laundering and financial crime** (Chapter 22), **multinational enterprises** (Chapter 23), **patents and trade secrets** (Chapter 24), **private equity** (Chapter 25), **private international law** (Chapter 26), and **private law aspects of finance** (Chapter 27).

The book also covers **project finance** (Chapter 28), **public international law** (Chapter 29), **international commercial arbitration** (Chapter 30), and advanced **legal research methods** (Chapter 31).

Further chapters examine specific legal areas such as **securities law** (Chapter 34), **strategic management** (Chapter 35), **taxation principles** (Chapter 36), **telecommunications law** (Chapter 37),

corporate governance (Chapter 38), **devolution law in Wales** (Chapter 39), and **maritime security** (Chapter 40).

The final chapters include detailed studies on **cargo transportation law** (Chapter 41), **socio-legal studies** (Chapter 42), **trademarks** (Chapter 43), **technology transfer law** (Chapter 44), **transitional justice** (Chapter 45), **transnational business instruments** (Chapter 46), **transnational corporate law** (Chapter 47), **corporate restructuring** (Chapter 48), **UN international laws** (Chapter 49), and **world trade law** (Chapter 50).

Chapters 51 and 52 complete the book with an examination of the **key principles of the legal systems of Asian countries** (Japan, Singapore, South Korea, Taiwan, Malaysia, Thailand) and **EU countries** (Germany, France, Italy, Belgium, Netherlands, Poland, Spain, and others). Each chapter provides an overview of the legal systems, comparative constitutional structures, key legal institutions, and business and corporate law in the respective regions.

Book Cover:

Global Master of International Law GMIL-LLM

Embark on a comprehensive journey through the intricate world of international law with "Global Master of International Law GMIBL-LLM." This essential volume is meticulously crafted to cater to legal professionals, scholars, and students seeking a profound understanding of global legal systems and specialized legal fields. Dive into detailed explorations of diverse legal traditions, from Islamic Business Transaction Law to the complexities of Takaful and Sharia compliance. Examine the unique principles governing the legal landscapes of Australia, China, the Gulf/Middle East, USA/Canada, Pakistan, and SAARC countries. Delve into specialized areas such as financial crime, international taxation, maritime law, and digital copyright issues.

Authored by leading experts in the field, each chapter offers in-depth analyses, practical case studies, and comparative perspectives that bridge theoretical concepts with real-world applications. Whether you are navigating the nuances of international finance, unravelling the complexities of project finance, or exploring the future of Legal Tech, this book provides unparalleled insights and practical guidance.
"Global Master of International Law GMIBL-LLM" is not just a book; it is an indispensable resource that equips you with the knowledge and skills to excel in the dynamic and ever-evolving landscape of international law. Your journey to mastering global legal systems starts here.

Preface:

"Global Master of International Law: An Extensive & In-Depth Exploration of Diverse Legal Systems and Specialized Fields for the Modern Legal Professional GMIL-LLM" offers a comprehensive insight into global legal systems, providing the ultimate guide to understanding and navigating the complexities of international legal practices. This book serves as an essential resource for legal professionals, scholars, and students, equipping them with the knowledge and skills necessary to excel in a globalized world. Through detailed explorations of regional legal traditions and specialized fields, readers gain a profound understanding of the principles, frameworks, and case studies that define contemporary international law. By bridging theory and practice, this book empowers its audience to navigate the dynamic and ever-evolving landscape of global legal systems with confidence and expertise, making it an indispensable tool for anyone committed to mastering international law.

The "Global Master of International Law GMIL-LLM" is a culmination of extensive research, in-depth analysis, and a deep understanding of various legal systems and specialized fields within international law. This book is designed to be a comprehensive resource for legal scholars, practitioners, and students, offering an unparalleled breadth of knowledge and insight into the multifaceted world of international law. The primary aim of this book is to bridge the gap between theoretical principles and practical applications, providing readers with a robust foundation in both the fundamentals and the advanced aspects of global legal systems.

This book is organized into meticulously crafted chapters that cover a wide array of topics, beginning with the principles of Islamic finance and the unique aspects of Sharia-compliant business transactions. Islamic Business Transaction Law, as explored in Chapter 1, introduces readers to the ethical and operational frameworks that distinguish Islamic finance from conventional systems. It underscores the significance of adhering to Sharia principles, such as the prohibition of riba (interest) and the emphasis on risk-sharing and ethical investments. This chapter sets the stage for a broader understanding of how Islamic principles permeate various aspects of business and finance. Chapter 2 delves into Islamic Insurance, or Takaful, highlighting the principles of mutual assistance and shared responsibility that underpin this system. By examining the operational models and regulatory frameworks of Takaful, and comparing them with conventional insurance systems, this chapter provides readers with a nuanced understanding of the ethical and practical differences that define Islamic insurance.

The subsequent chapters shift focus to regional legal systems, offering comprehensive overviews and detailed analyses of the legal landscapes in Australia, China, the Gulf/Middle East, the USA/Canada, Pakistan, and SAARC countries. Each regional chapter is designed to provide a thorough understanding of the historical development, constitutional frameworks, judicial systems, and business laws specific to these regions. By examining these diverse legal systems, readers gain valuable insights into the unique challenges and opportunities that characterize each jurisdiction.

Chapters 3 through 9 meticulously cover the key principles and operational specifics of these regional legal systems. The chapter on the Australian legal system, for instance, provides an in-depth look at the constitutional framework, judicial system, and key legal institutions, offering a comprehensive understanding of how business and corporate law operate within this context. Similarly, the chapter on the Chinese legal system delves into the historical evolution of Chinese law, the structure of its legal system, and the key legislation and regulatory bodies that govern business and trade law in China.

As the book progresses, it transitions into specialized legal fields, beginning with financial crime in Chapter 10. This chapter explores the several types of financial crime, the legal frameworks designed to combat them, and the importance of international cooperation in addressing these issues. It also includes case studies that provide practical examples of how financial crimes are detected and prosecuted.

Chapters 11 and 12 cover syndicated loans and international project finance, respectively. These chapters provide a detailed examination of the principles, legal frameworks, and risk management strategies associated with these complex financial instruments. By including case studies, these chapters offer practical insights into the real-world applications and challenges of syndicated loans and project finance.

International taxation is the focus of Chapter 13, which explores the principles of international taxation, double taxation treaties, transfer pricing regulations, and tax planning and compliance. This chapter provides readers with a comprehensive understanding of how tax laws are applied across borders and the strategies used to navigate the complexities of international tax systems.

The book also addresses maritime law, WTO law, and investment entities in Chapters 14, 15, and 16. Each chapter provides a thorough exploration of the principles, legal frameworks, and regulatory challenges associated with these areas of law. The inclusion of case studies helps to illustrate the practical applications and implications of these legal principles.

Chapter 17 emphasizes the importance of legal research skills and methods. This chapter guides readers through the fundamentals of legal research, including research methodologies, legal writing and analysis, and the presentation of legal research. By equipping readers with these essential skills, this chapter lays the groundwork for effective legal scholarship and practice.

The intersection of technology and law is explored in Chapter 18, which focuses on Legal Tech and FinTech. This chapter examines the legal issues and regulatory frameworks associated with these rapidly evolving fields, as well as the innovations and future trends that are shaping the landscape of legal technology.
Marine insurance law is the subject of Chapter 19, which covers the principles, legal frameworks, and risk and liability issues associated with marine insurance. This chapter also includes case studies that provide practical insights into the complexities of marine insurance law.

Chapter 20 addresses the intersection of medicine, law, and society, exploring legal issues in medical practice, patient rights and medical ethics, and the regulation of medical professionals. This chapter provides a comprehensive overview of the legal principles that govern the medical field and the ethical considerations that underpin medical practice.
Modern copyright law is the focus of Chapter 21, which examines the fundamentals of copyright law, digital copyright issues, international copyright treaties, and case studies in copyright law. This chapter provides readers with a comprehensive understanding of the legal principles that protect creative works and the challenges associated with digital copyright.

Chapters 22 through 24 delve into money laundering and financial crime, multinational enterprises, patents, and trade secrets. Each chapter provides a detailed examination of the principles, legal frameworks, and case studies associated with these areas of law, offering practical insights into their real-world applications.
Private equity, private international law, and private law aspects of finance are covered in Chapters 25 through 27. These chapters provide a thorough exploration of the principles, legal frameworks, and regulatory issues associated with these areas, as well as case studies that illustrate their practical applications.

The book also includes chapters on project finance, public international law, international commercial arbitration, and advanced legal research methods. Each chapter provides a comprehensive examination of the principles, legal frameworks, and case studies associated with these areas, offering readers a thorough understanding of their complexities and applications. Additional chapters cover securities law, strategic management, taxation principles, telecommunications law, corporate governance, devolution law in Wales, maritime security, cargo transportation law, socio-legal studies, trademarks, technology transfer law, transitional justice, transnational business instruments, transnational corporate law, corporate restructuring, UN international laws, and world trade law. Each chapter provides a detailed examination of the principles, legal frameworks, and case studies associated with these areas, offering practical insights into their real-world applications.

The final chapters of the book focus on the key principles of the legal systems of Asian countries and EU countries. Each chapter provides an overview of the legal systems, comparative constitutional structures, key legal institutions, and business and corporate law in the respective regions, offering readers a comprehensive understanding of the legal landscapes in these regions.

Overall, "Global Master of International Law GMIBL-LLM" is an essential resource for anyone seeking a comprehensive understanding of international law. By covering a wide array of topics and regions, this book provides readers with the knowledge and skills needed to navigate the complexities of global legal systems and specialized legal fields. Whether you are a legal scholar, practitioner, or student, this book is an invaluable tool for advancing your understanding of international law and its applications.

Introduction to "Global Master of International Law: GMIL-LLM"

"Global Master of International Law: An Extensive & In-Depth Exploration of Diverse Legal Systems and Specialized Fields for the Modern Legal Professional GMIL-LLM" offers a comprehensive insight into global legal systems, providing the ultimate guide to understanding and navigating the complexities of international legal practices. This book serves as an essential resource for legal professionals, scholars, and students, equipping them with the knowledge and skills necessary to excel in a globalized world. Through detailed explorations of regional legal traditions and specialized fields, readers gain a profound understanding of the principles, frameworks, and case studies that define contemporary international law. By bridging theory and practice, this book empowers its audience to navigate the dynamic and ever-evolving landscape of global legal systems with confidence and expertise, making it an indispensable tool for anyone committed to mastering international law.

To the comprehensive exploration of international law encapsulated within the pages of "Global Master of International Law: GMIBL-LLM." This book is not merely a collection of legal doctrines and principles but a journey through the intricate tapestry of global legal systems, designed to equip legal scholars, practitioners, and students alike with a deep understanding of the complexities and nuances of international law.

Navigating Global Legal Systems
The study of international law is a multifaceted endeavour that requires a nuanced understanding of legal systems across various jurisdictions. This book begins by delving into foundational principles such as Islamic Business Transaction Law and Sharia Compliance (Chapter 1), providing readers with insights into ethical frameworks that underpin Islamic finance and business practices. This exploration serves as a gateway to

understanding how cultural and religious norms shape legal practices and commercial interactions.

Comparative Analysis and Specialized Fields
One of the hallmarks of this book is its emphasis on comparative analysis. Each chapter not only explores the intricacies of a specific legal system but also juxtaposes it with others to highlight similarities, differences, and the evolving nature of legal norms. For instance, Chapters 3 to 9 offer detailed examinations of legal systems in regions ranging from Australia and China to the Gulf/Middle East, USA/Canada, Pakistan, and SAARC countries. These chapters illuminate the historical, constitutional, and regulatory frameworks that govern business and corporate law within these diverse jurisdictions.

Moving beyond regional analyses, the book delves into specialized fields crucial to modern legal practice. Chapters such as Financial Crime (Chapter 10), International Taxation (Chapter 13), and Maritime Law (Chapter 14) provide deep dives into complex legal areas, offering insights into the legal frameworks, international regulations, and case studies that illustrate their application in real-world scenarios.

Emerging Trends and Technologies
In today's interconnected world, legal practice is increasingly influenced by technological advancements and global trends. Therefore, this book includes chapters dedicated to emerging fields such as Legal Tech (Chapter 18) and Telecommunications Law (Chapter 37), which explore the intersection of law and technology and the regulatory challenges posed by rapid innovation.

Practical Applications and Case Studies
Throughout "Global Master of International Law: GMIL-LLM," practical applications are underscored through case studies. These case studies serve not only to illustrate theoretical concepts but also to provide readers with practical insights into navigating legal complexities. Whether examining syndicated loans (Chapter 11), project finance (Chapter 12), or intellectual

property issues (Chapter 24), the inclusion of real-world examples enhances the reader's understanding and prepares them for the challenges of legal practice in a global context.

Bridging Theory and Practice
At its core, this book aims to bridge the gap between theoretical knowledge and practical application. It is designed to empower legal professionals with the tools and insights needed to navigate the complexities of international law, whether advising multinational corporations, engaging in cross-border transactions, or advocating for justice in global forums. By equipping readers with a comprehensive understanding of legal systems, specialized fields, and emerging trends, "Global Master of International Law: GMIBL-LLM" serves as an indispensable resource for anyone navigating the dynamic landscape of international law.

Conclusion
As you embark on this journey through "Global Master of International Law: GMIL-LLM," prepare to deepen your understanding of global legal systems, expand your knowledge of specialized legal fields, and explore the transformative impact of emerging technologies. Whether you are a seasoned legal practitioner, a scholar delving into international law, or a student aspiring to specialize in global legal affairs, this book promises to be an invaluable companion in your quest for mastery of international law.

Chapter 1: Islamic Business Transaction Law

1.1 Principles of Islamic Finance

Islamic finance, rooted in Sharia law, represents a unique system of fiscal management that differs fundamentally from conventional finance. At its core, Islamic finance is governed by principles derived from the Quran and the Hadith, aiming to promote fairness, transparency, and ethical conduct in financial transactions. One of the most distinguishing features of Islamic finance is the prohibition of riba, or interest, which is considered exploitative and unjust. Instead of earning money on loans through interest, Islamic finance institutions engage in profit-and-loss sharing arrangements, equity participation, and asset-backed financing.

The principle of risk-sharing is central to Islamic finance, ensuring that both the lender and borrower share the risks and rewards of a business venture. This is operationalized through contracts such as Mudarabah (profit-sharing) and Musharakah (joint venture). In a Mudarabah contract, the investor provides capital while the entrepreneur manages the project, with profits shared according to a pre-agreed ratio. In a Musharakah contract, all partners contribute capital and share profits and losses in proportion to their respective investments. These arrangements encourage ethical investing and active partnership, fostering a sense of collective responsibility and mutual benefit.

Another foundational principle is the requirement for asset-backing in financial transactions. This ensures that all financial dealings are linked to tangible assets or services, promoting real economic activity, and preventing speculative behaviour. Contracts such as Murabaha (cost-plus financing) and Ijara (leasing) exemplify this principle. In a Murabaha transaction, the bank buys an asset and sells it to the client at a marked-up price, with the payment made in instalments. This contract structure not only provides financing but also ensures that the transaction is based on real assets. Similarly, Ijara involves leasing an asset to a client for a fixed period, with ownership remaining with the lessor. These contracts provide transparency and security, aligning financial practices with Islamic ethical standards.

The prohibition of gharar (excessive uncertainty) is another key principle. Islamic finance requires full disclosure and transparency in all transactions to avoid any element of uncertainty or deception. This principle safeguards the interests of all parties involved and promotes trust and integrity in financial dealings. Contracts are meticulously detailed to ensure that all terms and conditions are clear and agreed upon, reducing the risk of disputes, and fostering a stable financial environment.

Furthermore, Islamic finance emphasizes social justice and welfare, directing investments towards socially responsible projects that benefit the community. Instruments like Zakat (almsgiving) and Qard al-Hasan (benevolent loan) exemplify this commitment to social welfare. Zakat is a form of mandatory charity aimed at redistributing wealth and supporting the needy, while Qard al-Hasan involves lending money without interest to help those in financial distress. These practices reflect the broader ethical and moral objectives of Islamic finance, promoting a just and equitable society.

In summary, the principles of Islamic finance—prohibition of riba, risk-sharing, asset-backing, avoidance of gharar, and social justice—create a distinctive financial system that emphasizes ethical conduct, fairness, and real economic activity. By adhering to these principles, Islamic finance offers an alternative to conventional financial practices, fostering a more inclusive and responsible financial environment that aligns with the moral and ethical values of Islam.

1.2 Sharia Compliance in Business Transactions

Sharia compliance in business transactions ensures that all financial and commercial activities adhere to Islamic law principles, which emphasize justice, equity, and ethical conduct. Achieving Sharia compliance involves rigorous adherence to prohibitions against riba (interest), gharar (excessive uncertainty), and haram (forbidden) activities, such as investing in businesses related to alcohol, gambling, or pork. Financial institutions, particularly Islamic banks, have established internal Sharia boards comprising scholars and experts in Islamic law to oversee and ensure compliance in their operations.

Central to Sharia compliance is the concept of halal (permissible) activities and earnings. Businesses must engage in ethically sound activities and refrain from any form of exploitation or deceit. Transparency and full disclosure are mandatory, ensuring that all parties involved have a clear understanding of the terms and conditions. Additionally, transactions should be grounded in real economic activity, meaning they must involve tangible assets or services rather than speculative or purely financial activities.

Sharia-compliant financial products are designed to reflect these principles. For instance, in a Murabaha (cost-plus financing) transaction, the bank purchases an asset and sells it to the customer at a profit margin, allowing the customer to pay in instalments. The transaction must be transparent, with the cost and profit margin disclosed. Similarly, in an Ijara (leasing) agreement, the bank leases an asset to a customer for a fixed period, after which ownership may be transferred to the customer. These products ensure compliance with Sharia principles while meeting the financing needs of clients.

The role of Sharia boards is crucial in maintaining compliance. These boards review and approve financial products, contracts, and business practices, ensuring they align with Islamic principles. They also conduct regular audits and provide guidance on complex Sharia issues, helping institutions navigate the intricacies of Islamic law in a modern business context. By upholding these standards, Sharia boards play a vital role in maintaining the integrity and trust of Islamic financial institutions.

1.3 Contracts in Islamic Law

Contracts in Islamic law, or aqd, are fundamental to conducting business transactions in a manner that adheres to Sharia principles. Islamic contracts emphasize mutual consent, clear terms, and the fulfilment of obligations by all parties involved. The validity of a contract under Islamic law is contingent upon several key elements: the presence of offer and acceptance, the capacity of parties, lawful subject matter, and the absence of coercion or deceit.

There are several types of contracts unique to Islamic finance, each serving different purposes while ensuring compliance with Sharia. Murabaha, as previously mentioned, involves a sale contract where the seller discloses the cost and profit margin. This contract is widely used in asset financing and home purchases. Mudarabah (profit-sharing) is an investment partnership where one party provides capital and the other provides expertise, with profits shared according to a pre-agreed ratio. This contract is essential for venture capital and investment projects.

Musharakah (joint venture) is another significant contract where all partners contribute capital and share profits and losses. This contract is prevalent in business startups and project financing. Ijara (leasing) involves renting an asset while retaining ownership, with the option for the lessee to purchase the asset at the end of the lease period. This contract is common in equipment and property financing.

Islamic law also encompasses benevolent contracts, such as Qard al-Hasan (benevolent loan), which is an interest-free loan provided to those in need. This contract embodies the spirit of social justice and charity central to Islamic finance. Istisna (manufacturing contract) and Salam (forward sale) are contracts designed for manufacturing and agricultural financing, respectively. They allow for the purchase of goods and commodities to be delivered in the future, providing flexibility for producers and buyers.

1.4 Comparative Analysis with Conventional Business Law

The comparative analysis between Islamic business law and conventional business law reveals fundamental differences in principles, objectives, and practices. While both systems aim to facilitate commerce and finance, their underlying philosophies and operational mechanisms diverge significantly.

One of the most prominent differences is the prohibition of riba in Islamic finance, contrasted with the conventional practice of interest-based lending. Islamic finance operates on profit-and-loss sharing, asset-backed financing, and leasing, promoting risk-sharing and ethical investment. Conventional finance, on the other hand, relies heavily on interest as a cost of borrowing, often leading to risk transfer rather than risk sharing.

Another critical distinction is the emphasis on ethical and socially responsible investing in Islamic finance. Islamic law prohibits investment in industries deemed harmful or unethical, such as alcohol, gambling, and pork. Conventional finance does not impose such restrictions, allowing investments across a broader spectrum of industries without moral considerations.

Contracts in Islamic law are designed to ensure transparency, fairness, and mutual consent, with specific structures like Murabaha, Mudarabah, and Ijara tailored to meet these requirements. Conventional business contracts, while also emphasizing transparency and fairness, do not adhere to the same religiously mandated structures and are often more flexible in terms of terms and conditions.

The approach to uncertainty and speculation further differentiates the two systems. Islamic finance prohibits excessive uncertainty (gharar) and speculative transactions, promoting stability and real economic activity. Conventional finance allows a higher degree of speculation and derivative trading, which can lead to volatility and financial instability.

In terms of regulatory frameworks, Islamic finance is overseen by Sharia boards ensuring compliance with religious principles, adding a layer of governance. Conventional financial institutions are regulated by secular legal frameworks and financial authorities, focusing primarily on financial stability and consumer protection without religious considerations.

Overall, while both Islamic and conventional business laws aim to facilitate efficient and fair transactions, their methodologies and guiding principles reflect distinct worldviews and objectives. Islamic business law integrates religious ethics and social justice into its framework, whereas conventional business law prioritizes economic efficiency and market dynamics.

Chapter 2: Islamic Insurance (Takaful)

2.1 Principles of Takaful

Takaful, derived from the Arabic word "kafalah" meaning "guaranteeing each other," represents the Islamic approach to insurance, rooted in the principles of mutual assistance, cooperation, and shared responsibility. Unlike conventional insurance, which operates on a profit-based model, Takaful is structured as a cooperative system where participants contribute to a common pool, providing financial protection and support to one another against specified risks. This system aligns with Sharia law, emphasizing ethical conduct, social solidarity, and the prohibition of riba (interest), gharar (excessive uncertainty), and haram (forbidden) activities.

At the core of Takaful is the concept of mutual guarantee, where participants (policyholders) agree to protect each other from loss or damage. This principle is operationalized through a Takaful contract, where each participant contributes a sum of money (premium) into a pool or fund, managed by a Takaful operator. The contributions are considered donations (Cabarrus) intended to support those among the participants who suffer a loss. This pooling of resources embodies the spirit of mutual aid and cooperation, foundational to Takaful.

One of the distinguishing features of Takaful is the absence of riba. In conventional insurance, premiums are invested in interest-bearing instruments, and the insurer earns profits from the interest. Takaful, however, strictly avoids such practices. The funds collected are invested in Sharia-compliant avenues, excluding industries such as alcohol, gambling, and pork, which are considered unethical in Islam. The profits generated from these investments are distributed among the participants and the Takaful operator, according to pre-agreed ratios, ensuring that the entire system operates within the bounds of Islamic ethics.

Gharar, or excessive uncertainty, is also meticulously avoided in Takaful. Conventional insurance contracts often involve elements of uncertainty and ambiguity regarding premium payments and claim payouts. Takaful addresses this by ensuring transparency and clarity in all contractual terms. The participants have a clear understanding of their contributions, the risks covered, and the conditions under which payouts are made. This reduces uncertainty and enhances trust among participants, aligning the operation with Sharia principles.

Another key principle of Takaful is the ethical management of funds. The Takaful operator acts as a manager (wakil) or entrepreneur (mudarib), responsible for overseeing the contributions and investments on behalf of the participants. The operator's fees and profit-sharing arrangements are clearly defined and agreed upon in advance, ensuring transparency and fairness. Any surplus remaining in the Takaful fund after claims and expenses can be distributed back to the participants or retained to reduce future contributions, depending on the specific model of Takaful being implemented.

Takaful operates under several models, each reflecting different arrangements of risk-sharing and management. The most common models are the Mudarabah model and the Wakalah model. In the Mudarabah model, the Takaful operator acts as an entrepreneur, sharing the profit from investments with the participants. In the Wakalah model, the operator acts as an agent, earning a fee for managing the funds. Hybrid models combining elements of both are also prevalent, tailored to meet the specific needs and preferences of the participants.

The ethical and social objectives of Takaful extend beyond financial protection, aiming to enhance social solidarity and economic justice. By pooling resources and sharing risks, Takaful promotes a sense of community and mutual support, reflecting the Islamic values of brotherhood and social responsibility. This collective approach ensures that the benefits of insurance are accessible to all members of society, including those who might be marginalized or disadvantaged.

In summary, the principles of Takaful—mutual guarantee, prohibition of riba, avoidance of gharar, ethical fund management, and social solidarity—establish a unique and ethically grounded system of insurance. By adhering to these principles, Takaful provides a Sharia-compliant alternative to conventional insurance, fostering a financial environment that aligns with Islamic values and promotes the well-being of the community.

2.2 Operational Models of Takaful

The operational models of Takaful are designed to facilitate cooperation and shared responsibility among participants, ensuring compliance with Sharia principles while providing financial protection. The main models are Mudarabah (profit-sharing), Wakalah (agency), and hybrid models that combine elements of both. Each model has distinct characteristics and mechanisms for managing contributions, investments, and claims.

Mudarabah Model: In the Mudarabah model, the Takaful operator acts as an entrepreneur (mudarib) who manages the Takaful fund on behalf of the participants (rabb-ul-mal). The participants contribute to the fund, which is then invested in Sharia-compliant ventures. Profits generated from these investments are shared between the operator and the participants according to a pre-agreed ratio. Losses, if any, are borne by the participants as the operator does not guarantee the capital. This model emphasizes profit-sharing and risk-sharing, aligning with the principles of Islamic finance.

Wakalah Model: The Wakalah model operates on an agency basis where the Takaful operator acts as an agent (wakil) for the participants. The operator charges a fixed fee for managing the Takaful fund, known as the Wakalah fee. The contributions are pooled and invested in Sharia-compliant assets, and the profits from these investments belong entirely to the participants, after deducting the management fee. The Wakalah model ensures transparency and aligns the operator's incentives with the participants' interests, as the operator's earnings are fixed and not dependent on investment performance.

Hybrid Models: Hybrid models combine elements of both Mudarabah and Wakalah, offering flexibility to meet diverse participant needs. In such models, the operator may charge a Wakalah fee for management services and also share in the profits as a mudarib. This approach allows for tailored arrangements that can balance the benefits of both models, enhancing the efficiency and appeal of Takaful products.

2.3 Regulatory Framework for Takaful

The regulatory framework for Takaful is essential to ensure the industry operates within Sharia principles while maintaining stability, transparency, and consumer protection. Various jurisdictions have established regulatory bodies and frameworks to oversee Takaful operations, ensuring compliance and fostering industry growth.

Sharia Governance: A cornerstone of Takaful regulation is Sharia governance. This involves the establishment of Sharia boards or committees comprising scholars and experts in Islamic law who review and approve Takaful products and operations. These boards ensure that all aspects of the Takaful business, from contracts to investments, comply with Sharia principles, providing credibility and trust in the industry.

Regulatory Bodies: In many countries, regulatory bodies such as central banks or dedicated Islamic finance authorities oversee Takaful operations. These bodies issue guidelines and standards for Takaful companies, covering aspects like capital adequacy, risk management, investment practices, and transparency. They also conduct regular audits and inspections to ensure compliance and protect the interests of participants.

International Standards: International organizations, such as the Accounting and Auditing Organization for Islamic Financial Institutions (AAOIFI) and the Islamic Financial Services Board (IFSB), have developed standards and guidelines for Takaful. These standards address various aspects of Takaful operations, including accounting practices, governance, and risk management, promoting harmonization and best practices across the industry.

Consumer Protection: Regulatory frameworks also emphasize consumer protection, ensuring that Takaful operators provide clear and accurate information to participants. This includes transparent disclosure of fees, investment strategies, and risk factors. Mechanisms for dispute resolution and participant feedback are also integral to protecting consumer interests and maintaining trust in the Takaful system.

2.4 Comparative Analysis with Conventional Insurance

Comparing Takaful with conventional insurance highlights significant differences in principles, structure, and operational mechanisms, reflecting their distinct philosophical foundations.

Principles and Objectives: Takaful is based on the principles of mutual cooperation, shared responsibility, and ethical conduct, aiming to provide financial protection while promoting social solidarity and justice. Conventional insurance, in contrast, operates on a profit-driven model where the insurer assumes risk in exchange for premiums, with the primary objective of profit maximization.

Risk Management: In Takaful, the risk is shared among participants who contribute to a common pool, providing mutual support in case of loss. Conventional insurance transfers risk from the insured to the insurer, who manages it through actuarial calculations and reinsurance. This fundamental difference in risk management reflects the cooperative nature of Takaful versus the risk transfer mechanism in conventional insurance.

Investment Practices: Takaful funds are invested in Sharia-compliant assets, excluding industries and activities deemed unethical in Islam. Conventional insurers, however, invest premiums in a wide range of assets, including interest-bearing instruments, which are prohibited in Takaful. This difference ensures that Takaful operations align with Islamic ethical standards.

Profit and Surplus Distribution: In Takaful, any surplus remaining in the fund after claims and expenses can be distributed back to participants or retained to reduce future contributions. In conventional insurance, profits generated from underwriting and investments belong to the insurer and are distributed to shareholders. This reflects the mutual benefit approach of Takaful versus the profit-oriented approach of conventional insurance.

Transparency and Governance: Takaful emphasizes transparency, with clear disclosure of contributions, fees, and investment strategies. Sharia boards play a crucial role in ensuring compliance with Islamic principles. Conventional insurance is regulated by secular authorities focusing on financial stability and consumer protection but lacks the religious oversight integral to Takaful.

Ethical and Social Impact: Takaful's ethical framework promotes social welfare and economic justice, aligning financial protection with broader societal goals. Conventional insurance, while providing essential risk management services, does not inherently incorporate ethical considerations into its business model.

In conclusion, Takaful offers a Sharia-compliant alternative to conventional insurance, grounded in mutual cooperation, ethical conduct, and social solidarity. Its unique principles and operational models provide a distinctive approach to financial protection, aligning with the values and needs of Muslim communities while also appealing to those seeking ethical financial solutions.

Chapter 3: Key Principles of the Australian Legal System

3.1 Overview of the Australian Legal System

The Australian legal system is a unique and complex amalgamation of historical influences, legislative frameworks, judicial interpretations, and constitutional principles. Its foundation is deeply rooted in the British common law tradition, reflecting Australia's colonial past, yet it has evolved to address the specific needs and circumstances of Australian society.

Historical Development: The Australian legal system traces its origins to the British legal system, established during the colonization period beginning in 1788. The initial legal framework was transplanted directly from Britain, applying English common law and statutes to the new colonies. Over time, as the colonies developed their own identities and administrative structures, a distinct Australian legal system began to emerge. The transition from a collection of British colonies to an independent nation culminated in the federation of the Australian states in 1901, with the creation of the Commonwealth of Australia under the Constitution.

Constitutional Framework: The Australian Constitution is the supreme law of the land, establishing the structure of government, the distribution of powers, and the relationship between the Commonwealth (federal government) and the states. It outlines the separation of powers into three branches: the legislative (Parliament), the executive (Government), and the judiciary (Courts). This separation ensures a system of checks and balances, preventing the concentration of power and protecting individual rights.

Legislative Branch: The Australian Parliament, composed of the House of Representatives and the Senate, is responsible for making laws. The House of Representatives, also known as the lower house, consists of members elected from electoral divisions based on population. The Senate, or upper house, represents the states and territories, with an equal number of senators from each state regardless of population, ensuring a balance between populous and less populous regions. Legislation must be passed by both houses and receive royal assent from the Governor-General to become law.

Executive Branch: The executive power is vested in the Governor-General, who acts as the representative of the monarch, and the Prime Minister and Cabinet. The Governor-General's role is largely ceremonial, with real executive power exercised by the Prime Minister and Cabinet, who are responsible for implementing laws and managing the day-to-day affairs of government. The executive is accountable to Parliament, ensuring democratic oversight and transparency.

Judicial Branch: The judiciary interprets and applies the law, ensuring justice and resolving disputes. The High Court of Australia is the apex court, with the authority to interpret the Constitution, review legislation, and hear appeals from lower courts. Below the High Court, the federal judicial system includes the Federal Court, the Family Court, and the Federal Circuit Court, each with specific jurisdictional responsibilities. Additionally, each state and territory has its own hierarchy of courts, including supreme courts, district, or county courts, and local or magistrates' courts.

Common Law Tradition: Australia follows the common law tradition, where legal principles are developed through judicial decisions and precedents. Courts interpret statutes and develop case law, which guides future judicial decisions. This system provides flexibility and adaptability, allowing the law to evolve with societal changes while ensuring consistency and predictability in legal outcomes.

Federal and State Laws: Australia operates under a federal system, with powers divided between the Commonwealth and the states. The Constitution enumerates specific powers for the Commonwealth, such as defence, foreign affairs, and trade, while residual powers remain with the states. Both levels of government can enact legislation within their respective jurisdictions, and in cases of conflict, federal law prevails. This dual system allows for local autonomy and governance while maintaining national cohesion.

Human Rights and Legal Protections: Australia lacks a comprehensive bill of rights, but human rights are protected through a combination of constitutional provisions, legislation, and common law principles. Key protections include the right to a fair trial, freedom of speech and assembly, and protection against discrimination. The judiciary plays a crucial role in interpreting these rights and ensuring they are upheld.

Legal Profession and Education: The legal profession in Australia is divided into solicitors and barristers. Solicitors provide general legal advice and services to clients, while barristers specialize in advocacy and appear in courts. Legal education is rigorous, with aspiring lawyers required to complete a law degree and practical legal training before being admitted to practice. Continuous professional development ensures that legal practitioners remain competent and up-to-date with legal developments.

In summary, the Australian legal system is a robust and dynamic framework that combines historical influences with contemporary legal principles. Its constitutional foundation, federal structure, adherence to the common law tradition, and commitment to justice and human rights make it a cornerstone of Australian democracy and governance. This system not only reflects Australia's legal heritage but also its ongoing evolution to meet the needs of a modern and diverse society.

3.2 Constitutional Framework

The constitutional framework of Australia is the bedrock of its legal and governmental systems. The Commonwealth of Australia Constitution Act 1900 (UK) established the legal foundation for the federation of the Australian colonies into a single nation, effective from January 1, 1901. The Constitution delineates the structure of government, the separation of powers, and the distribution of powers between the Commonwealth and the states.

Structure of Government: The Australian Constitution establishes a federal system of government, dividing authority between the national government (the Commonwealth) and the state and territorial governments. The Constitution also defines the structure and powers of the three branches of government: the legislative, executive, and judicial branches.

- **Legislative Branch:** The Parliament of Australia, consisting of the House of Representatives and the Senate, is responsible for making laws. The House of Representatives represents the people, with members elected based on population. The Senate represents the states, with an equal number of senators from each state, ensuring a balance of power between populous and less populous states.

- **Executive Branch:** The executive power is vested in the Queen, represented by the Governor-General, and exercised by the Prime Minister and Cabinet. The Governor-General's role is largely ceremonial, while the Prime Minister and Cabinet are responsible for policy-making and administration.

- **Judicial Branch:** The judiciary is independent and interprets the law. The High Court of Australia is the supreme court, with the authority to interpret the Constitution, adjudicate disputes between the Commonwealth and the states, and hear appeals from lower courts.

Separation of Powers: The Constitution establishes the separation of powers doctrine, ensuring that the legislative, executive, and judicial branches operate independently and provide checks and balances on each other. This separation prevents the concentration of power and protects individual liberties.

Division of Powers: The Constitution divides powers between the Commonwealth and the states. Section 51 enumerates the specific powers of the Commonwealth, including defence, foreign affairs, trade, and commerce. Residual powers, not explicitly mentioned in the Constitution, remain with the states. In case of conflict between state and federal laws, Section 109 of the Constitution provides that federal law prevails.

Amendment Process: Amending the Constitution requires a rigorous process outlined in Section 128. A proposed amendment must pass both houses of Parliament by an absolute majority. It is then submitted to the voters in a referendum, where it must receive a majority of votes in a majority of states, as well as a national majority.

3.3 Judicial System and Legal Institutions

Australia's judicial system is a cornerstone of its legal framework, ensuring justice, interpreting laws, and safeguarding rights. The system is hierarchical, with the High Court of Australia at its apex, followed by federal and state courts.

High Court of Australia: The High Court is the supreme court, with the authority to interpret the Constitution and adjudicate disputes between the Commonwealth and the states. It also hears appeals from federal, state, and territory courts. The High Court's decisions are binding on all other courts in Australia.

Federal Courts:

- **Federal Court of Australia:** Handles most civil disputes governed by federal law, including trade practices, native title, intellectual property, and industrial relations.

- **Family Court of Australia:** Specializes in family law matters such as divorce, child custody, and property disputes.
- **Federal Circuit Court of Australia:** Deals with less complex matters that would otherwise be heard in the Federal Court or the Family Court, offering a more streamlined process.

State and Territory Courts: Each state and territory has its own court system, typically consisting of:

- **Supreme Courts:** The highest courts in each state/territory, with jurisdiction over serious criminal and civil cases, and appeals from lower courts.
- **District/County Courts:** Intermediate courts handling serious criminal offences and civil cases involving larger sums of money.
- **Local/Magistrates' Courts:** Lower courts dealing with minor criminal offences, small civil disputes, and preliminary hearings for more serious cases.

Specialist Courts and Tribunals: Australia also has various specialist courts and tribunals, such as the Industrial Relations Commission and Administrative Appeals Tribunal, which handle specific types of legal matters and disputes.

Legal Institutions:

- **Attorney-General's Department:** Provides legal advice to the government, drafts legislation, and oversees the legal framework.
- **Commonwealth and State Directors of Public Prosecutions (DPPs):** Responsible for prosecuting criminal cases on behalf of the state.
- **Legal Aid Commissions:** Provide legal assistance to those unable to afford private legal services.

- **Law Societies and Bar Associations:** Regulate the legal profession, ensuring standards and professional conduct.

3.4 Business and Corporate Law in Australia

Australia's business and corporate law framework is comprehensive and designed to support a robust and fair business environment. It governs the formation, operation, and regulation of businesses, ensuring compliance, protecting stakeholders, and promoting economic growth.

Corporations Act 2001: The Corporations Act 2001 is the primary legislation regulating companies in Australia. It covers company formation, duties of directors and officers, financial reporting, takeovers, and insolvency. Administered by the Australian Securities and Investments Commission (ASIC), the Act ensures corporate transparency and accountability.

Australian Securities and Investments Commission (ASIC): ASIC is the regulatory body overseeing corporate conduct, financial markets, and financial services. It enforces the Corporations Act, ensuring companies comply with legal requirements, protecting investors, and enhancing market integrity.

Corporate Governance: Corporate governance in Australia emphasizes transparency, accountability, and fairness. The ASX Corporate Governance Council provides principles and recommendations to guide listed companies. Key principles include the structure of the board, integrity in financial reporting, and risk management.

Business Structures: Businesses in Australia can operate under various structures, including sole proprietorships, partnerships, companies, and trusts. Each structure has distinct legal and regulatory implications, affecting liability, taxation, and reporting obligations.

Consumer Protection: The Australian Consumer Law (ACL), part of the Competition and Consumer Act 2010, protects consumers and ensures fair trading. It covers areas such as product safety, unfair contract terms, and consumer rights against misleading or deceptive conduct.

Employment Law: Employment relationships are governed by a combination of statutes, awards, and agreements. The Fair Work Act 2009 establishes the framework for employment conditions, including minimum wages, working hours, and protections against unfair dismissal. The Fair Work Commission oversees disputes and ensures compliance with employment laws.

Intellectual Property: Intellectual property law protects creations of the mind, including inventions, literary works, and trademarks. Key legislation includes the Patents Act 1990, the Copyright Act 1968, and the Trade Marks Act 1995. IP Australia administers these laws, granting rights and resolving disputes.

Insolvency and Bankruptcy: The insolvency framework provides mechanisms for dealing with financially distressed companies and individuals. The Corporations Act outlines procedures for corporate insolvency, including liquidation and administration. The Bankruptcy Act of 1966 governs personal insolvency, providing for the distribution of assets and discharge from debts.

Mergers and Acquisitions: Mergers and acquisitions (M&A) are regulated to ensure fair competition and protect stakeholders. The Australian Competition and Consumer Commission (ACCC) oversees M&A activities, preventing anti-competitive practices. The Takeovers Panel resolves disputes relating to takeover bids, ensuring compliance with the Corporations Act.

Trade and Commerce: Australia's trade laws facilitate domestic and international commerce, promoting economic growth. The Customs Act 1901 and associated regulations govern import and export activities, ensuring compliance with international agreements and protecting local industries.

Environmental Law: Environmental regulations ensure sustainable business practices, balancing economic development with environmental protection. The Environment Protection and Biodiversity Conservation Act 1999 (EPBC Act) is the central legislation, requiring businesses to assess and mitigate environmental impacts.

Future Developments: Australia's business and corporate law continuously evolve, adapting to new challenges and global trends. Emerging areas such as digital commerce, data protection, and sustainable finance are shaping the future legal landscape, ensuring Australia remains a competitive and attractive destination for business.

Chapter 4: Key Principles of the Chinese Legal System

4.1 Historical Development of Chinese Law

The historical development of Chinese law is a rich and intricate journey that spans several millennia, reflecting the country's complex socio-political evolution and its philosophical underpinnings. Chinese legal history can be broadly divided into several distinct periods: ancient and imperial China, the early modern period, the Republican era, the Maoist period, and the reform era post-1978. Each period contributed uniquely to the present-day legal system in China.

Ancient and Imperial China:
Chinese law has its roots in the ancient philosophies of Confucianism and Legalism. Confucianism, established by Confucius around the sixth century BCE, emphasized moral virtues, social harmony, and the importance of familial relationships. It advocated for a society governed by ethical norms and humaneness (Ren), rather than stringent laws and punishments. Conversely, Legalism, which gained prominence during the Warring States period (475-221 BCE), promoted the idea of a strong, centralized state where laws and strict enforcement were pivotal for maintaining order. The first unification of China under the Qin Dynasty (221-206 BCE) saw Legalism becoming the foundation of governance. The harsh and autocratic nature of Qin's legal practices, however, led to its quick demise.

The subsequent Han Dynasty (206 BCE - 220 CE) saw a synthesis of Confucianism and Legalism, where Confucian ideals were promoted within the framework of a centralized legal system. This blend persisted through many dynasties, with the Tang Code (established in 624 CE) becoming a significant legal document. The Tang Code combined penal law with administrative regulations and remained influential through the Song (960-1279), Yuan (1271-1368), and Ming (1368-1644) Dynasties. The Qing Dynasty (1644-1912) further refined this code, which underpinned Chinese law until the early 20th century.

Early Modern Period and Republican Era:
The fall of the Qing Dynasty and the establishment of the Republic of China in 1912 marked a significant shift towards modernization and Westernization of the legal system. Under the influence of legal scholars educated abroad, particularly in Japan and Europe, the Republic introduced a series of reforms inspired by German, Japanese, and Soviet legal principles. The Nationalist government enacted numerous laws, including the 1929 Civil Code, the Criminal Code, and various commercial laws, aiming to build a modern legal framework.

Maoist Period (1949-1978):
The founding of the People's Republic of China (PRC) in 1949 under the leadership of the Chinese Communist Party (CCP) initiated a new era of legal transformation. Mao Zedong's vision for China placed less emphasis on formal legal institutions and more on revolutionary ideals and class struggle. The legal system during this period was characterized by mass campaigns, political trials, and the use of law as a tool for consolidating socialist policies. The formal legal institutions were either dismantled or severely weakened, especially during the Cultural Revolution (1966-1976) when law was largely subordinated to the whims of political movements.

Reform Era Post-1978:
The death of Mao Zedong and the rise of Deng Xiaoping in the late 1970s marked the beginning of significant legal reforms. The reform era emphasized the rule of law as essential for economic development and modernization. The 1982 Constitution, which remains in effect today (albeit with numerous amendments), laid the foundation for rebuilding China's legal system. This period saw the re-establishment of courts, the reinstatement of legal education, and the drafting of comprehensive laws in areas such as civil, economic, administrative, and criminal law.

One of the key developments in the reform era was the adoption of the General Principles of Civil Law in 1986, which laid the groundwork for the Civil Code enacted in 2021. The reform period also introduced significant legal frameworks for business, such as the Company Law (1993), the Contract Law (1999), and the Anti-Monopoly Law (2007), aligning China more closely with international legal standards.

Contemporary Developments:
In recent years, China has continued to refine its legal system, focusing on issues like intellectual property protection, environmental law, and social governance. The Xi Jinping era has seen a strong emphasis on legal reforms to support the anti-corruption campaign and ensure the CCP's control. The legal system today is characterized by a blend of modern statutory laws and traditional legal principles, heavily influenced by the overarching authority of the CCP.

The historical development of Chinese law reflects the country's continuous adaptation and integration of diverse legal traditions to meet the changing needs of its society. From ancient philosophical doctrines to modern legal reforms, China's legal system remains a dynamic and integral part of its governance and socio-economic development.

4.2 Structure of the Chinese Legal System

The Chinese legal system is a complex and multifaceted framework that integrates various legal traditions and modern legislative practices, all under the overarching control of the Chinese Communist Party (CCP). The system is hierarchical and consists of a range of institutions and bodies that perform legislative, judicial, and administrative functions.

Legislative Structure:
The National People's Congress (NPC) is the highest legislative authority in China. It has the power to enact and amend fundamental laws, including the Constitution. The NPC Standing Committee (NPCSC), a permanent body of the NPC, handles legislative functions when the NPC is not in session, including interpreting laws and the Constitution. Below the NPC, local people's congresses at provincial, municipal, and county levels have the authority to pass local laws and regulations, which must align with national laws.

Executive Structure:
The executive branch is headed by the State Council, which functions as the central government and is responsible for implementing laws and regulations. It oversees various ministries and commissions that manage specific areas such as finance, education, and public health. At the local level, provincial, municipal, and county governments implement laws and policies within their jurisdictions, following directives from higher levels of government.

Judicial Structure:
The Chinese judicial system comprises several levels of courts, including the Supreme People's Court (SPC), which is the highest judicial authority. Below the SPC are the Higher People's Courts at the provincial level, Intermediate People's Courts at the municipal level, and Basic People's Courts at the county or district level. Additionally, there are specialized courts such as military courts and maritime courts. The judicial system also includes the People's Procuratorate, which is responsible for public prosecution and legal supervision.

Legal Profession and Institutions:
The legal profession in China includes judges, prosecutors, lawyers, and legal academics. The Ministry of Justice oversees legal education and the legal profession, including the licensing of lawyers. The All China Lawyers Association (ACLA) is the official body representing Chinese lawyers and plays a significant role in regulating the profession.

Party Control:
The CCP maintains considerable influence over the legal system. Party committees at all levels of government and judiciary ensure that the legal system aligns with party policies and directives. The Central Political and Legal Affairs Commission of the CCP oversees legal and law enforcement institutions, ensuring that party leadership is integrated into the judicial process.

4.3 Key Legislation and Regulatory Bodies

China's legal system is underpinned by a range of key legislation and regulatory bodies that govern various aspects of social, economic, and political life.

Constitution:
The Constitution of the People's Republic of China, adopted in 1982 and subsequently amended, is the supreme law of the land. It outlines the fundamental principles of governance, the structure of government, and the rights and duties of citizens.

Civil and Commercial Law:
The General Principles of Civil Law (1986) and the Civil Code (2021) form the backbone of civil law in China. The Civil Code consolidates previous laws on property, contracts, torts, family, and inheritance into a single comprehensive legal framework. The Company Law (1993, revised 2018), the Contract Law (1999), and the Partnership Enterprise Law (1997, revised 2006) are critical for regulating business activities.

Criminal Law:
The Criminal Law (1979, revised 1997) and the Criminal Procedure Law (1979, revised 2018) outline offences and procedures for prosecution, trial, and sentencing. The Anti-Corruption Law and various other regulations address specific crimes such as bribery and economic offences.

Administrative Law:
The Administrative Procedure Law (1989, revised 2017) and the Administrative Penalty Law (1996, revised 2021) regulate the actions of administrative authorities and provide mechanisms for citizens to challenge administrative decisions.

Regulatory Bodies:
- **Ministry of Justice:** Oversees the legal profession, legal education, and prison administration.
- **Supreme People's Court (SPC):** The highest judicial authority, interpreting laws and overseeing lower courts.
- **Supreme People's Procuratorate (SPP):** Supervises public prosecution and legal enforcement.
- **National Development and Reform Commission (NDRC):** Oversees economic and social development policies.

- **China Securities Regulatory Commission (CSRC):** Regulates the securities market.
- **China Banking and Insurance Regulatory Commission (CBIRC):** Supervises banking and insurance sectors.
- **State Administration for Market Regulation (SAMR):** Enforces competition law and oversees market regulation.

4.4 Business and Trade Law in China

Business and trade laws in China are governed by a complex set of regulations designed to facilitate economic growth, ensure fair competition, and integrate China into the global economy. These laws cover various aspects of business operations, from company formation and management to trade practices and intellectual property protection.

Company Formation and Regulation:
The Company Law (1993, revised 2018) is the primary legislation governing the establishment, operation, and dissolution of companies in China. It outlines the requirements for company registration, capital contributions, shareholder rights, and corporate governance. The law distinguishes between limited liability companies (LLCs) and joint-stock companies (JSCs), each with specific regulatory requirements.

Contract Law:
The Contract Law (1999) regulates contractual relationships, ensuring that contracts are legally binding and enforceable. It covers several types of contracts, including sales, leases, services, and technology transfers, providing a framework for resolving disputes.

Foreign Investment:
The Foreign Investment Law (2020) replaced previous laws governing foreign investment, streamlining the regulatory framework, and providing greater protection for foreign investors. It emphasizes the principle of equal treatment for foreign and domestic investors and includes provisions for intellectual property protection, dispute resolution, and investment promotion.

Trade Regulations:
China is a member of the World Trade Organization (WTO) and adheres to international trade agreements and standards. The Foreign Trade Law (1994, revised 2016) governs import and export activities, ensuring compliance with WTO rules. Customs Law, anti-dumping regulations, and export control laws further regulate international trade.

Intellectual Property:
China has significantly strengthened its intellectual property (IP) laws to align with international standards. The Patent Law (1984, revised 2020), Trademark Law (1982, revised 2019), and Copyright Law (1990, revised 2020) provide robust protections for IP rights. The National Intellectual Property Administration (CNIPA) oversees IP registration and enforcement.

Competition Law:
The Anti-Monopoly Law (2007) aims to prevent anti-competitive practices, such as monopolies, cartels, and abuse of market dominance. The State Administration for Market Regulation (SAMR) enforces competition law and oversees mergers and acquisitions to ensure fair competition.

Dispute Resolution:
China offers various mechanisms for business dispute resolution, including litigation, arbitration, and mediation. The China International Economic and Trade Arbitration Commission (CIETAC) is a prominent institution for resolving international commercial disputes. The courts also play a significant role in enforcing contracts and resolving business disputes.

Corporate Social Responsibility:
Chinese law encourages companies to adopt corporate social responsibility (CSR) practices. Environmental protection laws, labour laws, and corporate governance regulations require businesses to operate sustainably and ethically, addressing issues such as pollution control, worker rights, and corporate transparency.

Recent Developments:
Recent legal developments focus on enhancing the business environment, improving regulatory efficiency, and fostering innovation. The introduction of the Civil Code in 2021, reforms

in the financial sector, and efforts to strengthen IP enforcement reflect China's commitment to creating a more predictable and fairer legal framework for businesses.

The Chinese business and trade law landscape is continually evolving, influenced by domestic economic policies, international trade obligations, and the need to foster a competitive, innovative, and sustainable economy. This dynamic legal environment presents both opportunities and challenges for domestic and international businesses operating in China.

Chapter 5: Key Principles of the English Legal System

5.1 Historical Foundations of English Law

The historical foundations of English law are deeply rooted in a complex tapestry of historical events, cultural influences, and legal evolutions. English law, known for its unique system of common law, has developed over centuries through a combination of judicial decisions, statutory enactments, and customary practices. This section delves into the key historical milestones that have shaped the English legal system as we know it today.

1. Early Beginnings and Roman Influence:
The origins of English law can be traced back to the early Anglo-Saxon period (circa 500-1066 AD). During this time, tribal customs and oral traditions formed the basis of the legal system. Each tribe had its own set of rules and practices, which were primarily unwritten and passed down through generations. The arrival of the Romans in 43 AD brought significant changes to the legal landscape. Roman law introduced concepts such as written statutes, legal documentation, and a more formalized legal system. Although Roman rule in Britain ended in the early fifth century, the influence of Roman legal principles persisted and mingled with existing Anglo-Saxon customs.

2. Norman Conquest and the Formation of Common Law:
The Norman Conquest of 1066 was a pivotal moment in the development of English law. William the Conqueror centralized legal authority and introduced the feudal system, which significantly altered land ownership and governance. One of the most significant contributions of the Norman period was the establishment of common law. Common law emerged as a unified legal system that applied uniformly across the realm, replacing the disparate local customs and laws.
The royal courts, such as the King's Bench and the Court of Common Pleas, played a crucial role in the development of

common law. Judges in these courts began to record their decisions, setting precedents that would guide future cases. This practice of stare decisis, or adhering to precedent, became a cornerstone of the common law system. The use of itinerant judges, who travelled across the country to hear cases, further ensured the consistency and uniformity of legal principles.

3. Magna Carta and the Development of Constitutional Principles:

The signing of the Magna Carta in 1215 was a landmark event that had a profound impact on the English legal system. Forced upon King John by rebellious barons, the Magna Carta established the principle that the king was subject to the law and not above it. It laid the foundation for the development of constitutional law by guaranteeing certain fundamental rights and liberties, such as the right to a fair trial and protection against arbitrary imprisonment.

Magna Carta also introduced the concept of due process and limited the powers of the monarchy, paving the way for the establishment of parliamentary democracy. Over time, its principles were reaffirmed and expanded through subsequent legal documents, such as the Petition of Right (1628) and the Bill of Rights (1689), which further entrenched the rule of law and the separation of powers.

4. Development of Equity and the Court of Chancery:

By the late medieval period, the rigid application of common law principles sometimes led to injustices. To address these shortcomings, the Court of Chancery was established, which administered justice based on principles of equity. Equity aimed to provide remedies that were more flexible and just, taking into account the specifics of each case.

The development of equity introduced important legal concepts such as trusts, injunctions, and specific performance, which complemented the common law system. The integration of common law and equitable principles ensured that the legal system could provide comprehensive and fair remedies.

5. The Influence of Legal Scholars and the Renaissance:

The Renaissance period brought a renewed interest in classical learning and the works of ancient legal scholars. The writings of legal philosophers such as Sir Edward Coke and Sir William Blackstone played a significant role in shaping English law. Coke's commentaries on common law and Blackstone's "Commentaries on the Laws of England" provided comprehensive legal treatises that systematized and clarified legal principles.

Blackstone's Commentaries, in particular, became a foundational text for legal education and practice, not only in England but also in other common law jurisdictions, including the United States. These scholarly works contributed to the intellectual development of the legal system and reinforced the importance of legal precedent and the rule of law.

6. Industrial Revolution and Legal Reforms:

The Industrial Revolution of the 18th and 19th centuries brought about profound social and economic changes, necessitating significant legal reforms. The rise of industrialization led to new legal challenges related to labour rights, property laws, and commercial regulations. The judiciary and legislature responded with a series of reforms aimed at modernizing the legal system.

Key legal reforms included the Judicature Acts of 1873 and 1875, which reorganized the court system and streamlined legal procedures. These acts merged the common law and equity courts, creating a unified judiciary and improving access to justice. The introduction of various statutory laws also addressed emerging issues related to industrialization, such as worker protection and corporate regulation.

7. Modern Era and the Evolution of English Law:

In the 20th and 21st centuries, English law continued to evolve to address contemporary challenges and global developments. The incorporation of European Union law, particularly during the UK's membership in the EU, introduced new legal concepts and standards. The Human Rights Act 1998 incorporated the European Convention on Human Rights into domestic law, enhancing the protection of individual rights.

The legal system also adapted to technological advancements and globalization, addressing issues such as cybercrime, intellectual property, and international trade. Despite these changes, the core principles of common law, equity, and the rule of law remain fundamental to the English legal system. The historical foundations of English law reflect a dynamic and adaptive legal tradition that has evolved over centuries. From its early beginnings in tribal customs and Roman influence on the development of common law, equity, and constitutional principles, the English legal system has continually adapted to meet the needs of society. Its rich history and enduring principles continue to shape modern legal practices and influence legal systems around the world.

5.2 Common Law System

The English legal system is renowned worldwide for its foundation in common law principles. Common law, rooted in judicial decisions and precedents established through court cases, forms the bedrock of the legal framework in England. Unlike civil law systems that rely heavily on codified statutes, common law evolves primarily through judges' interpretations and applications of legal principles to specific cases. This evolutionary process ensures flexibility and adaptability, allowing the law to respond dynamically to changing societal norms and circumstances.

The doctrine of stare decisis, or the principle of precedent, is fundamental to the common law system. Under this doctrine, lower courts must follow the legal principles established by higher courts in previous decisions when faced with similar issues. This ensures consistency and predictability in judicial outcomes while maintaining respect for established legal norms.

5.3 Key Legal Institutions and Their Roles

The English legal system operates through a network of institutions that collectively administer justice and uphold the rule of law. At the apex is the Supreme Court of the United

Kingdom, established in 2009 to replace the Appellate Committee of the House of Lords as the highest court of appeal. The Supreme Court hears cases of the greatest public or constitutional importance and provides authoritative interpretations of the law.

Below the Supreme Court are the Court of Appeal, which handles appeals from lower courts and certain tribunals, and the High Court of Justice, which is divided into three divisions: the Queen's Bench Division, the Chancery Division, and the Family Division. Each division specializes in diverse types of cases, such as civil disputes, commercial matters, and family law issues.

The judiciary in England and Wales is independent and impartial, ensuring judicial decisions are made free from political influence or interference. Judges are appointed based on their legal expertise and experience, upholding the highest standards of professionalism and integrity in dispensing justice.

5.4 Business and Corporate Law in England

Business and corporate law in England is characterized by a robust legal framework that promotes commerce and protects the rights of stakeholders. The Companies Act 2006, a comprehensive statute governing company law, outlines the formation, management, and dissolution of companies. It sets out directors' duties, shareholder rights, and corporate governance principles to ensure transparency and accountability within corporate entities.

Commercial law encompasses various aspects of business transactions, including contract law, sale of goods, and commercial dispute resolution. English contract law, based on common law principles, emphasizes the enforcement of agreements and the sanctity of contractual obligations. The Sale of Goods Act 1979 regulates the sale and purchase of goods, providing remedies for breaches of contract and establishing consumer protections.

In recent years, English law has adapted to accommodate developments in global commerce and finance. The City of London, as a leading international financial centre, attracts businesses from around the world seeking to benefit from its legal expertise and institutional infrastructure. Legal practitioners specializing in business and corporate law play a crucial role in advising clients on regulatory compliance, risk management, and strategic business decisions.

In conclusion, the English legal system's adherence to common law principles, coupled with its independent judiciary and specialized legal institutions, underpins its reputation as a beacon of legal excellence. Business and corporate law in England continues to evolve to meet the challenges of a dynamic global economy while upholding principles of fairness, equity, and justice.

Chapter 6: Key Principles of the Gulf (UAE/Saudi Arabia)/Middle East Legal System

6.1 Legal Traditions in the Gulf and Middle East

The legal systems of the Gulf and Middle East region are richly diverse, reflecting a blend of Islamic law principles, local customs, and influences from both historical and contemporary legal traditions. This section explores the foundational legal principles and institutions that shape the legal landscape in countries such as the United Arab Emirates (UAE), Saudi Arabia, and other Gulf Cooperation Council (GCC) states.

Islamic Law (Sharia)

Islamic law, or Sharia, serves as a primary source of legislation and jurisprudence in many Gulf and Middle Eastern countries. Sharia is derived from the Quran, Hadith (sayings and actions of Prophet Muhammad), Ijma (consensus among Islamic scholars), and Qiyas (analogical reasoning). Its application varies across jurisdictions but generally governs personal status matters, family law, and aspects of commercial transactions.

Civil Law Influence

While Islamic law provides the foundation, several Gulf and Middle Eastern countries have integrated aspects of civil law systems, particularly in commercial and contractual matters. Civil codes codify rules related to contracts, torts, and obligations, drawing on European legal traditions adapted to local contexts. This dual legal system approach aims to balance religious principles with modern legal frameworks necessary for economic development and international trade.

Customary Law

Customary law, rooted in local traditions and practices, plays a significant role in resolving disputes, particularly in rural or tribal communities. Customary laws govern issues such as property rights, inheritance, and social relationships, reflecting historical norms and community consensus. In some jurisdictions, customary law operates alongside formal legal systems, offering alternative dispute resolution mechanisms and ensuring cultural sensitivity in legal proceedings.

Legal Institutions and Judicial System

The Gulf and Middle East regions feature distinct legal institutions responsible for interpreting and administering the law. Sharia courts, often presided over by Islamic scholars (Qadis), specialize in matters concerning family law, inheritance, and personal status. Civil courts handle commercial disputes, contractual matters, and civil rights cases, operating under statutes and regulations derived from civil law principles.

Modernization and Legal Reforms

In recent decades, countries in the Gulf and Middle East have embarked on ambitious legal reforms to enhance judicial efficiency, promote transparency, and attract foreign investment. Initiatives include the establishment of specialized commercial courts, the adoption of international legal standards, and the modernization of legal infrastructure to accommodate the demands of a globalized economy.

Challenges and Future Directions

Despite progress, challenges remain in harmonizing diverse legal systems, ensuring equitable access to justice, and reconciling traditional values with evolving societal norms. The ongoing evolution of Gulf and Middle Eastern legal systems reflects a delicate balance between preserving cultural heritage and embracing legal innovations necessary for sustainable development and international integration.

In conclusion, the legal traditions of the Gulf and Middle East region embody a blend of Islamic principles, civil law frameworks, and customary practices. These legal systems play a crucial role in shaping societal norms, resolving disputes, and fostering economic growth. As countries continue to navigate the complexities of globalization and legal harmonization, understanding the foundational principles and institutions of Gulf and Middle Eastern legal systems is essential for legal professionals and stakeholders alike.

6.2 Sharia Law and Its Application

Sharia law holds a pivotal position in the legal systems of the Gulf and Middle East, influencing various aspects of personal and commercial law. Sharia, derived from Islamic principles and jurisprudence, governs matters such as family law, inheritance, and contracts. In practice, Sharia courts, guided by Islamic scholars (Qadis), adjudicate cases involving marriage, divorce, child custody, and inheritance rights based on Quranic teachings and Hadith.

While Sharia serves as a fundamental source of law, its application varies across jurisdictions within the Gulf and Middle East region. Some countries, such as Saudi Arabia, apply Sharia comprehensively in both personal and criminal law, adhering strictly to Islamic principles. In contrast, countries like the UAE have adopted a dual legal system approach, where Sharia courts handle family and personal status matters, while civil courts manage commercial and contractual disputes under codified civil law.

6.3 Legal Reforms and Modernization Efforts

In response to the demands of globalization and economic diversification, Gulf and Middle Eastern countries have embarked on comprehensive legal reforms and modernization initiatives. These efforts aim to enhance judicial efficiency, promote transparency, and align legal frameworks with international standards to attract foreign investment and support sustainable development.

Key reforms include the establishment of specialized commercial courts equipped to handle complex commercial disputes swiftly and impartially. Legal reforms also focus on streamlining business regulations, enhancing intellectual property rights protection, and strengthening corporate governance frameworks to foster a conducive environment for business growth and innovation.

Moreover, legal modernization efforts extend to procedural reforms, such as the digitization of court systems and the introduction of alternative dispute resolution mechanisms to expedite case resolution and reduce litigation costs. These reforms underscore a commitment to enhancing legal certainty, promoting investor confidence, and ensuring equitable access to justice within the Gulf and Middle Eastern legal systems.

6.4 Business and Corporate Law in the Gulf Region

Business and corporate law in the Gulf region reflect a blend of traditional Islamic principles and modern legal frameworks tailored to support economic development and international trade. Countries such as the UAE, Qatar, and Bahrain have enacted comprehensive company laws and regulations that govern the formation, operation, and dissolution of companies, ensuring transparency, accountability, and investor protection. Corporate governance standards have been strengthened to align with global best practices, emphasizing board accountability, shareholder rights, and ethical business conduct. Regulatory bodies, such as securities commissions and financial authorities, oversee capital markets and enforce compliance with regulatory requirements to maintain market integrity and investor confidence.

The Gulf region's strategic geographic location and robust legal infrastructure have positioned it as a hub for international business and investment. Legal professionals specializing in business and corporate law play a crucial role in advising multinational corporations, negotiating commercial agreements, and navigating regulatory complexities to facilitate cross-border transactions and strategic investments.

In conclusion, the Gulf and Middle Eastern legal systems, anchored in Sharia principles and supported by modern legal reforms, play a vital role in shaping economic governance and fostering regional integration. As countries continue to evolve their legal frameworks to meet global standards, understanding the foundational principles and contemporary developments in business and corporate law is essential for legal practitioners and stakeholders engaged in the region's dynamic business environment.

Chapter 7: Key Principles of the USA/Canada Legal System

7.1 Overview of the US Legal System
The legal systems of the United States and Canada are characterized by their adherence to principles of federalism, common law, and constitutionalism, each contributing distinctively to their legal frameworks. This chapter provides an insightful exploration of the foundational principles and institutions that define the legal landscapes of both nations.

United States Legal System
The legal system of the United States is rooted in the principles of federalism and separation of powers, as outlined in the U.S. Constitution. At its core, the Constitution establishes a federal system of government, dividing powers between the federal government and individual states. This division ensures that certain powers are reserved for the federal government, while others are reserved for the states, promoting a balance of authority and autonomy.

Common Law Tradition
The U.S. legal system operates primarily under a common law tradition, where judicial decisions and precedents play a crucial role in shaping legal interpretations and applications. Courts at both the federal and state levels interpret statutes and constitutional provisions, establishing legal principles that guide future rulings. The doctrine of stare decisis, or precedent, ensures consistency and predictability in judicial decisions, promoting stability within the legal system.

Key Legal Institutions
Legal institutions in the United States include federal and state courts, each with distinct jurisdictions and functions. The federal judiciary comprises the Supreme Court of the United States, appellate courts (Circuit Courts of Appeals), and district courts. The Supreme Court, as the highest judicial authority, interprets the Constitution and resolves disputes involving federal laws and constitutional rights. State courts, organized

into trial courts and appellate courts, handle cases involving state laws and regulations.

Canada Legal System
Canada's legal system shares similarities with the United States, influenced by common law principles and constitutional frameworks. The Constitution Act, of 1867, divides powers between the federal government and provincial governments, establishing a federal system of governance. The Constitution Act, of 1982, includes the Canadian Charter of Rights and Freedoms, which guarantees fundamental rights and freedoms to all Canadians.

Civil Law Influence
While both countries primarily operate under common law traditions, Canada also incorporates elements of civil law, particularly in Quebec, where civil law principles derived from French and Roman law traditions apply to private law matters. This dual legal system approach ensures legal diversity and accommodates regional differences within the Canadian legal framework.

Business and Corporate Law
Business and corporate law in the United States and Canada encompass a broad range of statutes and regulations governing commercial activities, corporate governance, and investor protections. Both countries have robust legal frameworks that promote business innovation, protect shareholder rights, and regulate market activities to ensure fair competition and consumer protection.

In conclusion, the legal systems of the United States and Canada embody a commitment to constitutional governance, legal pluralism, and the rule of law. Understanding the foundational principles and institutional frameworks of these legal systems is essential for legal practitioners, policymakers, and stakeholders engaged in navigating the complexities of North American law and promoting legal certainty in diverse areas of practice.

7.2 Overview of the Canadian Legal System

Canada's legal system is rooted in principles of federalism, common law, and civil law, reflecting its historical and constitutional foundations. The Constitution Act, of 1867, established Canada as a federal state, dividing powers between the federal government and provincial governments. This division ensures that the federal government has authority over matters such as criminal law, immigration, and trade, while provinces manage areas such as education, health care, and local governance.

Common Law and Civil Law Traditions

Canada operates under a dual legal system, influenced by both common law and civil law traditions. Common law principles, inherited from English law, form the basis of legal principles and judicial decisions in most provinces and territories. Quebec, however, follows a civil law system based on the Civil Code of Quebec, derived from French legal traditions. This dual legal heritage allows for legal diversity and accommodates regional differences within the Canadian legal framework.

Legal Institutions

Canada's legal institutions include federal and provincial courts, each with distinct jurisdictions and functions. The Supreme Court of Canada serves as the highest appellate court, interpreting the Constitution and resolving disputes involving federal laws and constitutional rights. Provincial courts handle matters related to provincial laws, including civil disputes, family law, and criminal offences under provincial statutes.

7.3 Constitutional and Federal Structures

The Constitution Act, of 1867, and the Constitution Act, 1982 (which includes the Canadian Charter of Rights and Freedoms), form the constitutional framework of Canada. These documents outline the division of powers between federal and provincial governments, establish fundamental rights and freedoms for Canadian citizens, and provide a mechanism for amending the Constitution.

Federalism ensures a balance of powers between the federal government and provinces, allowing each level of government to legislate on matters within their jurisdiction. This structure promotes autonomy for provinces while maintaining a cohesive national legal framework under federal authority.

7.4 Business and Corporate Law in North America

Business and corporate law in North America encompasses a comprehensive set of regulations and statutes governing commercial activities, corporate governance, and investor protections. In the United States and Canada, business laws aim to foster economic growth, protect shareholder interests, and ensure fair competition in domestic and international markets.

Both countries have robust legal frameworks that regulate corporate formation, operation, mergers and acquisitions, securities offerings, and corporate governance practices. Regulatory agencies such as the U.S. Securities and Exchange Commission (SEC) and the Canadian Securities Administrators (CSA) oversee capital markets and enforce compliance with securities laws to safeguard investor confidence and market integrity.

The North American Free Trade Agreement (NAFTA), and its successor, the United States-Mexico-Canada Agreement (USMCA), facilitate cross-border trade and investment by harmonizing trade regulations, reducing barriers to market entry, and providing dispute resolution mechanisms for trade disputes.

In conclusion, the legal systems of the United States and Canada embody principles of constitutional governance, legal pluralism, and the rule of law. Understanding the foundational principles and institutional frameworks of these legal systems is essential for legal practitioners, policymakers, and stakeholders engaged in navigating the complexities of North American law and promoting legal certainty in diverse areas of practice.

Chapter 8: Key Principles of the Pakistan Legal System

8.1 Historical Development of Pakistani Law

The legal system of Pakistan is deeply rooted in a rich historical and cultural context, shaped by various influences over centuries. Understanding its evolution provides crucial insights into the principles and institutions that define contemporary Pakistani law.

Pre-Partition Influences

Before the partition of British India in 1947, the region now comprising Pakistan was governed under British colonial rule. The British introduced a common law system, heavily influenced by English legal principles and judicial precedents. This legal framework laid the foundation for the development of modern legal institutions and practices in Pakistan.

Post-Independence Legal Framework

Following independence, Pakistan adopted a legal system that blends elements of Islamic law (Sharia), common law, and statutory law. The Constitution of Pakistan, promulgated in 1956 and subsequently amended, serves as the supreme law of the land, establishing a federal parliamentary democratic republic.

Islamic Law (Sharia)

Islamic law, derived from the Quran and Sunnah (teachings and practices of Prophet Muhammad), plays a significant role in Pakistan's legal system, particularly in matters concerning family law, inheritance, and personal status. Sharia courts, known as Qazi courts, adjudicate cases involving Islamic principles under the supervision of religious scholars (Ulema).

Legal Institutions and Judiciary
Pakistan's judiciary comprises a hierarchical system of courts, including the Supreme Court of Pakistan as the apex judicial authority. The judiciary interprets laws, safeguards constitutional rights, and resolves disputes between federal and provincial governments. Lower courts, including high courts and district courts, handle civil, criminal, and constitutional matters based on their respective jurisdictions.

Business and Corporate Law
Business and corporate law in Pakistan encompasses regulations governing corporate formation, governance, and commercial transactions. The Securities and Exchange Commission of Pakistan (SECP) regulates securities markets, ensuring transparency, investor protection, and market stability. Company laws prescribe requirements for corporate governance, shareholder rights, and financial reporting, aligning with international standards to promote investment and economic growth.

Challenges and Reforms
Pakistan's legal system faces challenges related to judicial efficiency, access to justice, and legal reforms. Efforts are ongoing to enhance judicial independence, streamline court procedures, and improve legal education and training. Legislative reforms aim to address socioeconomic disparities, strengthen the rule of law, and uphold constitutional rights and freedoms for all citizens.

In conclusion, the Pakistan legal system reflects a blend of historical influences, Islamic principles, and modern legal institutions. Understanding its foundational principles and contemporary developments is essential for legal professionals, policymakers, and stakeholders engaged in navigating Pakistan's dynamic legal landscape and promoting socio-economic development through effective legal governance.

8.2 Constitutional Framework

The constitutional framework of Pakistan provides the fundamental principles and structure of governance for the country. Pakistan's current constitution, adopted in 1973, outlines the rights and duties of citizens, the distribution of powers between federal and provincial governments, and the establishment of key institutions of state.

The Constitution of Pakistan is based on Islamic principles while also incorporating democratic norms and fundamental rights. It establishes a federal parliamentary system with a President as the head of state and a Prime Minister as the head of government. The constitution delineates the powers and functions of the executive, legislative, and judicial branches, ensuring a system of checks and balances.

8.3 Judicial System and Legal Institutions

Pakistan's judicial system consists of a hierarchical structure with multiple tiers of courts at the federal and provincial levels. At the apex is the Supreme Court of Pakistan, which serves as the final court of appeal and adjudicates constitutional matters. The Supreme Court interprets the constitution, resolves disputes between federal and provincial governments, and safeguards fundamental rights.

Below the Supreme Court are high courts in each province, which have jurisdiction over civil and criminal cases within their respective territories. District and session courts operate at the district level, handling trials and adjudicating cases under both civil and criminal law. Specialized courts, such as family courts and anti-terrorism courts, address specific legal issues and ensure expedient justice.

Legal institutions in Pakistan also include the Federal Shariat Court, which interprets laws following Islamic principles, and the Judicial Commission, responsible for judicial appointments and overseeing the judiciary's functioning.

8.4 Business and Corporate Law in Pakistan

Business and corporate law in Pakistan encompasses regulations governing commercial activities, corporate governance, and investor protections. The Securities and Exchange Commission of Pakistan (SECP) regulates corporate entities and capital markets, ensuring transparency, investor confidence, and market integrity.

Company law in Pakistan prescribes requirements for the formation, management, and dissolution of companies, protecting shareholder rights and regulating corporate transactions. The Companies Act, of 2017, modernizes corporate governance practices, enhances transparency, and aligns Pakistan's regulatory framework with international standards.

Pakistan's legal framework for business also includes laws on contracts, taxation, intellectual property, and competition, providing a conducive environment for investment and economic growth. Legal reforms continue to address challenges in corporate governance, streamline regulatory processes, and promote sustainable development.

In conclusion, Pakistan's legal system is shaped by its constitutional framework, judicial institutions, and laws governing business and corporate affairs. Understanding these key principles is essential for legal professionals, policymakers, and investors seeking to navigate Pakistan's evolving legal landscape and contribute to its socio-economic development.

Chapter 9: Key Principles of the SAARC Countries (India, Bangladesh, Nepal, Sri Lanka) Legal System

9.1 Overview of SAARC Legal Systems

The legal systems of the South Asian Association for Regional Cooperation (SAARC) countries—India, Bangladesh, Nepal, and Sri Lanka—reflect diverse historical, cultural, and legal influences. Despite these variations, commonalities exist in their legal frameworks, shaped by shared colonial legacies and Indigenous legal traditions.

Colonial Legacy and Common Law

Most SAARC countries inherited a common law system from their former colonial rulers, primarily British colonialism. This legal tradition emphasizes judicial precedents, case law, and principles derived from English legal doctrines. India and Sri Lanka, for instance, retain common law principles in their legal systems, influencing judicial decisions and legal interpretations.

Civil Law Traditions

In contrast, Bangladesh and Nepal predominantly follow civil law systems, rooted in codified laws and statutes derived from continental European legal traditions. Civil law systems emphasize legislative enactments and written laws, with judges interpreting laws based on statutory provisions rather than relying heavily on judicial precedents.

Islamic Law (Sharia) Influence

Islamic law (Sharia) significantly influences legal systems in SAARC countries with substantial Muslim populations, such as India and Bangladesh. Sharia governs personal status matters, including marriage, divorce, inheritance, and religious practices, operating alongside secular laws in family courts and religious institutions.

Constitutional Frameworks

Each SAARC country has a unique constitutional framework that establishes the structure of government, defines the separation of powers, and guarantees fundamental rights and freedoms. India, the largest SAARC member, has a federal system with a written constitution, ensuring the division of powers between the central government and states.

Judicial Systems

SAARC countries maintain hierarchical judicial systems with apex courts serving as the final arbiters of legal disputes and constitutional matters. The Supreme Court of India, for instance, interprets the constitution, safeguards fundamental rights, and resolves disputes between states and the central government.

Business and Corporate Law

Business and corporate law in SAARC countries regulates commercial activities, corporate governance, and investor protection. These legal frameworks aim to promote economic growth, attract foreign investment, and ensure fair competition in regional and global markets. Regulations governing company formation, mergers and acquisitions, securities markets, and intellectual property rights vary across SAARC jurisdictions, reflecting national priorities and international standards.

Challenges and Reforms

SAARC countries face challenges related to judicial delays, access to justice, and legal reforms aimed at enhancing judicial efficiency, transparency, and accountability. Efforts to modernize legal institutions, harmonize laws across borders, and strengthen the rule of law are essential for fostering regional cooperation and socio-economic development within the SAARC region.

In conclusion, understanding the key principles of SAARC legal systems provides insights into the complexities and nuances of legal governance in diverse cultural and socio-economic contexts. Legal professionals, policymakers, and stakeholders benefit from this knowledge to navigate legal landscapes, promote regional integration, and advance justice and development goals across SAARC countries.

9.2 Comparative Constitutional Structures

SAARC countries exhibit diverse constitutional structures that reflect their historical, cultural, and political contexts.

India, as the largest SAARC member, operates under a federal system with a written constitution. The Constitution of India, adopted in 1950, delineates powers between the central government and states, ensuring a balance of authority and autonomy. The Supreme Court of India interprets the constitution, resolves disputes, and upholds fundamental rights.

Bangladesh follows a unitary parliamentary democracy with a written constitution. The Constitution of Bangladesh, adopted in 1972 and amended multiple times, establishes the President as the head of state and the Prime Minister as the head of government. The judiciary, led by the Supreme Court of Bangladesh, safeguards constitutional rights and ensures legal stability.

Nepal embraces a federal democratic republic under its constitution adopted in 2015. Nepal's constitution divides powers between federal, provincial, and local governments, promoting decentralization and inclusivity. The Supreme Court of Nepal oversees constitutional interpretations, upholding the rule of law and protecting fundamental freedoms.

Sri Lanka operates under a semi-presidential system with a written constitution. The Constitution of Sri Lanka, enacted in 1978 and amended thereafter, balances executive authority between the President and Prime Minister. The judiciary, including the Supreme Court of Sri Lanka, safeguards constitutional rights and adjudicates legal disputes.

9.3 Key Legal Institutions in SAARC Countries

Legal institutions in SAARC countries play pivotal roles in administering justice, interpreting laws, and ensuring legal certainty.

In **India**, the legal system includes the Supreme Court as the highest judicial authority, high courts in states, and district courts at the grassroots level. The judiciary upholds constitutional principles, resolves disputes, and safeguards civil liberties.

Bangladesh's legal institutions encompass the Supreme Court, which includes the Appellate Division and High Court Division. Specialized tribunals address specific legal issues, promoting judicial efficiency and access to justice.

Nepal's legal framework includes the Supreme Court, appellate courts, and district courts. The judiciary interprets laws, protects fundamental rights, and resolves legal disputes through constitutional review and appellate jurisdiction.

Sri Lanka's legal system comprises the Supreme Court, Court of Appeal, and district courts. The judiciary upholds the rule of law, safeguards constitutional rights, and ensures judicial independence in adjudicating legal matters.

9.4 Business and Corporate Law in SAARC Region

Business and corporate law in SAARC countries regulates commercial activities, corporate governance, and investor protections to promote economic growth and regional integration.

India's business and corporate laws encompass the Companies Act, Securities and Exchange Board of India (SEBI) regulations, and intellectual property laws. These frameworks govern company formation, corporate governance practices, securities markets, and competition law.

Bangladesh's legal framework includes the Companies Act, Securities and Exchange Commission (SEC) regulations, and intellectual property laws. These laws aim to enhance corporate transparency, protect investor rights, and facilitate business operations.

Nepal's business and corporate laws govern company registration, corporate governance norms, and commercial transactions. Legal reforms aim to attract foreign investment, promote entrepreneurship, and ensure regulatory compliance in business activities.

Sri Lanka's legal regime encompasses company law, securities regulations, and intellectual property rights protection. These laws foster a conducive environment for business expansion, safeguard investor interests, and uphold corporate accountability.

In conclusion, understanding the comparative constitutional structures, key legal institutions, and business and corporate laws in SAARC countries provides insights into legal governance, regional cooperation, and economic development. Legal professionals, policymakers, and stakeholders benefit from this knowledge to navigate legal landscapes, promote cross-border trade, and foster harmonious relations within the SAARC region.

Chapter 10: Law of Financial Crime

10.1 Types of Financial Crime

Financial crime encompasses a broad spectrum of illicit activities that undermine financial systems, exploit vulnerabilities, and harm individuals, businesses, and economies. Understanding the types of financial crime is crucial for effective detection, prevention, and enforcement within legal frameworks globally.

Fraud: Fraud involves deceit or misrepresentation for financial gain. Common types include investment fraud, insurance fraud, and credit card fraud. Perpetrators use false information or schemes to deceive victims and unlawfully obtain money or assets.

Money Laundering: Money laundering is the process of concealing the origins of illegally obtained money, typically through complex financial transactions. It involves three stages: placement (introducing illicit funds into the financial system), layering (conducting multiple transactions to obscure the source), and integration (legitimizing illicit funds through investments or purchases).

Bribery and Corruption: Bribery entails offering, giving, receiving, or soliciting something of value to influence the actions of an individual in a position of authority. Corruption involves misuse of public office for personal gain, undermining public trust and economic stability.

Insider Trading: Insider trading occurs when individuals trade stocks or securities based on non-public, material information about a company. It gives traders an unfair advantage and can harm market integrity and investor confidence.

Tax Evasion: Tax evasion involves illegally avoiding paying taxes owed to government authorities. Methods include underreporting income, inflating deductions, and using offshore accounts to conceal assets.

Cybercrime: Cybercrime includes various financial offences committed using digital technologies. These may involve hacking, phishing, identity theft, and ransomware attacks targeting financial institutions, businesses, or individuals.

Counterfeiting: Counterfeiting involves producing fake goods or currency to deceive consumers or defraud financial systems. It undermines intellectual property rights and poses risks to public safety and economic stability.

Embezzlement: Embezzlement occurs when individuals entrusted with managing funds or assets misappropriate them for personal use. It often involves breaches of trust within organizations or financial institutions.

Market Manipulation: Market manipulation involves illegal practices that distort market prices or trading volume. Examples include pump-and-dump schemes, where false information inflates stock prices for profit before selling off shares.

Terrorist Financing: Terrorist financing involves providing financial support to terrorist organizations or activities. It includes fundraising, money transfers, and illicit donations used to carry out terrorist acts or operations.

Conclusion

Addressing financial crime requires robust legal frameworks, international cooperation, and proactive measures from financial institutions and regulatory authorities. Effective enforcement, transparency in financial transactions, and compliance with anti-money laundering (AML) and counter-terrorism financing (CTF) regulations are essential to combatting financial crime and safeguarding global financial stability. Understanding the diverse types of financial crime equips legal professionals and policymakers with the tools to mitigate risks, protect stakeholders, and uphold the integrity of financial systems worldwide.

10.2 Legal Framework for Combating Financial Crime

The legal framework for combating financial crime involves comprehensive laws, regulations, and enforcement mechanisms designed to detect, investigate, and prosecute offenders. Key elements of this framework include:

Anti-Money Laundering (AML) Laws: AML laws require financial institutions to verify the identity of customers, monitor transactions for suspicious activity, and report suspicious transactions to authorities. These laws aim to prevent the integration of illicit funds into the financial system.

Counter-Terrorist Financing (CTF) Measures: CTF measures focus on disrupting financial support to terrorist organizations and activities. They include monitoring financial transactions, freezing assets linked to terrorism, and implementing sanctions against individuals and entities involved in terrorist financing.

Fraud and Corruption Laws: Laws against fraud and corruption criminalize deceptive practices, bribery, embezzlement, and other forms of financial misconduct. They establish penalties for offenders and mechanisms for recovering the proceeds of crime.

Securities and Insider Trading Regulations: Regulations governing securities markets aim to ensure transparency, fairness, and investor protection. Insider trading laws prohibit trading based on non-public, material information, promoting market integrity and preventing unfair advantages.

Cybercrime Legislation: Cybercrime laws address financial offences committed through digital platforms. They criminalize hacking, phishing, identity theft, and other cyber threats targeting financial institutions and individuals.

10.3 International Cooperation and Regulation

International cooperation and regulation are critical in addressing transnational financial crime, which often crosses borders and jurisdictions. Key aspects include:

Mutual Legal Assistance Treaties (MLATs): MLATs facilitate cooperation between countries in investigating and prosecuting financial crimes. They enable the sharing of information, evidence, and assets across borders to combat money laundering, fraud, and corruption.

Financial Action Task Force (FATF): FATF sets international standards and promotes effective implementation of AML and CTF measures globally. It conducts evaluations of countries' compliance with these standards and issues recommendations to strengthen national frameworks.

Regional and Bilateral Agreements: Regional organizations and bilateral agreements enhance collaboration in combating financial crime. They establish frameworks for information exchange, joint investigations, and coordinated enforcement actions against financial criminals.

Regulatory Harmonization: Harmonizing regulatory frameworks across jurisdictions facilitates the consistent application of laws and regulations. It reduces regulatory arbitrage, enhances legal certainty for businesses, and strengthens global efforts to combat financial crime.

10.4 Case Studies in Financial Crime

Case studies illustrate real-world examples of financial crime investigations, legal challenges, and enforcement actions. Examples include:

Enron Scandal (United States): The Enron scandal involved corporate fraud and accounting irregularities that led to the bankruptcy of Enron Corporation in 2001. It highlighted weaknesses in corporate governance and regulatory oversight.

Libor Manipulation (Global): The manipulation of the London Interbank Offered Rate (Libor) involved financial institutions falsely reporting interest rates to profit from derivative trades. It resulted in significant fines and regulatory reforms to enhance benchmark rate integrity.

1MDB Scandal (Malaysia): The 1Malaysia Development Berhad (1MDB) scandal involved allegations of embezzlement and money laundering, implicating high-level officials and financial institutions in Malaysia and internationally. It underscored the risks of corruption and illicit financial flows.

Conclusion

Effective legal frameworks, international cooperation, and case studies play crucial roles in combating financial crime and promoting global financial integrity. Strengthening regulatory compliance, enhancing transparency, and fostering collaboration among stakeholders is essential in addressing evolving threats and safeguarding financial systems worldwide. Understanding the complexities and impacts of financial crime equips legal professionals and policymakers with the tools needed to mitigate risks, protect stakeholders, and uphold the rule of law in the global financial landscape.

Chapter 11: Law of International Finance Syndicated Loans

11.1 Principles of Syndicated Loans

Syndicated loans are pivotal instruments in international finance, facilitating large-scale funding for corporations, governments, and other entities. Understanding the principles governing syndicated loans is essential for legal professionals navigating the complexities of global finance.

Definition and Structure: Syndicated loans involve multiple lenders jointly providing funds to a borrower under a single loan agreement. This structure allows lenders to share the risk and liquidity requirements associated with financing large projects or acquisitions.

Key Parties Involved: The primary parties in syndicated loans include the borrower, lead arrangers (who structure and arrange the loan), syndicate members (lenders participating in the loan), and administrative agents (responsible for managing the loan post-closing).

Loan Documentation: Syndicated loan agreements detail terms such as loan amount, interest rates, repayment schedules, covenants, and default provisions. Documentation is complex, reflecting negotiations among lenders and borrowers to balance risk allocation and borrower needs.

Legal Framework: Syndicated loans are governed by comprehensive legal frameworks encompassing contract law, banking regulations, securities laws (if applicable), and international finance conventions. Jurisdictional considerations and choice of law clauses are crucial in resolving disputes and enforcing contractual obligations across borders.

Risk Management: Legal professionals play a critical role in assessing and mitigating risks associated with syndicated loans. They ensure compliance with regulatory requirements, negotiate favourable terms for clients, and address legal implications of default or restructuring.

Market Practices and Standards: Syndicated loan markets operate under established practices and standards, influenced by market conditions, borrower creditworthiness, and lender preferences. Legal professionals monitor market developments to advise clients on optimal financing strategies.

Challenges and Innovations: Evolving regulatory landscapes, economic conditions, and technological advancements present challenges and opportunities in syndicated lending. Legal expertise is vital in navigating regulatory changes, leveraging fintech solutions, and structuring innovative financing arrangements.

Conclusion

Syndicated loans are integral to international finance, providing flexible and efficient financing solutions for diverse global transactions. Legal professionals specializing in syndicated loans navigate intricate legal frameworks, facilitate transactional efficiencies, and safeguard client interests in a dynamic and competitive global financial environment. Understanding the principles, practices, and legal complexities of syndicated loans equips professionals to effectively support clients in achieving their strategic financial objectives and managing risks inherent in complex international finance transactions.

11.2 Legal Framework for Syndicated Lending

Syndicated lending operates within a robust legal framework that spans international, national, and contractual laws. This framework ensures clarity, enforceability, and protection of rights for all parties involved in syndicated loan transactions.

Contractual Arrangements: Syndicated loans are governed by detailed loan agreements that outline the rights, obligations, and responsibilities of the borrower and syndicate members.

These agreements incorporate legal principles such as contract law, specifying loan terms, repayment schedules, interest rates, and conditions precedent.

Banking and Financial Regulations: Regulatory requirements impact syndicated lending, influencing aspects such as capital adequacy, disclosures, and lender responsibilities. Compliance with banking regulations ensures transparency, stability, and fairness in financial markets, enhancing investor confidence and borrower protection.

Securities and Exchange Laws: In cases where syndicated loans involve securities, securities laws regulate issuance, trading, and disclosure requirements. Compliance with these laws mitigates risks associated with securities-linked syndicated loans and ensures investor protection.

Jurisdiction and Choice of Law: Syndicated loans often involve parties from different jurisdictions, requiring careful consideration of jurisdictional rules and choice of law provisions. Legal professionals navigate these complexities to determine applicable laws for contract interpretation, dispute resolution, and enforcement of rights.

11.3 Risk Management in Syndicated Loans

Risk management is pivotal in syndicated lending to safeguard lender interests, manage borrower risks, and ensure loan repayment. Key aspects of risk management include:

Credit Risk Assessment: Legal professionals assess borrower creditworthiness through due diligence, financial analysis, and evaluation of industry trends. This helps mitigate default risks and informs loan structuring decisions.

Documentation and Covenants: Comprehensive loan documentation includes financial covenants, reporting requirements, and default provisions. Legal oversight ensures alignment with lender expectations and facilitates timely detection and response to potential risks.

Market and Operational Risks: Legal advisors monitor market conditions, regulatory changes, and operational risks affecting syndicated loans. They provide strategic counsel to mitigate risks associated with interest rate fluctuations, currency exchange, and geopolitical factors.

Collateral and Security Arrangements: Legal expertise is crucial in negotiating and structuring collateral and security arrangements to secure lender interests. This includes assessing the value and enforceability of collateral assets and optimizing security structures to enhance loan recoverability.

11.4 Case Studies in International Syndicated Loans

Case studies illustrate real-world applications and legal implications of syndicated lending across diverse sectors and jurisdictions. Examples include:

Airline Industry Financing: Syndicated loans support aircraft acquisitions and fleet expansions, requiring legal expertise in aviation regulations, cross-border financing, and aircraft collateralization.

Infrastructure Projects: Large-scale infrastructure projects, such as energy facilities and transportation networks, utilize syndicated loans to fund construction and operational phases. Legal advisors navigate project finance structures, regulatory approvals, and environmental considerations.

Cross-Border Mergers and Acquisitions: Syndicated loans facilitate financing for cross-border mergers and acquisitions, involving complex legal due diligence, antitrust regulations, and compliance with international transaction laws.

Conclusion

Syndicated lending plays a pivotal role in global finance, offering flexible financing solutions for complex transactions and projects. Legal professionals specializing in syndicated loans navigate intricate legal frameworks, mitigate risks, and optimize financing structures to support client objectives and uphold regulatory compliance. Understanding the legal framework, risk management strategies, and practical applications of syndicated loans empowers professionals to facilitate successful transactions and foster sustainable economic growth in a dynamic global marketplace.

Chapter 12: Law of International Project Finance

12.1 Fundamentals of Project Finance

Project finance is a specialized funding mechanism essential for large-scale infrastructure and development projects worldwide. It involves structuring financial arrangements that are uniquely tailored to the specific project's risks and revenue streams rather than solely relying on the creditworthiness of the project sponsors. Understanding the fundamentals of project finance is crucial for legal professionals navigating the complexities of international finance and infrastructure development.

Key Components of Project Finance:

1. **Project Cash Flow:** Project finance relies on the projected cash flows generated by the project itself to repay debt and provide returns to investors. Legal advisors analyze revenue forecasts, cost estimates, and financial models to assess the project's viability and financial sustainability.

2. **Special Purpose Vehicle (SPV):** Projects are often structured through an SPV, a legal entity created solely to own, operate, and finance the project. SPVs ring-fence project risks and liabilities from sponsors and investors, enhancing project bankability and creditworthiness.

3. **Risk Allocation:** Project finance involves meticulous risk assessment and allocation among stakeholders, including lenders, sponsors, contractors, and government entities. Legal frameworks and contractual agreements define risk-sharing mechanisms, insurance requirements, and dispute-resolution procedures to mitigate project risks effectively.

4. **Legal and Regulatory Environment**: Legal advisors navigate diverse legal systems, regulatory frameworks, and government policies impacting project finance. They ensure compliance with environmental regulations, permitting requirements, tax laws, and international treaties to facilitate project development and financing.
5. **Financing Structures**: Project finance structures vary based on project complexity, industry sector, and financing sources. Common structures include debt financing, equity investments, mezzanine financing, and hybrid instruments tailored to optimize capital structure and financial returns.

Legal Challenges and Considerations:
1. **Complex Contracts**: Project finance involves intricate contractual arrangements, including loan agreements, concession agreements, off-take agreements, and construction contracts. Legal professionals draft, negotiate, and enforce these contracts to protect client interests and ensure project viability.
2. **Political and Sovereign Risks**: International projects face political instability, regulatory changes, and sovereign risks that impact project finance. Legal advisors assess geopolitical risks, negotiate political risk insurance, and structure legal protections to safeguard investor interests and project continuity.
3. **Cross-Border Transactions**: Project finance transactions span multiple jurisdictions, requiring expertise in cross-border legal issues, jurisdictional conflicts, and choice of law considerations. Legal advisors facilitate transactional efficiency, resolve legal uncertainties, and mitigate cross-border legal risks.

Case Studies in International Project Finance:

1. **Renewable Energy Projects**: Solar, wind, and hydropower projects utilize project finance to fund infrastructure investments and achieve renewable energy targets. Legal advisors navigate regulatory incentives, environmental permits, and power purchase agreements to secure project financing.
2. **Infrastructure Development**: Transportation, telecommunications, and healthcare infrastructure projects rely on project finance to modernize infrastructure networks and enhance public services. Legal professionals negotiate public-private partnerships (PPP), infrastructure concessions, and funding mechanisms to accelerate project implementation.
3. **Natural Resource Exploitation**: Mining, oil, and gas exploration projects utilize project finance to fund capital-intensive operations and mitigate resource extraction risks. Legal advisors address environmental compliance, community engagement, and revenue-sharing agreements to promote sustainable resource development.

Conclusion

Project finance is pivotal in financing transformative infrastructure projects and driving economic growth globally. Legal professionals specializing in international project finance play a crucial role in structuring transactions, managing legal risks, and fostering public-private collaborations to support sustainable development goals. Understanding the fundamentals, legal complexities, and practical applications of project finance equips professionals to navigate diverse legal landscapes, facilitate successful project financing, and contribute to global infrastructure advancement and economic prosperity.

12.2 Legal and Regulatory Framework

The legal and regulatory framework underpinning international project finance encompasses a complex interplay of laws, regulations, and governmental policies across multiple jurisdictions. Understanding these frameworks is essential for legal professionals navigating the intricacies of financing large-scale infrastructure and development projects globally.

Jurisdictional Considerations: Project finance transactions often involve stakeholders from different jurisdictions, each with distinct legal systems and regulatory requirements. Legal advisors analyze jurisdictional issues, choice of law provisions, and regulatory compliance to ensure alignment with project goals and mitigate legal risks.

Governmental Approvals and Permits: International projects require various governmental approvals, permits, and licenses to proceed with construction and operation. Legal experts facilitate regulatory approvals, environmental assessments, and compliance with local laws to secure project viability and mitigate regulatory risks.

Contractual Agreements: Project finance relies on comprehensive contractual agreements, including loan agreements, concession agreements, construction contracts, and off-take agreements. Legal professionals draft, negotiate, and enforce these agreements to define rights, obligations, and responsibilities among project stakeholders, ensuring project bankability and investor confidence.

Financial Regulations: Regulatory compliance in project finance encompasses financial reporting standards, capital adequacy requirements, and banking regulations impacting lenders and investors. Legal advisors navigate financial regulations to optimize project financing structures, mitigate financial risks, and enhance project sustainability.

12.3 Risk Allocation and Management

Effective risk allocation and management are critical to the success of international project finance. Legal professionals collaborate with stakeholders to identify, assess, and mitigate project risks through strategic risk management frameworks and contractual arrangements.

Risk Assessment: Legal advisors conduct comprehensive risk assessments, analyzing technical, environmental, political, and economic risks impacting project feasibility and financial viability. They develop risk mitigation strategies tailored to project-specific challenges, ensuring proactive risk management throughout the project lifecycle.

Contractual Risk Allocation: Project finance involves intricate risk allocation mechanisms within contractual agreements. Legal experts negotiate risk-sharing provisions, force majeure clauses, and indemnification terms to protect parties against unforeseen events, minimize financial exposure, and facilitate dispute resolution.

Insurance and Guarantees: Legal advisors facilitate insurance coverage and guarantees to mitigate project risks, including political risk insurance, construction insurance, and performance guarantees. They negotiate insurance terms, coverage limits, and claims procedures to safeguard investor interests and ensure project continuity.

Project Monitoring and Compliance: Legal oversight includes monitoring project performance, compliance with regulatory requirements, and contractual obligations. Legal professionals provide ongoing counsel, review project milestones, and address legal challenges to support project execution and mitigate operational risks.

12.4 Case Studies in Project Finance

Case studies illustrate real-world applications and legal complexities of international project finance across diverse sectors and regions. Examples include:

1. **Infrastructure Development**: Public-private partnerships (PPPs) finance transportation, energy, and healthcare infrastructure projects, leveraging legal expertise in concession agreements, regulatory approvals, and financing structures.
2. **Renewable Energy Investments**: Solar and wind energy projects utilize project finance to fund capital-intensive installations, requiring legal navigation of renewable energy incentives, power purchase agreements (PPAs), and environmental regulations.
3. **Natural Resource Exploration**: Mining and oil & gas projects secure project finance for resource exploration and development, involving legal negotiations of resource concessions, environmental permits, and revenue-sharing agreements.

Conclusion

International project finance plays a pivotal role in funding transformative infrastructure projects worldwide. Legal professionals specializing in project finance navigate complex legal and regulatory landscapes, facilitate stakeholder collaborations, and mitigate risks to promote sustainable economic development. Understanding the legal framework, risk management strategies, and practical applications of project finance equips professionals to drive successful project outcomes, foster investor confidence, and contribute to global infrastructure advancement and prosperity.

Chapter 13: Law of International Taxation

13.1 Principles of International Taxation

International taxation encompasses the principles, rules, and regulations governing the taxation of cross-border transactions, investments, and income flows between different countries. Legal professionals specializing in international taxation navigate a complex landscape shaped by domestic tax laws, bilateral tax treaties, and international tax norms to facilitate compliant and efficient tax planning strategies for multinational corporations, individuals, and entities engaged in global commerce.

Key Principles:

1. **Residency and Sourcing Rules**: International taxation hinges on determining the tax residency of individuals and entities and the sourcing of income across jurisdictions. Legal advisors apply residency rules to establish tax liabilities and obligations based on where income is earned or derived.

2. **Double Taxation Treaties**: Bilateral and multilateral tax treaties play a pivotal role in preventing double taxation and promoting international trade and investment. Legal professionals interpret treaty provisions, including definitions of permanent establishment, withholding tax rates, and dispute resolution mechanisms, to optimize tax outcomes and mitigate tax burdens for taxpayers engaged in cross-border activities.

3. **Transfer Pricing Regulations**: Transfer pricing rules govern the pricing of transactions between related parties in different tax jurisdictions. Legal advisors ensure compliance with transfer pricing regulations, including documentation requirements, arm's length principles, and contemporaneous documentation, to

align intercompany transactions with market realities and prevent tax base erosion.

4. **Tax Treatments of Cross-Border Transactions**: International tax law addresses the tax implications of various cross-border transactions, such as mergers and acquisitions, cross-border investments, and international trade. Legal experts analyze transaction structures, tax implications, and treaty benefits to optimize tax efficiency, minimize tax risks, and ensure regulatory compliance across jurisdictions.

5. **Tax Planning and Compliance**: Legal professionals collaborate with clients to develop strategic tax planning initiatives tailored to their business operations and international footprint. They guide tax-efficient structures, repatriation strategies, and compliance with global tax reporting obligations to mitigate tax exposure and enhance corporate governance.

Legal Challenges and Considerations:

1. **BEPS and Global Tax Transparency**: Base Erosion and Profit Shifting (BEPS) initiatives by the OECD and global tax transparency requirements pose challenges for multinational enterprises (MNEs) in managing tax risks and compliance obligations. Legal advisors navigate evolving BEPS regulations, country-by-country reporting requirements, and automatic exchange of information to ensure regulatory compliance and reputational risk management.

2. **Digital Economy and E-commerce**: The digital economy presents unique challenges in international taxation, including the taxation of digital services, remote sales, and data-driven business models. Legal professionals monitor digital tax reforms, nexus rules, and digital permanent establishment concepts to

address tax challenges posed by digital transactions and e-commerce activities.
3. **Cross-Border Tax Disputes**: International tax disputes arise from conflicting interpretations of tax laws, transfer pricing adjustments, and treaty interpretations between tax authorities and taxpayers. Legal advisors employ dispute resolution mechanisms, including mutual agreement procedures (MAPs) under tax treaties and competent authority negotiations, to resolve cross-border tax disputes and avoid double taxation.

Case Studies in International Taxation:
1. **Global Transfer Pricing Disputes**: Transfer pricing disputes involving multinational corporations and tax authorities highlight the complexities of applying arm's length principles and resolving intercompany pricing disputes across multiple jurisdictions.
2. **Tax Treaty Benefits in Cross-Border Investments**: Case studies demonstrate the application of tax treaty benefits, including reduced withholding tax rates on dividends, interest, and royalties, in facilitating cross-border investments and promoting economic cooperation between treaty countries.
3. **Tax Planning Strategies for MNEs**: Successful tax planning strategies adopted by multinational enterprises illustrate the importance of proactive tax risk management, compliance with anti-avoidance rules, and leveraging tax incentives and exemptions to optimize global tax outcomes.

Conclusion
International taxation is integral to global economic integration and corporate strategy, shaping cross-border investments, trade flows, and multinational operations. Legal professionals specializing in international taxation play a critical role in

navigating regulatory complexities, mitigating tax risks, and optimizing tax efficiency for clients operating in diverse jurisdictions. Understanding the foundational principles, legal challenges, and practical applications of international taxation equips professionals to provide strategic tax advice, ensure compliance with evolving tax regulations, and support sustainable business growth in the interconnected global marketplace.

13.2 Double Taxation Treaties

Double taxation treaties (DTTs) are bilateral agreements between countries aimed at eliminating the potential for double taxation of income earned by residents of one country in another country. These treaties establish rules for allocating taxing rights between jurisdictions to prevent income from being taxed twice—once in the country where it is earned (source country) and again in the country where the taxpayer resides (residence country). Key aspects of double taxation treaties include:

- **Residency Rules**: DTTs define criteria for determining an individual's or entity's tax residency status, which is crucial in allocating taxing rights and entitlement to treaty benefits.
- **Allocation of Taxing Rights**: They specify which country has the primary right to tax certain types of income, such as dividends, interest, royalties, and capital gains. This allocation helps ensure that income is taxed only once, either in the source country or the residence country.
- **Withholding Tax Rates**: DTTs often include provisions for reducing or eliminating withholding taxes on cross-border payments of dividends, interest, and royalties.

These reduced rates promote international trade and investment by lowering the cost of capital flows between treaty partners.
- **Dispute Resolution Mechanisms**: They provide procedures for resolving disputes between tax authorities from different countries concerning the application or interpretation of treaty provisions. These mechanisms typically include mutual agreement procedures (MAPs) and arbitration, ensuring that taxpayers have the means to resolve disputes and avoid double taxation.

13.3 Transfer Pricing Regulations

Transfer pricing regulations govern the pricing of transactions between related entities within multinational enterprises (MNEs). These regulations ensure that transactions are conducted at arm's length—that is, under conditions that would prevail in independent transactions between unrelated parties. Key aspects of transfer pricing regulations include:

- **Arm's Length Principle**: The cornerstone of transfer pricing rules, requiring that transactions between related entities be priced as if they were between unrelated parties. This principle prevents MNEs from artificially shifting profits to low-tax jurisdictions or improperly reducing taxable income in high-tax jurisdictions.
- **Documentation Requirements**: Tax authorities impose documentation requirements on MNEs to demonstrate compliance with transfer pricing rules. Documentation typically includes an expert file, local file, and country-by-country report detailing the MNE's global operations, intercompany transactions, and transfer pricing policies.

- **Advance Pricing Agreements (APAs)**: APAs allow MNEs to obtain certainty regarding the transfer pricing methods and pricing arrangements for specific transactions in advance. APAs reduce compliance costs, mitigate transfer pricing risks, and provide tax authorities and taxpayers with a transparent framework for determining arm's length pricing.
- **Transfer Pricing Audits and Adjustments**: Tax authorities conduct transfer pricing audits to assess compliance with transfer pricing rules and may adjust profits or prices if they determine that transactions do not meet the arm's length standard. Legal advisors assist MNEs in preparing for audits, responding to tax authority inquiries, and appealing transfer pricing adjustments.

13.4 Tax Planning and Compliance

Tax planning and compliance strategies are essential for multinational corporations, individuals, and entities to manage tax liabilities effectively while complying with domestic and international tax laws. Key elements of tax planning and compliance include:

- **Structuring Cross-Border Transactions**: Legal advisors assist clients in structuring cross-border transactions, investments, and operations to optimize tax efficiency while ensuring compliance with applicable tax laws and regulations.
- **Tax Optimization Strategies**: They develop tax optimization strategies tailored to the client's business objectives, industry dynamics, and geographic footprint. These strategies may include leveraging tax incentives, deductions, credits, and exemptions available under domestic laws and tax treaties.

- **Compliance with Regulatory Requirements**: Legal professionals ensure that clients comply with ongoing tax reporting obligations, including filing tax returns, disclosing foreign assets, and complying with anti-avoidance measures and substance requirements.
- **Risk Management and Contingency Planning**: They assess and mitigate tax risks associated with international operations, transfer pricing arrangements, and cross-border transactions. Legal advisors develop contingency plans and strategies to address potential tax disputes, audits, and regulatory challenges.

Conclusion

International taxation is a dynamic field shaped by evolving regulatory frameworks, bilateral agreements, and compliance requirements. Legal professionals specializing in international tax law play a pivotal role in advising clients on double taxation treaties, transfer pricing regulations, and tax planning strategies to optimize tax outcomes, ensure compliance, and mitigate risks in an increasingly interconnected global economy. Understanding the complexities of these areas equips legal practitioners with the expertise needed to navigate international tax challenges, support cross-border transactions, and foster sustainable business growth in a competitive global marketplace.

Chapter 14: Law of the Sea

14.1 Principles of Maritime Law

Maritime law, also known as admiralty law, encompasses a comprehensive framework of legal principles and regulations governing activities and issues related to the sea. It addresses various aspects crucial to maritime commerce, navigation, and environmental protection. Key principles of maritime law include:

- **Freedom of Navigation**: Fundamental to maritime law is the principle of freedom of navigation, ensuring that vessels have the right to sail across seas and navigate international waters without undue interference, subject to international law and regulations.
- **Maritime Zones and Boundaries**: Maritime law delineates different zones, including territorial waters, contiguous zones, exclusive economic zones (EEZs), and the high seas. Each zone has specific jurisdictional boundaries and rights concerning navigation, exploitation of resources, and environmental protection.
- **Sovereignty and Jurisdiction**: States exercise sovereignty over their territorial waters, enforcing laws and regulations within these zones. Additionally, states have jurisdiction over vessels flying their flag, subject to international conventions and treaties governing maritime activities.
- **Maritime Pollution and Environmental Protection**: Maritime law establishes rules and standards to prevent pollution of the marine environment, including regulations on oil spills, dumping of wastes, and protection of marine biodiversity. International agreements such as the International Convention for

the Prevention of Pollution from Ships (MARPOL) outline obligations for ship operators and states.
- **Maritime Contracts and Liability**: Admiralty law governs contracts and disputes related to maritime commerce, including charter parties, bills of lading, salvage, and marine insurance. It also addresses liability for maritime accidents, collisions, and cargo damage, determining responsibilities and compensation for losses.
- **International Conventions and Treaties**: The legal framework of maritime law is largely shaped by international conventions and treaties, such as the United Nations Convention on the Law of the Sea (UNCLOS). UNCLOS sets forth rules for maritime boundaries, navigation rights, jurisdictional limits, and environmental conservation, serving as a cornerstone of modern maritime governance.

Conclusion

Maritime law plays a crucial role in facilitating global trade, protecting marine resources, and ensuring maritime security. Legal practitioners specializing in this field navigate complex international regulations, represent clients in maritime disputes, and promote compliance with environmental standards and safety protocols. Understanding the principles of maritime law equips legal professionals with the knowledge and expertise to address diverse challenges in maritime commerce, contribute to sustainable development, and uphold the rights and responsibilities of stakeholders in the global maritime domain.

14.2 UNCLOS and Its Implications

The United Nations Convention on the Law of the Sea (UNCLOS), adopted in 1982, is a comprehensive international legal framework governing maritime affairs. UNCLOS establishes rules and principles concerning maritime boundaries, navigation rights, exploitation of marine resources, environmental protection, and dispute resolution. Key implications of UNCLOS include:

- **Maritime Zones**: UNCLOS defines various maritime zones, including territorial waters, contiguous zones, exclusive economic zones (EEZs), and the continental shelf. Each zone carries distinct rights and responsibilities for coastal states and international shipping.
- **Freedom of Navigation**: UNCLOS upholds the principle of freedom of navigation, ensuring that vessels of all nations have the right to sail through international waters and transit through straits used for international navigation.
- **Marine Resource Management**: UNCLOS provides guidelines for the management and exploitation of marine resources within national jurisdictions and the high seas. It establishes rights and obligations regarding fishing, seabed mining, and the protection of marine biodiversity.
- **Environmental Protection**: UNCLOS includes provisions for the conservation and sustainable use of marine resources, pollution prevention, and liability for environmental damage caused by maritime activities. It sets standards for ship pollution, marine scientific research, and the establishment of marine protected areas.

14.3 Maritime Boundaries and Jurisdiction

Maritime boundaries and jurisdiction under international law are crucial aspects of maritime disputes and governance. Key principles include:

- **Delimitation of Maritime Boundaries**: States use UNCLOS principles to determine maritime boundaries, especially in areas where overlapping claims exist. Delimitation involves factors such as geographic features, equitable principles, and historical maritime usage.
- **Exclusive Economic Zones (EEZs)**: Coastal states have sovereign rights within their EEZs, including jurisdiction over natural resources and the authority to regulate economic activities such as fishing, mining, and environmental protection.
- **Continental Shelf**: UNCLOS establishes criteria for the extension of a coastal state's continental shelf beyond its EEZ, based on geological and geomorphological factors. States must submit scientific data to the Commission on the Limits of the Continental Shelf for review and approval.
- **International Dispute Resolution**: UNCLOS provides mechanisms for resolving disputes between states concerning maritime boundaries, including negotiation, mediation, and compulsory dispute settlement procedures before international courts or arbitral tribunals.

14.4 Case Studies in Maritime Disputes

Maritime disputes under UNCLOS involve complex legal, geopolitical, and environmental issues. Case studies include:

- **South China Sea Disputes**: Multiple states claim sovereignty over islands, reefs, and maritime features in

the South China Sea, leading to disputes over maritime boundaries, EEZs, and the interpretation of historical rights under UNCLOS.
- **Arctic Ocean Claims**: States bordering the Arctic Ocean, including Russia, Canada, Denmark (Greenland), Norway, and the United States, assert territorial claims over the Arctic continental shelf, affecting access to natural resources and navigation rights.
- **Marine Environmental Disputes**: Cases involving pollution, illegal fishing, and environmental degradation in maritime areas highlight the importance of UNCLOS provisions on marine environmental protection and liability.

Conclusion

UNCLOS remains the cornerstone of international maritime law, providing a framework for cooperation, conflict resolution, and sustainable ocean governance. Legal practitioners specializing in the law of the sea navigate UNCLOS provisions, represent states and stakeholders in maritime disputes, and promote compliance with international standards for marine resource management and environmental conservation. Understanding UNCLOS implications and case studies equip legal professionals with the knowledge and tools to address contemporary challenges in maritime affairs and contribute to global efforts towards maritime security and sustainable development.

Chapter 15: Law of the World Trade Organization

15.1 Principles of WTO Law

The World Trade Organization (WTO) is a global international organization that deals with the rules of trade between nations. It operates a system of trade rules that govern international trade relations, covering goods, services, and intellectual property. Key principles of WTO law include:

- **Most-Favored-Nation (MFN) Principle**: Under WTO law, member countries must treat all other members equally, granting the same trade advantages and not discriminating between trading partners.
- **National Treatment**: WTO members must treat foreign goods, services, and nationals no less favourable than their own once goods and services have entered their market.
- **Tariffs and Trade Restrictions**: WTO law regulates the use of tariffs, quotas, and other trade restrictions to ensure they are transparent, predictable, and not arbitrarily applied.
- **Dispute Settlement**: The WTO has a comprehensive dispute settlement mechanism to resolve trade disputes between member countries, ensuring adherence to WTO agreements and resolving conflicts peacefully.
- **Trade Liberalization**: WTO agreements aim to reduce barriers to international trade through negotiations, fostering global economic integration and promoting fair competition among member states.
- **Special and Differential Treatment**: Recognizing the varying development levels of member countries, WTO law allows developing countries to receive special

treatment and flexibility in implementing trade agreements.
- **Intellectual Property Rights (TRIPS Agreement)**: The Agreement on Trade-Related Aspects of Intellectual Property Rights (TRIPS) sets international standards for the protection of intellectual property rights, ensuring minimum standards of protection and enforcement.
- **Trade in Services (GATS)**: The General Agreement on Trade in Services (GATS) regulates international trade in services, promoting transparency, openness, and non-discrimination in service sectors.
- **Trade and Environment**: WTO law addresses the relationship between trade and environmental protection, encouraging sustainable development and ensuring that trade measures do not undermine environmental objectives.
- **Trade and Development**: WTO agreements include provisions to support the development objectives of developing and least-developed countries, facilitating their integration into the global trading system.

Conclusion

The principles of WTO law form the foundation of international trade relations, promoting a rules-based system that facilitates predictable and mutually beneficial trade among nations. Legal practitioners specializing in WTO law navigate complex trade rules, represent member countries in dispute settlement proceedings, and advise on compliance with WTO agreements. Understanding the principles of WTO law equips legal professionals with the knowledge and expertise to address contemporary challenges in global trade, promote economic growth, and contribute to the advancement of international trade law and policy.

15.2 Dispute Settlement Mechanism

The dispute settlement mechanism of the World Trade Organization (WTO) is a cornerstone of international trade law, ensuring members abide by WTO agreements and resolve disputes in a timely and orderly manner. Key aspects of the WTO dispute settlement mechanism include:

- **Panel Establishment**: Disputes are adjudicated by panels composed of independent experts chosen by the disputing parties or appointed by the WTO Director-General. Panels examine the facts of the case and issue findings based on WTO agreements.
- **Appellate Body Review**: Appeals from panel decisions are heard by the WTO Appellate Body, a standing body of seven members. The Appellate Body reviews legal interpretations and findings of the panels and issues final rulings, which are binding on the parties involved.
- **Enforcement of Rulings**: WTO rulings are enforceable and binding. If a member country fails to bring its measures into compliance with WTO agreements within a reasonable period, the complaining party may seek authorization to retaliate through trade sanctions.
- **Transparency and Monitoring**: The dispute settlement process is transparent, with proceedings and rulings made publicly available. The WTO Secretariat monitors the implementation of rulings and reports on member countries' compliance with WTO decisions.
- **Preventative and Remedial Function**: The dispute settlement mechanism not only resolves disputes but also serves a preventative function by clarifying WTO rules and discouraging unilateral trade actions that could lead to disputes.

15.3 Trade Liberalization and Regulation

WTO law aims to promote trade liberalization while allowing member countries to regulate trade to achieve legitimate policy objectives. Key aspects of trade liberalization and regulation under WTO law include:

- **Market Access Commitments**: WTO agreements include commitments by member countries to reduce tariffs and other trade barriers through negotiations, promoting market access for goods and services.
- **Non-Discrimination Principles**: The MFN and national treatment principles ensure that member countries do not discriminate against foreign goods, services, or nationals in favour of domestic products, promoting fair competition.
- **Trade Remedies**: WTO agreements allow member countries to impose temporary trade remedies, such as anti-dumping duties and countervailing measures, to address unfair trade practices and protect domestic industries.
- **Technical Barriers to Trade (TBT)**: WTO agreements on TBT aim to ensure that technical regulations, standards, and conformity assessment procedures do not create unnecessary trade barriers while allowing countries to pursue legitimate objectives such as consumer protection and public health.
- **Sanitary and Phytosanitary Measures (SPS)**: The WTO SPS Agreement regulates food safety and animal and plant health measures, balancing the need to protect human, animal, and plant life to facilitate trade.

15.4 Case Studies in WTO Law

Case studies in WTO law illustrate the application of WTO principles and the resolution of trade disputes under the WTO dispute settlement mechanism. Examples include:

- **The US-China Trade Disputes**: Cases involving tariffs, subsidies, and intellectual property rights between the United States and China highlight disputes over market access, unfair trade practices, and the interpretation of WTO rules.
- **EU-US Airbus-Boeing Dispute**: Long-standing disputes between the European Union and the United States regarding subsidies to Airbus and Boeing have resulted in multiple WTO rulings and ongoing negotiations to achieve compliance with WTO decisions.
- **Trade Disputes in Agriculture**: Cases involving agricultural subsidies, import quotas, and sanitary measures illustrate the challenges of balancing trade liberalization with domestic policy objectives in agriculture.
- **Intellectual Property Rights Disputes**: WTO cases on intellectual property rights, including patent protection and copyright enforcement, demonstrate the role of WTO rules in balancing innovation incentives with access to essential medicines and cultural goods.

Conclusion

The World Trade Organization plays a crucial role in facilitating international trade, resolving disputes, and promoting economic growth through a rules-based system. Legal practitioners specializing in WTO law navigate complex trade rules, represent member countries in dispute settlement proceedings, and advise on compliance with WTO agreements. Case studies in WTO law provide valuable insights into the application of WTO principles in resolving trade disputes and advancing global trade relations. Understanding the dispute settlement mechanism, trade liberalization principles, and case studies equips legal professionals with the knowledge and expertise to address contemporary challenges in international trade law and contribute to the development of global trade policy.

Chapter 16: Law on Investment Entities

16.1 Types of Investment Entities

Investment entities play a pivotal role in global finance, facilitating capital flows and investment opportunities across various sectors and jurisdictions. Understanding the types of investment entities is essential for legal professionals specializing in investment law. Key types include:

1. **Investment Funds**: These are collective investment schemes that pool money from multiple investors to invest in securities or other assets. Types of investment funds include mutual funds, hedge funds, and exchange-traded funds (ETFs), each subject to specific regulatory frameworks.

2. **Private Equity Funds**: Private equity funds raise capital from institutional investors and high-net-worth individuals to acquire equity in private companies. They aim to enhance company performance, achieve capital appreciation, and eventually sell investments for a profit.

3. **Venture Capital Funds**: Venture capital funds provide financing to startups and small businesses with high growth potential. They typically invest in early-stage companies in exchange for equity stakes and play a crucial role in fostering innovation and entrepreneurship.

4. **Real Estate Investment Trusts (REITs)**: REITs are investment vehicles that own, operate, or finance income-producing real estate properties. They enable investors to access real estate assets without directly owning physical properties and benefit from potential rental income and property appreciation.

5. **Infrastructure Funds**: Infrastructure funds invest in public infrastructure projects such as transportation,

energy, and utilities. They provide long-term financing for essential infrastructure developments and contribute to economic growth and sustainability.

6. **Pension Funds**: Pension funds manage retirement savings and investments on behalf of pension beneficiaries. They invest in a diversified portfolio of assets, aiming to generate returns that ensure long-term pension obligations are met.
7. **Sovereign Wealth Funds (SWFs)**: SWFs are state-owned investment funds that manage a country's wealth derived from surplus revenues, such as oil or trade surpluses. They invest globally across various asset classes to diversify national wealth and generate returns for future generations.

Regulatory Framework for Investment Entities

Each type of investment entity operates within a specific regulatory framework designed to protect investors, ensure market integrity, and promote financial stability. Regulatory aspects include:

- **Securities Regulation**: Investment entities are subject to securities laws governing the issuance, trading, and reporting of securities to protect investors from fraud and ensure transparency in financial markets.
- **Investment Adviser Regulation**: Regulations govern the conduct and responsibilities of investment advisers who manage investment funds and provide investment advice to clients, ensuring fiduciary duties are upheld.
- **Compliance and Disclosure Requirements**: Investment entities must comply with disclosure requirements to provide investors with accurate and timely information about investment strategies, risks, and performance.

- **Risk Management and Governance**: Regulatory frameworks emphasize robust risk management practices and governance structures within investment entities to mitigate risks and safeguard investor interests.

Case Studies in Investment Law
Case studies in investment law illustrate the application of regulatory frameworks and legal principles in addressing complex issues faced by investment entities. Examples include:
- **Madoff Investment Scandal**: A case of securities fraud perpetrated by Bernard Madoff, highlighting failures in regulatory oversight and investor protection measures.
- **SEC v. Goldman Sachs**: A high-profile case involving allegations of securities fraud and misleading investors about mortgage-backed securities, leading to regulatory scrutiny and legal proceedings.
- **The Rise of ESG Investing**: Case studies on environmental, social, and governance (ESG) investing practices, showcasing how investment entities integrate sustainability criteria into investment decision-making.
- **Cross-Border Investment Disputes**: Cases involving disputes over foreign investment protection agreements (BITs) and investor-state arbitration illustrate challenges in enforcing investment protections and resolving disputes between investors and host states.

Conclusion
Understanding the types of investment entities, regulatory frameworks, and case studies in investment law is essential for legal professionals navigating the dynamic landscape of global finance. Specializing in investment law enables lawyers to advise clients on compliance, manage risks, and navigate legal complexities in the pursuit of investment opportunities. Case

studies provide valuable insights into the application of legal principles and regulatory requirements, contributing to the advancement of investment law and practice globally.

16.2 Legal Framework for Investment Funds

Investment funds operate under a structured legal framework that governs their formation, operation, and management. Key components of the legal framework for investment funds include:

- **Formation and Structure**: Investment funds are typically structured as collective investment schemes regulated by securities laws. The formation process involves drafting offering documents such as prospectuses or private placement memoranda (PPMs) that disclose fund objectives, strategies, risks, and terms to potential investors.
- **Regulatory Oversight**: Regulatory bodies, such as the Securities and Exchange Commission (SEC) in the United States or the Financial Conduct Authority (FCA) in the UK, oversee investment funds to ensure compliance with securities laws. Regulatory requirements encompass registration, reporting, disclosure, and periodic audits to protect investor interests and maintain market integrity.
- **Investment Restrictions**: Legal frameworks impose investment restrictions on funds to mitigate risks and safeguard investor capital. Restrictions may include limits on asset allocation, leverage, derivatives usage, and exposure to specific sectors or asset classes.
- **Fiduciary Duties**: Fund managers owe fiduciary duties to investors, requiring them to act in the best interests of fund beneficiaries. Duties include duty of care,

loyalty, and prudence in investment decision-making, ensuring transparency and accountability in fund operations.
- **Investor Protections**: Legal frameworks incorporate investor protections, such as anti-fraud provisions, fair dealing rules, and mechanisms for handling investor complaints or disputes. These protections aim to enhance investor confidence and promote market efficiency.

16.3 Regulation of Investment Entities

Regulation of investment entities encompasses a broad spectrum of rules and guidelines aimed at promoting transparency, protecting investors, and maintaining financial stability. Key aspects of regulation include:

- **Securities Regulation**: Investment entities must comply with securities laws governing the issuance, trading, and sale of securities to the public. Regulations address disclosure requirements, registration processes, and ongoing reporting obligations to ensure transparency and investor protection.
- **Investment Adviser Regulation**: Regulation extends to investment advisers who provide investment advice and manage client assets. Advisers must register with regulatory authorities, adhere to fiduciary duties, and disclose conflicts of interest to clients.
- **Compliance and Governance**: Regulatory frameworks mandate robust compliance programs and governance structures within investment entities. Compliance entails adhering to internal policies, conducting audits, and implementing risk management practices to mitigate operational and financial risks.

Market Conduct Regulations: Regulations govern market conduct, prohibiting insider trading, market manipulation, and deceptive practices that undermine market integrity. Regulatory bodies enforce rules through inspections, investigations, and enforcement actions to maintain fair and orderly markets.

16.4 Case Studies in Investment Law

Case studies in investment law provide practical insights into legal issues, regulatory challenges, and best practices in the investment industry. Examples include:

- **Bernie Madoff Ponzi Scheme**: A landmark case of securities fraud where Bernie Madoff operated a Ponzi scheme, deceiving investors, and regulators for decades. The case highlighted deficiencies in regulatory oversight and investor protections.
- **Hedge Fund Long-Term Capital Management (LTCM)**: The LTCM collapse in 1998 underscored risks associated with excessive leverage and complex derivatives strategies employed by hedge funds. Regulatory responses focused on enhancing risk management and systemic risk monitoring.
- **Investor-State Disputes**: Case studies on investor-state arbitration under international investment agreements (IIAs), involving disputes between foreign investors and host states over treaty violations or expropriation. Cases illustrate the arbitration process, treaty interpretation, and enforcement challenges.
- **Emerging Trends in ESG Investing**: Case studies on environmental, social, and governance (ESG) investing practices, demonstrating how investment entities integrate sustainability criteria into investment

decision-making. Regulatory developments promote ESG disclosure and impact measurement.

Conclusion

Understanding the legal framework for investment funds, regulatory oversight of investment entities, and case studies in investment law is crucial for legal professionals navigating the complexities of global finance. Specializing in investment law enables lawyers to advise clients on compliance, manage regulatory risks, and advocate for investor protection. Case studies provide valuable insights into legal challenges, regulatory responses, and evolving industry practices, contributing to the advancement of investment law and regulatory reform globally.

Chapter 17: Legal Research Skills and Methods

17.1 Fundamentals of Legal Research

Legal research is a foundational skill for legal professionals, encompassing systematic investigation, analysis, and synthesis of legal principles and sources. Key fundamentals include:

- **Understanding Legal Sources**: Legal research involves identifying and accessing primary sources such as statutes, regulations, and case law, and secondary sources like legal commentaries, treatises, and scholarly articles. Mastery of legal databases and libraries facilitates efficient information retrieval.

- **Research Methodologies**: Effective legal research employs structured methodologies to frame research questions, conduct comprehensive searches, and evaluate sources for relevance, authority, and currency. Methodologies include Boolean searching, citation analysis, and the use of legal indexes.

- **Analytical Skills**: Legal research develops critical analytical skills to interpret and apply legal principles, identify precedent, distinguish between binding and persuasive authorities, and synthesize complex legal issues into coherent arguments or advice.

- **Legal Writing and Analysis**: Research findings inform legal writing and analysis, enabling lawyers to draft pleadings, memoranda, opinions, contracts, and briefs supported by well-reasoned arguments and authority citations. Clarity, precision, and persuasiveness are essential in communicating legal conclusions.

- **Presentation of Legal Research**: Effective presentation of legal research involves organizing findings, documenting sources, and attributing legal authority accurately. Presentation formats range from formal legal briefs and court submissions to oral advocacy and client advisories.

- **Ethical Considerations**: Legal research adheres to ethical standards, respecting confidentiality, avoiding conflicts of interest, and upholding professional integrity. Ethical conduct ensures the reliability and credibility of research outcomes in legal practice.

Importance in Legal Practice

Legal research skills are indispensable in guiding strategic decision-making, resolving disputes, advising clients, and shaping legal arguments in diverse practice areas. Mastery of research methodologies and resources equips legal professionals to navigate complex legal landscapes, contribute to legal scholarship, and advocate for justice and equity in society.

Challenges and Innovations

Challenges in legal research include information overload, evolving digital platforms, and globalized legal systems requiring cross-jurisdictional expertise. Innovations such as artificial intelligence (AI), data analytics, and legal tech tools enhance research efficiency, automate routine tasks, and predict legal outcomes, transforming legal practice in the digital age.

Conclusion

Legal research skills are fundamental to the practice of law, empowering legal professionals to navigate legal complexities, uphold justice, and advance legal scholarship. Continuous refinement of research techniques, adaptation to technological advancements, and adherence to ethical standards ensure effective legal research contributes to informed decision-making and the evolution of legal doctrine globally.

17.2 Research Methodologies

Legal research methodologies encompass systematic approaches to gather, analyze, and synthesize legal information effectively. Key methodologies include:

- **Formulating Research Questions**: Identifying precise research questions guides the scope and direction of legal research. Questions may pertain to statutory interpretation, case law analysis, regulatory compliance, or comparative legal analysis across jurisdictions.
- **Utilizing Legal Databases**: Accessing comprehensive legal databases such as Westlaw, LexisNexis, and Hein Online facilitates efficient information retrieval. Utilizing advanced search features, Boolean operators, and database filters enhances the accuracy and relevance of research outcomes.
- **Primary and Secondary Sources**: Evaluating primary sources (e.g., statutes, regulations, case law) and secondary sources (e.g., legal treatises, law reviews) ensures a comprehensive understanding and validation of legal principles and precedents.
- **Citation Analysis**: Analyzing legal citations verifies the authority and relevance of legal sources cited in judicial opinions, legal briefs, and scholarly articles. Citation analysis aids in tracking legal developments, identifying influential precedents, and assessing legal arguments.
- **Comparative Legal Analysis**: Conducting comparative legal research involves examining legal principles, doctrines, and judicial interpretations across different jurisdictions. Comparative analysis enhances understanding of international law, harmonization efforts, and cross-border legal implications.

17.3 Legal Writing and Analysis

Legal writing and analysis are integral to communicating research findings, constructing persuasive arguments, and drafting legal documents. Key aspects include:

- **Clear and Concise Communication**: Effective legal writing conveys complex legal concepts clearly and concisely to diverse audiences, including clients, judges, and legal peers. Structuring arguments logically and using plain language enhances readability and comprehension.
- **Analytical Reasoning**: Legal analysis involves critically evaluating legal issues, applying relevant laws and precedents to factual scenarios, and predicting potential outcomes. Analytical reasoning supports informed decision-making, strategic planning, and legal advocacy.
- **Drafting Legal Documents**: Drafting skills encompass preparing legal memoranda, contracts, briefs, opinions, and pleadings that adhere to legal standards and formatting conventions. Precision in drafting minimizes ambiguities and strengthens legal arguments.
- **Persuasive Argumentation**: Effective legal writing incorporates persuasive techniques, such as logical reasoning, analogical reasoning, and rhetorical strategies, to influence judicial decisions, negotiate settlements, and advocate for client interests.

17.4 Presentation of Legal Research

Presentation of legal research involves communicating findings comprehensively and professionally in various formats and contexts:

- **Oral Advocacy**: Presenting legal arguments orally in court hearings, arbitration proceedings, or client

consultations requires articulating complex legal concepts persuasively and responding to judicial inquiries effectively.
- **Written Advocacy**: Drafting written submissions, including legal briefs, motions, and appellate briefs, involves organizing legal arguments coherently, supporting assertions with evidence and precedent, and adhering to court rules and procedural requirements.
- **Client Advisories**: Providing concise and actionable advice to clients involves synthesizing complex legal research into practical recommendations that align with client objectives, risk tolerance, and compliance requirements.
- **Academic and Professional Presentations**: Presenting legal research at conferences, seminars, or academic forums requires preparing engaging presentations, addressing audience questions, and contributing to legal scholarship and professional discourse.

Conclusion

Legal research skills encompass research methodologies, legal writing and analysis, and presentation techniques essential for legal professionals to navigate complex legal issues, advocate effectively, and contribute to legal scholarship and professional development. Continuous refinement of research strategies, adaptation to technological advancements, and adherence to ethical standards ensure robust legal research outcomes that inform legal practice and advance justice globally.

Chapter 18: Legal Tech/FinTech

18.1 Introduction to Legal Tech

Legal technology (Legal Tech) and financial technology (FinTech) represent innovative sectors that have transformed traditional legal and financial practices through technological advancements.

Legal Tech

Legal Tech encompasses a range of technologies designed to enhance efficiency, accuracy, and accessibility in legal services. Key components include:

- **Legal Research and Analytics**: Advanced search algorithms and AI-powered platforms streamline legal research, offering lawyers comprehensive access to case law, statutes, and regulatory materials. Predictive analytics assist in case outcome forecasting and strategy development.
- **Document Automation and Management**: Software tools automate document drafting, contract review, and compliance checks, reducing manual errors and enhancing workflow efficiency. Document management systems ensure secure storage, version control, and retrieval of legal documents.
- **E-Discovery and Litigation Support**: E-discovery tools facilitate electronic document review and data analysis in litigation, identifying relevant evidence, conducting keyword searches, and ensuring compliance with discovery obligations.
- **Online Dispute Resolution (ODR)**: ODR platforms provide alternative dispute resolution mechanisms through online mediation, arbitration, and negotiation. ODR enhances access to justice, reduces litigation costs, and expedites resolution of disputes.

FinTech
FinTech revolutionizes financial services through technology-driven innovations, including:
- **Payment Solutions**: Mobile payments, peer-to-peer transfers, and digital wallets enable seamless financial transactions, enhancing convenience and accessibility for consumers and businesses.
- **Blockchain and Cryptocurrencies**: Distributed ledger technology (DLT) and cryptocurrencies like Bitcoin and Ethereum facilitate secure, decentralized transactions, tokenization of assets, and smart contract automation.
- **Robo-Advisors and Algorithmic Trading**: Automated investment platforms (robo-advisors) provide personalized financial advice based on algorithms, optimizing portfolio management and asset allocation. Algorithmic trading algorithms execute trades based on pre-defined criteria, leveraging market data and analytics.
- **RegTech**: Regulatory technology (RegTech) solutions ensure compliance with financial regulations through automated reporting, risk assessment, and monitoring of regulatory changes. RegTech mitigates compliance costs and operational risks for financial institutions.

Integration and Future Trends
The convergence of Legal Tech and FinTech presents opportunities for synergistic innovations, such as RegTech applications in financial compliance, blockchain-enabled smart contracts in legal agreements, and AI-driven analytics in risk management. Future trends include enhanced cybersecurity measures, the adoption of AI in legal research and predictive modelling, and regulatory developments to govern emerging technologies.

Conclusion

Legal Tech and FinTech continue to reshape legal and financial landscapes, offering transformative solutions that improve operational efficiency, enhance client service delivery, and foster innovation-driven growth. Legal professionals and financial stakeholders must adapt to technological advancements, embrace interdisciplinary collaboration, and uphold ethical standards to harness the full potential of Legal Tech and FinTech in a rapidly evolving global economy.

18.2 Legal Issues in FinTech

The intersection of technology and finance, known as FinTech, introduces several legal considerations that shape its regulatory landscape and operational framework:

- **Data Privacy and Security**: FinTech platforms collect and process vast amounts of consumer data, necessitating compliance with data protection laws such as GDPR and CCPA. Robust cybersecurity measures are crucial to safeguard sensitive financial information from unauthorized access and breaches.
- **Regulatory Compliance**: FinTech firms must navigate complex regulatory requirements governing financial services, including anti-money laundering (AML) regulations, know-your-customer (KYC) protocols, and consumer protection laws. Compliance ensures transparency, trustworthiness, and adherence to regulatory standards.
- **Cryptocurrency Regulation**: The proliferation of cryptocurrencies and blockchain technology prompts regulatory scrutiny to prevent fraud, ensure investor protection, and manage systemic risks. Regulatory approaches vary globally, impacting the issuance, trading, and taxation of digital assets.

- **Smart Contracts and Legal Validity:** Smart contracts, automated agreements executed on blockchain networks, challenge traditional contract law principles regarding enforceability, interpretation, and jurisdictional issues. Legal frameworks must evolve to accommodate technological innovations while upholding contractual integrity.

18.3 Regulatory Framework for FinTech

The regulatory landscape for FinTech is multifaceted, encompassing global, regional, and national frameworks that govern its operations:

- **Global Coordination:** International bodies like the Financial Stability Board (FSB) and the International Organization of Securities Commissions (IOSCO) collaborate to establish harmonized standards for FinTech regulation, promoting market stability and cross-border cooperation.
- **Regional Regulations:** Regional entities, such as the European Union's European Banking Authority (EBA) and the U.S. Securities and Exchange Commission (SEC), issue directives and guidelines tailored to regional market dynamics, ensuring compliance with regional laws, and fostering market integration.
- **National Oversight:** National regulators, including central banks and financial supervisory authorities, implement specific regulations tailored to local FinTech activities. Regulatory frameworks address licensing requirements, operational standards, and consumer protection measures to mitigate financial risks.
- **Innovation Sandboxes:** Regulatory sandboxes provide controlled environments for FinTech firms to test innovative products and services under regulatory

supervision. Sandboxes foster innovation, enable regulatory feedback, and facilitate compliance with regulatory requirements before full-scale market deployment.

18.4 Innovations and Future Trends in Legal Tech

The evolution of Legal Tech continues to drive transformative innovations within the legal industry, shaping future trends and operational efficiencies:

- **Artificial Intelligence (AI) and Machine Learning**: AI-powered legal technologies enhance contract review, legal research, and predictive analytics. Natural language processing (NLP) algorithms automate routine tasks, extract insights from legal documents, and improve decision-making accuracy.
- **Blockchain in Legal Transactions**: Blockchain technology facilitates secure and transparent legal transactions, including smart contracts, digital identity verification, and intellectual property rights management. Decentralized ledger systems enhance transactional trust, reduce intermediaries, and streamline dispute resolution.
- **RegTech Advancements**: Regulatory technology (RegTech) solutions integrate AI and big data analytics to automate regulatory compliance, monitor regulatory changes, and enhance risk management for financial institutions and legal entities. RegTech innovations promote operational efficiency and regulatory adherence.
- **Legal Practice Management Software**: Cloud-based legal practice management platforms optimize law firm operations, including case management, client billing, and document collaboration. Integrated software

solutions enhance productivity, client communication, and data security across legal practices.

Conclusion

The convergence of Legal Tech and FinTech represents a paradigm shift in legal and financial services, driving innovation, regulatory adaptation, and operational efficiency. As stakeholders navigate legal complexities, embrace technological advancements, and prioritize regulatory compliance, they harness the transformative potential of FinTech and Legal Tech to navigate a rapidly evolving global economy while upholding legal integrity and consumer trust.

Chapter 19: Marine Insurance Law

19.1 Principles of Marine Insurance

Marine insurance is a specialized branch of insurance law that addresses risks associated with maritime activities and cargo transportation. The principles governing marine insurance are essential to understanding its legal framework and operational dynamics:

- **Insurable Interest**: In marine insurance, insurable interest refers to the legal right of the insured party to insure against potential losses arising from marine perils. Insurable interest must exist at the time of the insurance contract's inception and throughout its duration to ensure the validity of claims.
- **Utmost Good Faith (Uberrimae Fidei)**: Marine insurance contracts are based on the principle of utmost good faith, requiring both the insured and insurer to disclose all material facts relevant to the risk. This principle ensures transparency, prevents misrepresentation, and facilitates fair risk assessment and premium determination.
- **Indemnity**: The principle of indemnity in marine insurance dictates that the insured party should be restored to the same financial position they were in before the occurrence of the insured peril. Insurers compensate for actual losses suffered by the insured, up to the policy limit, excluding any potential for profit from the insured event.
- **Proximate Cause**: In determining liability under marine insurance policies, the concept of proximate cause identifies the primary or dominant cause of loss or damage. Insurers assess whether the insured peril was

the proximate cause of the loss, impacting the validity and extent of insurance coverage.
- **Subrogation:** Subrogation grants insurers the right to pursue legal action against third parties responsible for the insured loss after compensating the insured. This principle aims to recover incurred losses and prevent unjust enrichment, ensuring equitable distribution of financial burdens related to marine risks.
- **Marine Perils and Risks:** Marine insurance covers a range of perils and risks associated with sea voyages and cargo transportation, including shipwrecks, piracy, collisions, and natural disasters. Policies may be tailored to specific maritime activities, cargo types, and operational contexts to mitigate financial losses.

Legal Framework and Regulations

Marine insurance operates within a regulatory framework governed by national laws, international conventions, and industry standards:

- **International Conventions:** The Hague-Visby Rules, York-Antwerp Rules, and other international maritime conventions establish uniform rules and liabilities for cargo transportation, insurance coverage, and maritime safety. These conventions ensure consistency and predictability in international trade and shipping practices.
- **National Legislation:** Each jurisdiction may enact marine insurance laws, regulations, and judicial precedents to govern insurance contracts, claims procedures, and dispute resolution mechanisms. National laws ensure compliance with international standards while addressing local maritime risks and insurance market practices.

- **Insurance Market Practices**: Marine insurance markets, such as Lloyd's of London and international insurance brokers, play a pivotal role in underwriting marine risks, negotiating policy terms, and settling insurance claims. Market practices reflect industry trends, risk assessments, and evolving regulatory requirements.

Challenges and Future Trends

Emerging trends in marine insurance include:
- **Cyber Risks**: Increasing reliance on digital technologies in maritime operations introduces cybersecurity risks, prompting insurers to develop policies covering cyber threats and data breaches in marine environments.
- **Climate Change Impacts**: Rising sea levels, extreme weather events, and environmental risks influence marine insurance underwriting and risk assessment. Insurers may adjust policies to mitigate climate-related losses and promote sustainable maritime practices.
- **Technological Innovations**: Blockchain technology, IoT (Internet of Things), and satellite imagery enhance risk assessment, claims management, and operational efficiency in marine insurance. These innovations streamline processes, reduce administrative costs, and improve transparency across the insurance value chain.

Conclusion

Marine insurance law is integral to global maritime commerce, offering essential protection against diverse risks encountered during sea voyages and cargo transportation. By adhering to fundamental principles of marine insurance, navigating regulatory landscapes, and embracing technological advancements, stakeholders in the marine insurance industry can enhance risk management, foster industry resilience, and sustainably support international trade and maritime activities in the 21st century.

19.2 Legal Framework for Marine Insurance

Marine insurance operates within a comprehensive legal framework that encompasses national laws, international conventions, and industry standards. Key aspects of the legal framework for marine insurance include:

- **National Legislation:** Each country may have specific laws governing marine insurance contracts, claims handling procedures, and regulatory oversight. These laws ensure compliance with international standards while addressing local market practices and maritime risks.

- **International Conventions:** Several international conventions establish uniform rules and principles governing marine insurance. The **Marine Insurance Act 1906** in the United Kingdom, for example, outlines fundamental principles such as utmost good faith, insurable interest, and indemnity. Additionally, global conventions like the **Hague-Visby Rules** and the **York-Antwerp Rules** provide guidelines for cargo transportation, liability, and insurance coverage in international maritime trade.

- **Industry Standards and Practices:** Marine insurance markets, including Lloyd's of London and international insurance brokers, adhere to industry standards and best practices in underwriting, risk assessment, and claims management. These standards promote transparency, consistency, and reliability in marine insurance transactions.

19.3 Risk and Liability in Marine Insurance

Marine insurance involves managing various risks and liabilities associated with sea voyages, cargo transportation, and maritime activities. Key aspects of risk and liability in marine insurance include:

- **Types of Risks Covered**: Marine insurance policies typically cover risks such as shipwrecks, collisions, piracy, natural disasters, and cargo damage or loss during transit. Policies may also extend to cover liabilities arising from environmental pollution or third-party claims related to maritime accidents.
- **Assessment and Underwriting**: Insurers assess marine risks based on factors such as vessel type, cargo value, voyage duration, geographical routes, and prevailing maritime conditions. Underwriters evaluate risk profiles to determine insurance premiums, coverage limits, and terms tailored to specific maritime risks.
- **Liability Coverage**: Marine insurance policies include provisions for liability coverage, addressing legal responsibilities and financial obligations incurred by shipowners, operators, and cargo owners. Liability coverage may encompass damages to third parties, salvage costs, general average contributions, and legal defence expenses in maritime claims.
- **Claims Settlement**: In the event of an insured loss or maritime incident, insurers facilitate claims settlement processes, ensuring timely compensation to policyholders for incurred losses or damages. Effective claims management involves verifying loss details, assessing coverage adequacy, and negotiating settlements in compliance with policy terms and regulatory requirements.

19.4 Case Studies in Marine Insurance

Case studies illustrate practical applications of marine insurance principles, legal frameworks, and risk management strategies in diverse maritime contexts:

- **Container Ship Casualty**: A case involving a container ship collision resulting in cargo damage and pollution liabilities. Marine insurers assess the extent of cargo loss, environmental impact, and third-party claims under applicable international conventions and insurance policies.
- **Piracy and Hostage Situation**: Insurers manage claims arising from piracy incidents, including ransom payments, vessel damage, crew injuries, and loss of revenue. Marine insurance policies cover piracy-related risks and provide financial protection against unforeseen maritime security threats.
- **Natural Disasters**: Following a severe storm affecting maritime operations, insurers process claims for vessel damage, cargo spoilage, and port infrastructure losses. Marine insurance policies mitigate financial losses caused by natural disasters, promoting resilience and recovery in maritime logistics and supply chains.

Conclusion

Marine insurance law encompasses a robust legal framework, risk management practices, and case-specific applications that safeguard stakeholders in global maritime commerce. By adhering to established principles, navigating regulatory landscapes, and leveraging case studies, marine insurers and industry stakeholders enhance operational resilience, mitigate financial risks, and sustainably support international trade and maritime activities worldwide.

Chapter 20: Medicine, Law, and Society

20.1 Legal Issues in Medical Practice

Medical practice intersects with a complex web of legal principles, ethical standards, and societal expectations, shaping the landscape of healthcare delivery and patient rights. Key legal issues in medical practice encompass:

- **Medical Malpractice**: Legal frameworks govern healthcare professionals' accountability for negligent acts or omissions that result in patient harm. Medical malpractice claims involve proving breach of duty, causation, and damages, often requiring expert testimony and adherence to procedural requirements.
- **Informed Consent**: Patients have the right to receive comprehensive information about treatment options, risks, benefits, and alternatives before consenting to medical procedures. Legal standards for informed consent vary by jurisdiction but universally prioritize patient autonomy and decision-making capacity.
- **Confidentiality and Privacy**: Healthcare providers must safeguard patient confidentiality and privacy under laws such as the Health Insurance Portability and Accountability Act (HIPAA) in the United States and similar regulations globally. Confidentiality breaches may result in legal liabilities and professional sanctions.
- **End-of-Life Care and Medical Ethics**: Legal frameworks address issues surrounding patient autonomy, euthanasia, palliative care, and advance directives. Laws may permit or restrict healthcare interventions based on patient wishes, ethical considerations, and cultural perspectives.
- **Regulatory Compliance**: Healthcare institutions and professionals must adhere to regulatory standards

governing licensure, accreditation, pharmaceutical practices, and clinical research. Regulatory bodies enforce compliance to ensure patient safety, quality of care, and ethical conduct.
- **Telemedicine and Digital Health**: Legal frameworks evolve to accommodate telemedicine practices, remote patient monitoring, electronic health records, and digital health innovations. Regulations address licensure, reimbursement, data security, and interstate practice for healthcare providers engaging in virtual care delivery.
- **Public Health Emergencies**: During pandemics or public health crises, legal frameworks enable emergency response measures, quarantine enforcement, vaccine distribution, and healthcare resource allocation. Public health laws balance individual rights with collective health priorities.
- **Medical Research and Ethics**: Research involving human subjects requires adherence to ethical guidelines, informed consent protocols, institutional review board oversight, and regulatory approvals. Legal frameworks protect research participants and uphold scientific integrity in biomedical and clinical studies.

Case Studies in Medical Law
- **Landmark Medical Malpractice Case**: Analysis of a high-profile medical malpractice lawsuit involving surgical errors and patient injury, highlighting legal precedents, expert testimony, and judicial interpretations of standard of care.
- **Ethical Dilemmas in End-of-Life Care**: A case study exploring legal and ethical dimensions of decisions regarding life-sustaining treatment withdrawal, patient

autonomy, and family consent in terminal illness scenarios.
- **Privacy Breach in Electronic Health Records**: Examination of legal repercussions following unauthorized access to patient medical records, emphasizing HIPAA violations, patient notification requirements, and healthcare provider liability.

Conclusion

Legal issues in medical practice reflect evolving societal norms, ethical standards, and regulatory landscapes that shape healthcare delivery, patient rights, and professional responsibilities. By navigating complex legal frameworks, healthcare stakeholders uphold the quality of care, protect patient interests, and advance public health outcomes in a dynamic global healthcare environment.

20.2 Patient Rights and Medical Ethics

Patient rights and medical ethics form the cornerstone of ethical medical practice, emphasizing principles such as autonomy, beneficence, non-maleficence, and justice. Key aspects include:

- **Autonomy**: Patients have the right to make informed decisions about their medical care, including treatment options, participation in research, and end-of-life choices. Informed consent processes ensure patients receive comprehensive information to make autonomous decisions.
- **Confidentiality**: Healthcare providers are legally obligated to protect patient information from unauthorized access or disclosure, maintaining confidentiality unless disclosure is required by law or necessary to protect public health.

- **Privacy**: Patients have the right to privacy in their medical information and treatment, ensuring confidentiality in healthcare settings and safeguarding personal health data from misuse or unauthorized access.
- **Dignity and Respect**: Medical ethics require healthcare providers to treat patients with dignity, respect cultural and religious beliefs, and promote a compassionate patient-provider relationship.
- **End-of-Life Care**: Legal and ethical frameworks guide decisions regarding withholding or withdrawing life-sustaining treatment, advance directives, and respecting patient wishes in terminal illness or incapacitation.

20.3 Regulation of Medical Professionals

Regulation of medical professionals ensures competency, ethical conduct, and patient safety through licensure, certification, and disciplinary mechanisms:

- **Licensure**: Medical professionals must obtain a license to practice, demonstrating education, training, and proficiency in medical standards. Licensure boards oversee qualifications and uphold professional standards.
- **Continuing Education**: Ongoing professional development and education are mandatory to maintain licensure, ensuring healthcare providers stay updated on medical advancements, ethics, and regulatory changes.
- **Professional Conduct**: Ethical codes and standards of conduct govern medical practice, addressing issues such as conflicts of interest, professional boundaries, and appropriate patient interactions.

- **Disciplinary Actions**: Regulatory bodies investigate complaints of professional misconduct or negligence, imposing sanctions such as license suspension, fines, or expulsion from professional associations.

20.4 Case Studies in Medical Law

- **Landmark Legal Case on Patient Privacy**: Analysis of a legal case involving a healthcare data breach, exploring legal responsibilities, patient notification requirements, and regulatory penalties for violating patient privacy laws.
- **Ethical Dilemma in Organ Transplantation**: A case study examining ethical considerations in organ allocation, informed consent for organ donation, and ensuring fairness and equity in transplant decisions.
- **Medical Malpractice Lawsuit**: Review of a medical malpractice lawsuit alleging surgical error, assessing the standard of care, expert testimony, and legal outcomes impacting patient safety and professional accountability.

Conclusion

Understanding patient rights, medical ethics, and regulatory frameworks is essential for medical professionals to navigate legal complexities, uphold ethical standards, and prioritize patient welfare. By integrating legal knowledge with ethical principles, healthcare providers promote patient autonomy, confidentiality, and quality care in a dynamic healthcare landscape.

Chapter 21: Modern Copyright Law

21.1 Fundamentals of Copyright Law

Copyright law serves as the foundation for protecting intellectual property rights in creative works, ensuring creators have exclusive rights to their original expressions. Key fundamentals include:

- **Scope of Protection**: Copyright protects original works of authorship fixed in a tangible medium, such as literary works, music, art, and software code. It grants creators exclusive rights to reproduce, distribute, perform, display, and create derivative works of their creations.
- **Copyright Ownership**: Creators automatically own copyright in their works upon creation, but may transfer or license their rights to others. Works created by employees in the course of employment may belong to the employer under the doctrine of work-for-hire.
- **Duration of Protection**: Copyright protection generally lasts for the life of the author plus 70 years. For works made for hire or anonymous/pseudonymous works, copyright protection endures for 95 years from publication or 120 years from creation, whichever is shorter.
- **Rights of Copyright Holders**: Copyright holders have exclusive rights to control the use of their works. These rights include the right to reproduce the work, prepare derivative works, distribute copies to the public, perform the work publicly, and display the work publicly.
- **Fair Use and Exceptions**: Fair use is a crucial exception to copyright protection, allowing limited use of copyrighted works without permission for purposes

such as criticism, commentary, news reporting, teaching, scholarship, or research. Courts consider factors like the purpose and character of the use, nature of the copyrighted work, amount used, and effect on the market.
- **International Copyright Law**: Treaties such as the Berne Convention and the TRIPS Agreement establish minimum standards of copyright protection among member countries, ensuring reciprocal protection for creators across borders.
- **Digital Copyright Issues**: Digital technology challenges traditional copyright enforcement with issues like online piracy, digital rights management (DRM), and file-sharing platforms. Legal responses include the Digital Millennium Copyright Act (DMCA), which provides safe harbours for online service providers while addressing copyright infringement.

Case Studies in Copyright Law
- **Napster and Peer-to-Peer File Sharing**: Analysis of legal challenges and court rulings surrounding Napster's peer-to-peer file-sharing platform, exploring implications for copyright infringement, digital distribution, and the evolution of online music consumption.
- **Fair Use in Digital Media**: Examination of landmark fair use cases involving transformative uses of copyrighted works in digital media, addressing issues of parody, remix culture, and the balance between copyright protection and free expression.
- **Digital Millennium Copyright Act (DMCA)**: A case study on the application of DMCA safe harbours and takedown notices in addressing online copyright

infringement, highlighting the legal responsibilities of online service providers and content creators.

Conclusion

Modern copyright law adapts to technological advancements and global challenges, balancing the rights of creators with the public interest in access to knowledge and innovation. Understanding copyright fundamentals, fair use principles, and digital copyright issues equips stakeholders—from creators to consumers and policymakers—with the knowledge to navigate and shape the evolving landscape of intellectual property protection.

21.2 Digital Copyright Issues

In the digital era, copyright law faces profound challenges and transformations due to rapid technological advancements and the internet's global reach. Key digital copyright issues include:

- **Digital Piracy**: The ease of copying and distributing digital content has intensified issues of piracy, posing significant challenges for copyright holders in protecting their works from unauthorized use.
- **Digital Rights Management (DRM)**: DRM technologies are employed to control access to digital content and protect copyright interests. However, DRM systems also raise concerns about user privacy, fair use, and interoperability across different platforms and devices.
- **Online Platforms and Liability**: Platforms that host user-generated content must navigate a complex legal landscape, balancing the facilitation of creativity and the obligation to prevent copyright infringement. Legal frameworks such as the Digital Millennium Copyright Act (DMCA) provide guidelines for platforms to handle copyright infringement claims and maintain safe harbour protections.

- **Fair Use in the Digital Age**: Courts worldwide are grappling with how traditional copyright exceptions like fair use apply in the digital context. Issues arise around transformative use, such as parody, commentary, and educational purposes, and their compatibility with copyright protections.
- **Emerging Technologies**: Advancements like artificial intelligence (AI) and machine learning pose new challenges for copyright law, particularly concerning the creation and ownership of AI-generated works and the implications for copyright ownership and infringement.

21.3 International Copyright Treaties

International copyright treaties play a crucial role in harmonizing copyright laws across borders and addressing global challenges in intellectual property protection. Key treaties and agreements include:

- **Berne Convention for the Protection of Literary and Artistic Works**: Established in 1886, the Berne Convention sets minimum standards for copyright protection among its member countries, promoting international recognition of copyright without the need for formal registration.
- **TRIPS Agreement**: Part of the World Trade Organization (WTO) framework, the Agreement on Trade-Related Aspects of Intellectual Property Rights (TRIPS) establishes standards for the protection and enforcement of intellectual property rights, including copyright, to facilitate international trade and investment.
- **WIPO Copyright Treaties**: The WIPO Copyright Treaty (WCT) and the WIPO Performances and Phonograms Treaty (WPPT) address digital copyright issues, ensuring

that creators and copyright holders receive adequate protection in the digital environment.
- **Bilateral and Regional Agreements**: Countries also engage in bilateral and regional agreements to enhance copyright protection and enforcement, addressing specific challenges in cross-border intellectual property rights and promoting cultural exchange.

21.4 Case Studies in Copyright Law

- **YouTube vs. Viacom**: This case highlighted issues of online copyright infringement liability when Viacom sued YouTube for hosting user-uploaded videos that infringed on Viacom's copyrights. The court's decision shaped interpretations of safe harbour provisions under the DMCA and the responsibilities of online platforms.
- **Disney Enterprises, Inc. v. VidAngel, Inc.**: Examined the legality of VidAngel's streaming service, which allowed users to filter and watch movies while circumventing digital rights management (DRM) protections. The case addressed questions about fair use, technological circumvention, and the application of copyright law to streaming services.
- **European Union Copyright Directive (Article 17)**: The EU Copyright Directive introduced Article 17 (formerly Article 13), requiring online platforms to obtain licenses for copyrighted content and implement measures to prevent unauthorized uploads. The directive aimed to rebalance the relationship between content creators, platforms, and users in the digital ecosystem.

Conclusion

Modern copyright law must continually evolve to address the challenges posed by digital technologies and global connectivity while ensuring a balance between the rights of creators, the interests of users, and the broader public domain. As digital copyright issues become increasingly complex, legal frameworks and international cooperation play pivotal roles in shaping the future of copyright protection and enforcement worldwide.

Chapter 22: Money Laundering and Financial Crime

22.1 Mechanisms of Money Laundering

Money laundering is a sophisticated process aimed at concealing the origins of illegally obtained funds, making them appear legitimate. The mechanisms involved in money laundering typically follow a series of stages to obscure the illicit source of funds:

1. **Placement**: In this initial stage, illicit funds are introduced into the legitimate financial system. This can be done through various means such as deposits into bank accounts, purchasing assets, or using currency exchanges. The goal is to integrate illicit funds into the financial system without raising suspicion.

2. **Layering**: Also known as structuring, this stage involves conducting multiple complex financial transactions to further distance the illicit funds from their source. Transactions may include wire transfers between accounts, international transactions, or purchasing and selling assets multiple times. Layering aims to create a complex web of transactions that make it difficult to trace the origin of the funds.

3. **Integration**: The final stage of money laundering involves reintroducing the laundered funds back into the economy as legitimate funds. This is typically done by investing in businesses, real estate, or other assets, or simply by using the laundered funds for everyday transactions. The laundered funds now appear to be clean and legitimate, making it challenging for law enforcement agencies to trace them back to their illegal origins.

Key Techniques and Challenges in Money Laundering:
- **Use of Financial Institutions**: Banks and other financial institutions are often unwittingly involved in the placement and layering stages of money laundering. Regulatory frameworks such as Know Your Customer (KYC) regulations aim to mitigate these risks by requiring institutions to verify the identity of their customers and monitor transactions for suspicious activities.
- **Shell Companies and Offshore Accounts**: Money launderers frequently use shell companies and offshore accounts in jurisdictions with lax regulations to obscure the ownership and movement of illicit funds. These entities can complicate investigations and make it challenging for authorities to uncover the true beneficiaries of the laundered funds.
- **Emerging Technologies**: The rise of digital currencies and decentralized financial systems presents new challenges for combating money laundering. Cryptocurrencies, for example, offer a degree of anonymity that can be exploited by criminals seeking to launder funds through online transactions.

Global Efforts and Regulations:
- **Financial Action Task Force (FATF)**: The FATF is an intergovernmental organization that sets international standards for combating money laundering and terrorist financing. Member countries are required to implement these standards, which include measures to enhance transparency, traceability, and accountability in financial transactions.
- **Anti-Money Laundering (AML) Laws**: Countries around the world have enacted AML laws and regulations to criminalize money laundering activities and impose

penalties on individuals and entities involved in illicit financial activities. These laws often require financial institutions to establish compliance programs and report suspicious transactions to authorities.

Case Studies in Financial Crime:
- **HSBC Money Laundering Scandal**: HSBC, one of the world's largest banks, faced allegations of facilitating money laundering activities for drug cartels and sanctioned entities. The case highlighted weaknesses in the bank's compliance and risk management practices, leading to significant regulatory fines and reputational damage.
- **Panama Papers**: The Panama Papers leak exposed the widespread use of offshore accounts and shell companies for money laundering and tax evasion purposes by wealthy individuals and public officials worldwide. The revelations prompted global investigations and calls for greater transparency in financial transactions.

Conclusion:
Money laundering remains a critical challenge for global financial systems, requiring ongoing efforts by governments, financial institutions, and international organizations to strengthen regulatory frameworks, enhance transparency, and combat illicit financial activities effectively. As financial crime evolves with technological advancements, continuous adaptation and collaboration across borders are essential to mitigate risks and protect the integrity of the financial system.

22.2 Legal Framework for Combating Money Laundering

The legal framework for combating money laundering involves a comprehensive set of laws, regulations, and enforcement measures aimed at detecting, preventing, and prosecuting financial crimes. Key components of this framework include:

- **Criminalization**: Money laundering is typically criminalized under national laws, which define offences related to the laundering of proceeds from criminal activities such as drug trafficking, corruption, and terrorism. These laws establish penalties for individuals and entities involved in laundering illicit funds.
- **Regulatory Requirements**: Financial institutions and designated non-financial businesses and professions (DNFBPs) are required to implement anti-money laundering (AML) measures, including customer due diligence (CDD), transaction monitoring, and reporting of suspicious activities. Regulatory authorities set standards and guidelines for compliance with these requirements.
- **Supervision and Enforcement**: Regulatory agencies oversee compliance with AML laws and regulations through inspections, audits, and enforcement actions. They have the authority to impose sanctions, fines, and other penalties on entities that fail to comply with AML requirements.
- **International Standards**: Countries adhere to international standards and recommendations set by bodies such as the Financial Action Task Force (FATF). These standards provide a framework for countries to develop and implement effective AML/CFT (Combating the Financing of Terrorism) regimes, promoting global cooperation and consistency in combating financial crime.

22.3 International Cooperation in Anti-Money Laundering

International cooperation is crucial in the fight against money laundering, given the transnational nature of financial crimes. Key aspects of international cooperation include:

- **Mutual Legal Assistance**: Countries exchange information and assist each other in criminal investigations and legal proceedings related to money laundering. Mutual legal assistance treaties (MLATs) facilitate cooperation by establishing procedures for requesting and obtaining evidence, seizing assets, and extraditing suspects.
- **Information Sharing**: Financial intelligence units (FIUs) and law enforcement agencies exchange information on suspicious transactions, trends, and typologies of money laundering. Information sharing enhances the ability to detect and disrupt illicit financial flows across borders.
- **International Organizations**: Organizations such as the FATF coordinate efforts to combat money laundering and terrorist financing globally. They conduct mutual evaluations of member countries' AML/CFT regimes, assess compliance with international standards, and provide technical assistance to strengthen national frameworks.
- **Sanctions and Measures**: International sanctions regimes target individuals, entities, and jurisdictions involved in money laundering and other illicit financial activities. These measures aim to disrupt illicit financial networks, prevent access to the international financial system, and deter financial crime.

22.4 Case Studies in Financial Crime

- **The Bernie Madoff Ponzi Scheme**: Bernie Madoff orchestrated one of the largest Ponzi schemes in history, defrauding investors of billions of dollars over several decades. The case highlighted failures in regulatory oversight and due diligence, prompting reforms in investor protection and financial market transparency.
- **The Danske Bank Money Laundering Scandal**: Danske Bank's Estonian branch was implicated in a vast money laundering scheme involving billions of euros from suspicious transactions. The scandal underscored weaknesses in AML controls, prompting regulatory investigations, executive resignations, and substantial fines.
- **The FinCEN Files**: The FinCEN Files leak exposed global banks' role in facilitating suspicious transactions worth trillions of dollars. The leak revealed deficiencies in AML compliance, regulatory oversight, and financial transparency, leading to calls for reforms to strengthen the global AML framework.

Conclusion

Effective measures to combat money laundering require a coordinated approach at national and international levels, integrating legal frameworks, regulatory oversight, and international cooperation. As financial crime evolves, continuous adaptation and collaboration among stakeholders are essential to safeguard the integrity of the global financial system and mitigate the risks posed by illicit financial activities.

Chapter 23: Multinational Enterprises and the Law

23.1 Legal Structure of Multinational Enterprises

Multinational enterprises (MNEs) are pivotal players in the global economy, operating across borders and navigating complex legal landscapes. The legal structure of MNEs encompasses various facets that define their operations, governance, and regulatory compliance:

- **Corporate Structure**: MNEs often adopt a decentralized corporate structure with subsidiaries, branches, and affiliates in multiple jurisdictions. This structure facilitates operational flexibility, tax optimization, and compliance with local laws and regulations.
- **Legal Entities**: MNEs establish legal entities such as corporations, partnerships, and limited liability companies (LLCs) in host countries to conduct business activities. Each entity operates under the legal framework of its jurisdiction, governing corporate governance, liability, and regulatory obligations.
- **Governance and Compliance**: MNEs adhere to corporate governance standards and compliance requirements mandated by national laws, international conventions, and industry regulations. Governance mechanisms ensure transparency, accountability, and ethical conduct in business operations.
- **Regulatory Compliance**: MNEs must comply with diverse regulatory regimes governing areas such as trade, competition, employment, environmental protection, and consumer rights in each jurisdiction of operation. Compliance frameworks mitigate legal risks and promote corporate responsibility.

- **Cross-Border Transactions**: MNEs engage in cross-border transactions, including mergers, acquisitions, joint ventures, and strategic alliances, which necessitate compliance with antitrust laws, foreign investment regulations, and tax treaties.
- **Intellectual Property (IP) Management**: MNEs manage IP rights across jurisdictions to protect innovations, trademarks, patents, and copyrights. IP strategies include licensing agreements, technology transfer, and enforcement of IP rights to safeguard proprietary assets.
- **Dispute Resolution**: MNEs resolve commercial disputes through litigation, arbitration, or alternative dispute resolution (ADR) mechanisms. International arbitration is favoured for its neutrality, enforceability of awards, and expertise in cross-border legal issues.
- **Corporate Social Responsibility (CSR)**: MNEs integrate CSR initiatives into their operations, addressing social, environmental, and ethical responsibilities. CSR practices promote sustainable development, community engagement, and stakeholder trust.

Case Studies in Multinational Enterprise Law
- **Shell Nigeria Oil Spill Case**: Royal Dutch Shell faced legal challenges and public scrutiny over environmental damage caused by oil spills in Nigeria. The case underscored the accountability of MNEs for environmental impacts and their obligations under international human rights and environmental laws.
- **Apple's Tax Practices in Europe**: Apple Inc. was involved in a legal dispute with the European Union (EU) over alleged tax avoidance practices in Ireland. The

case highlighted regulatory scrutiny of MNEs' tax planning strategies and efforts to prevent profit shifting.
- **Nike Sweatshops Controversy**: Nike encountered legal and ethical controversies regarding labour conditions in overseas sweatshops producing its products. The case prompted reforms in labour practices, supply chain management, and corporate governance within MNEs.

Conclusion

The legal framework governing multinational enterprises is multifaceted, encompassing corporate structure, governance, compliance, dispute resolution, and ethical responsibilities. As MNEs expand globally, adherence to legal norms, regulatory requirements, and stakeholder expectations is essential to foster sustainable business practices and mitigate legal risks across diverse jurisdictions.

23.2 Regulatory Challenges for Multinationals

Multinational enterprises (MNEs) face a myriad of regulatory challenges as they navigate diverse legal frameworks across countries:

- **Jurisdictional Variations**: MNEs must comply with distinct and sometimes conflicting regulations in each jurisdiction where they operate. This includes differences in labour laws, tax codes, environmental regulations, and consumer protection rules.
- **Compliance Costs**: Managing compliance across multiple jurisdictions can be costly and resource-intensive for MNEs. They must allocate resources to understand and adhere to local regulations, often necessitating legal counsel and compliance teams in each region.
- **Legal Risks**: MNEs are exposed to legal risks such as litigation, regulatory investigations, and sanctions for

non-compliance with local laws. Regulatory breaches can damage reputation, incur fines, and lead to operational disruptions.
- **Data Protection and Privacy**: Compliance with data protection laws, such as the GDPR in Europe or CCPA in California, poses challenges for MNEs handling customer and employee data across borders. Ensuring data security and privacy while meeting legal requirements is paramount.
- **Antitrust and Competition Laws**: MNEs must navigate antitrust laws that regulate market competition and prevent monopolistic practices. Compliance requires careful structuring of mergers, acquisitions, and pricing strategies to avoid regulatory scrutiny.
- **Trade and Tariffs**: Changes in international trade policies, tariffs, and trade agreements impact MNEs engaged in global supply chains and export-import activities. Tariff disputes and trade barriers require strategic planning to mitigate financial impacts.

23.3 Corporate Social Responsibility

Corporate social responsibility (CSR) is integral to MNEs' ethical practices and sustainability efforts:
- **Environmental Sustainability**: MNEs adopt sustainable practices to reduce carbon footprint, conserve resources, and comply with environmental regulations. Initiatives include renewable energy investments, waste reduction programs, and eco-friendly manufacturing processes.
- **Social Initiatives**: CSR programs support community development, education, healthcare, and poverty alleviation in regions where MNEs operate. These

initiatives foster goodwill, enhance brand reputation, and contribute to sustainable socio-economic growth.
- **Ethical Supply Chains**: MNEs uphold ethical standards in supply chain management, ensuring fair labour practices, human rights protection, and transparency in sourcing. Supplier audits and compliance assessments verify adherence to ethical guidelines.
- **Stakeholder Engagement**: MNEs engage with stakeholders including investors, employees, customers, and communities to address concerns, solicit feedback, and promote transparency in corporate governance and CSR initiatives.

23.4 Case Studies in Multinational Enterprise Law

- **Nestlé and Child Labor Allegations**: Nestlé faced legal and reputational challenges over allegations of child labour in cocoa supply chains. The case highlighted the importance of due diligence in supply chain management and adherence to international labour standards.
- **Google's Antitrust Cases in Europe**: Google encountered antitrust investigations and fines by the European Commission for alleged monopolistic practices related to online advertising and search engine dominance. The case underscored regulatory scrutiny of tech giants' market dominance.
- **IKEA and Sustainable Sourcing**: IKEA is committed to sustainable sourcing of wood products, and implementing forestry management practices and certifications to promote environmental stewardship. The case demonstrated MNEs' efforts to integrate sustainability into corporate strategies.

Conclusion

Multinational enterprises operate in a complex regulatory landscape characterized by diverse legal requirements, regulatory challenges, and expectations for corporate social responsibility. Adhering to legal norms, mitigating compliance risks, and embracing CSR initiatives are essential for MNEs to sustain ethical practices, foster stakeholder trust, and achieve long-term business success globally.

Chapter 24: Patents and Trade Secrets: Comparative and International Perspectives

24.1 Fundamentals of Patent Law

Patent law serves as a cornerstone for innovation protection across the globe, providing inventors with exclusive rights to their inventions. Understanding the fundamentals of patent law involves delving into several key aspects:

- **Definition and Scope**: Patents grant inventors exclusive rights to their inventions, preventing others from making, using, selling, or importing the patented invention without permission. This exclusivity typically lasts for a specified period, incentivizing innovation by ensuring inventors can reap rewards from their creations.

- **Requirements for Patentability**: To qualify for a patent, an invention must meet certain criteria, including novelty, inventive step (non-obviousness), and industrial applicability. These criteria vary slightly between jurisdictions but generally aim to protect inventions that are new, non-obvious, and useful.

- **Types of Patents**: Different jurisdictions recognize several types of patents, including utility patents for inventions with practical utility, design patents for ornamental designs, and plant patents for new plant varieties. Each type of patent offers protection tailored to the specific characteristics of the invention.

- **Patent Application Process**: Securing a patent involves filing a patent application with the relevant patent office, disclosing the invention in detail, and undergoing examination to assess patentability criteria. The

process may include responding to office actions and amendments to claims to meet legal standards.
- **Enforcement and Infringement**: Patents provide rights holders with the ability to enforce their exclusivity through legal action against infringers. Infringement occurs when someone makes, uses, sells, or imports a patented invention without authorization, leading to potential remedies such as injunctions, damages, and royalties.
- **International Treaties and Harmonization**: International treaties, such as the Paris Convention and the Patent Cooperation Treaty (PCT), facilitate the filing and recognition of patents across multiple jurisdictions. These treaties promote harmonization of patent laws, streamline patent application processes, and provide mechanisms for international protection.

Understanding the fundamentals of patent law is crucial for inventors, businesses, and legal professionals navigating the complexities of innovation protection in a globalized world. It underscores the importance of intellectual property rights in fostering creativity, technological advancement, and economic growth across diverse industries.

24.2 Legal Protection of Trade Secrets

Trade secrets represent a critical form of intellectual property that offers protection to confidential business information, providing competitive advantages to businesses. Understanding the legal framework surrounding trade secrets involves several key elements:
- **Definition and Scope**: Trade secrets encompass a broad range of confidential information, including formulas, processes, techniques, and business

strategies, which derive economic value from not being generally known or readily ascertainable by others.
- **Requirements for Protection**: Unlike patents, trade secrets do not require registration. Instead, protection hinges on maintaining secrecy through reasonable efforts. Businesses must implement measures to safeguard information from unauthorized disclosure or use.
- **Legal Remedies**: Legal protections for trade secrets vary across jurisdictions but commonly include civil remedies for misappropriation, such as injunctions, damages, and restitution. Some jurisdictions also recognize criminal penalties for egregious violations.
- **Challenges and Considerations**: Securing trade secret protection involves balancing confidentiality measures with operational transparency. Businesses must assess risks associated with potential leaks or breaches and implement robust internal policies and agreements to safeguard sensitive information.

24.3 Comparative Analysis of IP Rights

Comparative analysis of intellectual property (IP) rights provides insights into the diverse legal frameworks governing patents, trademarks, copyrights, and trade secrets globally. Key aspects include:
- **Legal Frameworks**: Different jurisdictions offer varying degrees of protection and enforcement mechanisms for IP rights. Understanding these frameworks is crucial for businesses operating in multiple countries to navigate regulatory compliance and mitigate risks.
- **Harmonization Efforts**: International treaties and agreements, such as the Berne Convention for copyrights and the Madrid Protocol for trademarks, aim

to harmonize IP laws across borders. These efforts streamline the process of securing and enforcing IP rights globally.
- **Emerging Trends**: Rapid advancements in technology and globalization have spurred discussions on emerging IP issues, such as digital piracy, cross-border enforcement challenges, and the intersection of IP rights with other areas like competition law and data protection.

24.4 International Treaties on IP Protection

International treaties play a pivotal role in promoting harmonized standards and facilitating cooperation in intellectual property protection. Key treaties include:
- **Paris Convention for the Protection of Industrial Property**: Established in 1883, the Paris Convention provides fundamental principles for protecting patents, trademarks, industrial designs, and trade secrets across member countries. It enables applicants to claim priority rights based on earlier filings in other member states.
- **Trade-Related Aspects of Intellectual Property Rights (TRIPS) Agreement**: Formulated under the World Trade Organization (WTO), the TRIPS Agreement sets minimum standards for IP protection and enforcement among member states. It mandates obligations on copyright, patent, trademark, and trade secret protections, ensuring compliance with global norms.
- **Patent Cooperation Treaty (PCT)**: Administered by the World Intellectual Property Organization (WIPO), the PCT simplifies the process of filing patent applications in multiple countries. It facilitates international patent

protection by providing a centralized application process and preliminary examination.

Understanding these international treaties is essential for stakeholders in the global economy seeking to protect and leverage their intellectual property assets effectively. It underscores the importance of navigating legal complexities and harnessing opportunities in the competitive landscape of innovation and creativity.

Chapter 25: Private Equity

25.1 Principles of Private Equity

Private equity is a specialized area of finance and investment that involves the acquisition and management of equity in companies that are not publicly traded on stock exchanges. It typically involves investment funds and firms that directly invest in private companies or engage in buyouts of public companies to take them private.

Key Principles:

1. **Investment Strategy**: Private equity firms develop specific investment strategies based on market conditions, sector expertise, and growth potential of target companies.
2. **Capital Structure**: The financing of private equity deals often involves a mix of equity and debt. This structure varies depending on the risk profile of the investment and the desired returns.
3. **Value Creation**: Private equity investors aim to enhance the value of their portfolio companies through various strategies such as operational improvements, strategic guidance, and financial restructuring.
4. **Exit Strategies**: Successful private equity investments typically involve exiting the investment within a defined time frame to realize returns. Common exit strategies include selling to strategic buyers, initial public offerings (IPOs), or secondary buyouts.
5. **Due Diligence**: Rigorous due diligence is conducted before making investments to assess the financial health, management capabilities, market position, and growth prospects of target companies.
6. **Risk and Return**: Private equity investments are characterized by higher risks compared to traditional

investments but offer the potential for higher returns, often through capital appreciation and operational efficiencies.
7. **Legal and Regulatory Considerations**: Private equity transactions involve navigating complex legal and regulatory environments, including compliance with securities laws, tax considerations, and contractual agreements.
8. **Ethical and Governance Standards**: Adherence to ethical standards and strong corporate governance practices are crucial in private equity to build trust with investors and stakeholders.
9. **Sector Focus**: Private equity firms often specialize in specific industries or sectors where they have expertise, allowing them to add significant value through industry knowledge and networks.
10. **Long-Term Perspective**: Private equity investments typically have a longer investment horizon compared to public market investments, allowing firms to implement strategic initiatives and realize value over time.

Understanding these principles is essential for both investors and professionals operating within the private equity industry. It provides a foundation for navigating the complexities and opportunities inherent in this dynamic field of finance and investment.

25.2 Legal Framework for Private Equity Investments

Private equity investments operate within a robust legal framework that governs various aspects of investment activities, transactions, and regulatory compliance. Key elements of the legal framework include:

1. **Formation of Funds**: The establishment and structuring of private equity funds involve legal

considerations such as fund documentation, partnership agreements, and compliance with securities laws.
2. **Investment Agreements**: Negotiation and drafting of investment agreements between private equity firms and portfolio companies, covering terms of investment, governance rights, and exit provisions.
3. **Due Diligence**: Legal due diligence is critical in assessing potential risks and liabilities associated with target companies, including regulatory compliance, intellectual property rights, and contractual obligations.
4. **Regulatory Compliance**: Private equity firms must adhere to securities regulations, anti-money laundering laws, and other regulatory requirements applicable to their operations and investments.
5. **Tax Considerations**: Structuring investments to optimize tax efficiency and compliance with tax laws in relevant jurisdictions is essential for maximizing returns and managing financial risk.
6. **Exit Strategies**: Legal frameworks for exit strategies include considerations for IPOs, sales to strategic buyers, secondary buyouts, or liquidation processes, ensuring compliance with legal and regulatory requirements.

Understanding and navigating these legal aspects are crucial for private equity professionals to mitigate risks, ensure compliance, and facilitate successful investment outcomes.

25.3 Regulatory Issues in Private Equity

Private equity investments face a range of regulatory challenges and considerations, including:
1. **Securities Regulations**: Compliance with securities laws governing the offer, sale, and transfer of securities,

particularly in relation to fundraising activities and investor disclosures.
2. **Antitrust Laws**: Potential antitrust issues arising from mergers and acquisitions, require scrutiny to ensure transactions do not create monopolies or restrict competition unfairly.
3. **Foreign Investment Regulations**: Restrictions or approvals are required for cross-border investments, navigating foreign ownership restrictions, national security reviews, and international trade laws.
4. **Environmental, Social, and Governance (ESG) Compliance**: Increasing focus on ESG factors requires private equity firms to integrate sustainability considerations into investment strategies and reporting practices.
5. **Taxation**: Tax implications of investment structures, profit repatriation, and compliance with local and international tax laws affecting fund performance and investor returns.

Navigating these regulatory issues requires a comprehensive understanding of applicable laws, proactive compliance measures, and strategic management of legal risks throughout the investment lifecycle.

25.4 Case Studies in Private Equity

Case studies provide practical insights into successful private equity transactions, illustrating strategies, challenges, and outcomes in real-world scenarios. Key elements typically covered in case studies include:
1. **Investment Thesis**: Rationale behind the investment decision, including market opportunities, competitive landscape, and potential for value creation.

2. **Due Diligence**: Analysis of financial, operational, and legal aspects of target companies to assess risks and opportunities for improvement.
3. **Execution**: Details of transaction structuring, negotiation of terms, and implementation of value enhancement strategies post-investment.
4. **Value Creation**: Initiatives undertaken to enhance company performance, including operational improvements, strategic repositioning, and governance enhancements.
5. **Exit Strategy**: Evaluation of exit options pursued, such as IPOs, sales to strategic buyers, or secondary market transactions, and factors influencing the chosen exit route.

Case studies offer valuable learning opportunities for private equity professionals, highlighting best practices, pitfalls to avoid, and strategies for maximizing returns and managing risks in dynamic investment environments.

Legal Framework, Regulatory Issues, and Case Studies in Private Equity

Private equity (PE) plays a pivotal role in global finance, involving the acquisition and management of equity in non-publicly traded companies. This sector operates within a multifaceted legal framework, navigates complex regulatory landscapes, and thrives on practical insights from case studies.

Legal Framework for Private Equity Investments

The legal framework underpinning private equity investments is comprehensive and crucial for structuring and executing transactions effectively. At its core, this framework encompasses several key elements:

Formation of Funds: PE firms establish investment vehicles through meticulous documentation, including partnership agreements and fund structuring that comply with securities regulations. These agreements outline governance structures, investment strategies, and the rights and responsibilities of stakeholders.

Investment Agreements: Negotiating and drafting precise investment agreements is essential. These agreements delineate terms such as capital contributions, management fees, exit strategies, and governance rights over portfolio companies.

Due Diligence: Legal due diligence is integral to PE transactions, ensuring a comprehensive assessment of target companies' financial health, regulatory compliance, intellectual property rights, and contractual obligations. Thorough due diligence mitigates risks and informs investment decisions.

Regulatory Compliance: Compliance with securities laws and regulations is paramount. PE firms must navigate complex regulatory requirements related to fundraising, investor disclosures, and cross-border investments. Antitrust laws also necessitate scrutiny to prevent monopolistic practices arising from mergers and acquisitions.

Tax Considerations: Structuring investments to optimize tax efficiency across jurisdictions requires careful planning. Tax implications influence fund performance, profit repatriation, and compliance with local and international tax laws.

Exit Strategies: Legal frameworks for exit strategies—such as initial public offerings (IPOs), sales to strategic buyers, or secondary buyouts—demand adherence to regulatory requirements. Structuring exits effectively ensures maximum returns for investors while managing legal complexities.

Regulatory Issues in Private Equity

PE investments confront diverse regulatory challenges that influence operational strategies and investment decisions:

Securities Regulations: Compliance with stringent securities laws governs the offer, sale, and transfer of securities. Regulatory compliance is essential for fundraising activities and investor protection.

Antitrust Laws: Mergers and acquisitions in PE transactions require scrutiny under antitrust laws to prevent anti-competitive practices and ensure fair market competition.

Foreign Investment Regulations: Cross-border investments necessitate navigating foreign ownership restrictions, national security reviews, and international trade laws. Compliance with foreign investment regulations mitigates legal risks associated with global investments.

ESG Compliance: Increasing focus on Environmental, Social, and Governance (ESG) factors necessitates integrating sustainability considerations into investment strategies. ESG compliance enhances corporate responsibility and mitigates reputational risks.

Taxation: Tax implications influence investment decisions and fund structuring. PE firms must navigate tax complexities to optimize returns and ensure compliance with evolving tax laws.

Case Studies in Private Equity

Case studies offer valuable insights into successful PE transactions, highlighting strategies, challenges, and outcomes:

Investment Thesis: Case studies articulate the rationale behind investment decisions, including market analysis, competitive positioning, and growth potential. A clear investment thesis guides strategic decision-making and aligns stakeholders' expectations.

Due Diligence: Detailed analysis of financial, operational, and legal aspects of target companies identifies risks and opportunities for value creation. Rigorous due diligence informs investment strategies and mitigates potential pitfalls.

Execution: Effective execution involves structuring transactions, negotiating terms, and implementing value enhancement strategies post-investment. Execution excellence translates investment thesis into actionable initiatives that drive company growth and profitability.

Value Creation: Initiatives to enhance company performance—such as operational efficiencies, strategic repositioning, and governance improvements—maximize portfolio value and investor returns.

Exit Strategy: Evaluation of exit options considers market conditions, investor preferences, and regulatory requirements. Optimal exit strategies—whether through IPOs, strategic sales, or secondary market transactions—realize investment gains and achieve liquidity for stakeholders.

Conclusion

Private equity thrives on a robust legal framework, strategic navigation of regulatory challenges, and insights gained from successful case studies. Effective management of legal and regulatory complexities ensures compliance, mitigates risks and enhances investor confidence. Case studies provide practical guidance, illustrating best practices, pitfalls to avoid, and strategies for achieving sustainable growth and profitability in dynamic market environments. As the PE landscape evolves, a deep understanding of legal intricacies, proactive regulatory compliance, and lessons learned from case studies remain essential for success in this competitive industry.

In summary, the synergy between legal acumen, regulatory diligence, and practical insights from case studies forms the bedrock of private equity's resilience and prosperity in today's global economy.

This section provides a comprehensive overview of private equity, covering its legal foundations, regulatory challenges, and practical applications through case studies.

Chapter 26: Private International Law in International Commercial Litigation

26.1 Principles of Private International Law

Private International Law, also known as conflict of laws, addresses legal issues that involve multiple jurisdictions. It provides rules and principles to determine which country's laws should apply when conflicts arise in international transactions or disputes. This field is crucial in international commercial litigation, where parties from different countries may have conflicting legal rights and obligations.

Key Principles:

1. **Choice of Law**: One of the fundamental principles of private international law is determining which jurisdiction's laws govern a particular dispute. This decision is often based on factors such as contractual agreements, the parties' domicile, the location of the transaction, or the nature of the legal issue.
2. **Jurisdiction**: Private international law defines rules for determining the jurisdiction of courts to hear a case. Jurisdictional issues arise when parties disagree on where a dispute should be litigated, considering factors such as the defendant's presence, forum selection clauses, and the location of assets or witnesses.
3. **Recognition and Enforcement of Judgments**: Once a court renders a judgment, private international law addresses the recognition and enforcement of that judgment in other jurisdictions. This involves evaluating whether the foreign judgment meets certain criteria, such as procedural fairness, jurisdictional competence, and public policy considerations.
4. **Conflict of Laws**: In cases involving multiple jurisdictions, private international law resolves conflicts

between different legal systems' laws. It provides methodologies, such as the "lex loci contracts" (law of the place where the contract was made) or "lex fori" (law of the forum), to determine applicable laws for specific issues like contract interpretation or tort liability.

5. **Public Policy Considerations**: Private international law incorporates public policy considerations to prevent enforcement of judgments that violate fundamental principles of justice or morality in the enforcing jurisdiction. This ensures that international legal cooperation respects fundamental rights and values across borders.

6. **International Treaties and Conventions**: Many countries have ratified international treaties and conventions that harmonize the rules of private international law. These treaties facilitate legal certainty and predictability in international transactions by providing uniform rules for jurisdiction, choice of law, and recognition of foreign judgments.

7. **Comity and Cooperation**: Private international law promotes principles of comity and international judicial cooperation. Courts in different jurisdictions may recognize each other's judgments and cooperate in sharing evidence or conducting cross-border proceedings to resolve disputes efficiently.

8. **Arbitration and Alternative Dispute Resolution**: Private international law governs international arbitration and alternative dispute resolution mechanisms. It addresses issues such as arbitrability, enforcement of arbitral awards, and the relationship between arbitration and judicial proceedings in different jurisdictions.

Importance in International Commercial Litigation:
In the context of international commercial litigation, private international law plays a crucial role in ensuring fairness, predictability, and efficiency in resolving disputes involving parties from diverse legal systems. By providing clear rules for determining applicable law, jurisdictional competence, and enforcement of judgments, private international law facilitates cross-border trade and investment while safeguarding legal rights and promoting international legal cooperation.

Conclusion:
Private international law is indispensable in navigating the complexities of international commercial litigation. Its principles provide a framework for resolving conflicts of laws, determining jurisdiction, and enforcing judgments across borders. As globalization continues to connect economies and legal systems worldwide, a robust understanding of private international law is essential for legal professionals involved in international transactions and disputes, promoting legal certainty, and facilitating equitable resolution of cross-border disputes.

This discipline remains pivotal in maintaining the balance between national sovereignty and international legal cooperation, ensuring that businesses and individuals can engage in global commerce with confidence in the predictability and fairness of the legal framework governing their transactions and disputes.

26.2 Jurisdiction and Choice of Law

Jurisdiction and choice of law are pivotal in international commercial litigation, governed by principles of private international law.

Jurisdiction: Determining which court has the authority to adjudicate a dispute involves complex considerations. Courts typically assess factors such as the defendant's presence, contractual forum selection clauses, and the location of assets or witnesses. The principle of forum non-convenience allows courts to decline jurisdiction if another jurisdiction is more appropriate for adjudicating the dispute.

Choice of Law: When parties from different jurisdictions are involved in a dispute, the choice of law determines which jurisdiction's laws govern the substantive issues. Common methodologies include the "lex loci contracts" (law of the place where the contract was made), "lex fori" (law of the forum), or the "proper law" chosen by the parties in their contract. Courts apply these principles to ensure consistency and predictability in resolving conflicts of laws.

26.3 Enforcement of Foreign Judgments

Enforcement of foreign judgments is essential for the effectiveness of international commercial litigation.

Recognition Criteria: Courts evaluate foreign judgments based on criteria such as jurisdictional competence, procedural fairness, and public policy considerations. The principle of comity guides courts in recognizing foreign judgments to promote international judicial cooperation and respect for the legal systems of other jurisdictions.

Enforcement Mechanisms: Mechanisms for enforcing foreign judgments vary by jurisdiction but commonly involve domestication procedures where foreign judgments are recognized as enforceable within the local jurisdiction. International treaties and conventions, such as the New York Convention on the Recognition and Enforcement of Foreign Arbitral Awards, facilitate the enforcement of foreign judgments and arbitral awards across multiple jurisdictions.

26.4 Case Studies in International Commercial Litigation

Case studies provide practical insights into the application of private international law in resolving complex international commercial disputes.

Example 1: Contractual Dispute: In a contract dispute between a German supplier and a French distributor, the choice of law clause stipulated German law. Despite the dispute being litigated in French courts, the court applied German law based on the parties' agreement, illustrating the primacy of contractual choice of law provisions.

Example 2: Jurisdictional Challenge: A multinational corporation faces a jurisdictional challenge in a product liability lawsuit filed in the United States by foreign plaintiffs. The corporation argues forum non convenience, advocating for the case to be heard in a more appropriate jurisdiction where witnesses and evidence are more accessible, highlighting the flexibility of jurisdictional principles in international litigation.

Example 3: Enforcement of Arbitral Award: Following a successful arbitration in Singapore between a Chinese investor and a Malaysian company, the investor seeks enforcement of the arbitral award in China. Despite initial challenges, the New York Convention facilitates the recognition and enforcement of the arbitral award in China, underscoring the international framework's role in promoting arbitration as an effective alternative dispute resolution mechanism.

Conclusion

Private international law in international commercial litigation encompasses jurisdictional determinations, choice of law considerations, and enforcement of foreign judgments critical for resolving disputes across borders. Case studies illustrate the practical application of these principles, showcasing how legal frameworks harmonize conflicting laws, uphold contractual agreements, and facilitate equitable outcomes in global business disputes. As global commerce expands, a nuanced understanding of private international law remains essential for legal practitioners and businesses navigating the complexities of international transactions and disputes.

Chapter 27: Private Law Aspects of the Law of Finance

27.1 Legal Principles in Financial Transactions

Financial transactions are governed by a set of legal principles that ensure clarity, enforceability, and fairness in the realm of finance. These principles form the backbone of regulatory frameworks and contractual agreements that underpin global financial markets.

Key Legal Principles:

1. **Contractual Freedom**: Central to financial transactions is the principle of contractual freedom, which allows parties to negotiate and agree upon terms that govern their financial relationships. This principle supports the autonomy of parties in defining rights, obligations, and remedies in financial contracts.

2. **Disclosure and Transparency**: Financial transactions require transparency and full disclosure of material information to all parties involved. This principle ensures that stakeholders make informed decisions based on accurate and comprehensive information, mitigating risks, and promoting market integrity.

3. **Legal Certainty**: Financial transactions rely on legal certainty, where laws and regulations provide clear guidelines and enforceable rights and obligations. This principle fosters stability and predictability in financial markets, enhancing investor confidence and facilitating efficient capital allocation.

4. **Enforceability of Contracts**: Contracts in financial transactions must be enforceable under applicable laws and regulations. This principle ensures that parties can seek legal remedies in case of breach or non-performance, thereby protecting their interests and promoting compliance with contractual obligations.

5. **Protection of Investors and Consumers**: Regulatory frameworks in financial law aim to protect investors and consumers from unfair practices, fraud, and market manipulation. This principle emphasizes market integrity, investor confidence, and equitable treatment of all participants in financial transactions.
6. **Risk Management and Prudence**: Financial transactions involve inherent risks, necessitating principles of risk management and prudence. Financial institutions and market participants are required to adopt measures to assess, monitor, and mitigate risks effectively, ensuring financial stability and resilience.
7. **Compliance with Regulatory Requirements**: Financial transactions must comply with applicable regulatory requirements, including securities laws, banking regulations, and anti-money laundering measures. This principle promotes market transparency, integrity, and adherence to legal standards.
8. **International Cooperation**: In the globalized financial landscape, principles of international cooperation are crucial. International agreements, treaties, and standards facilitate cross-border transactions, harmonize regulatory frameworks, and resolve legal conflicts arising from multinational financial activities.

Importance in Financial Law:

Legal principles in financial transactions are fundamental in shaping regulatory policies, contractual agreements, and market practices. They uphold fairness, accountability, and efficiency in financial markets while safeguarding stakeholders' interests and promoting economic stability. By providing a robust legal framework, these principles support innovation, investment, and sustainable growth in the global financial sector.

Conclusion:
The legal principles governing financial transactions underscore the importance of integrity, transparency, and compliance in global financial markets. They guide the conduct of parties, ensure the enforceability of contracts, and foster trust and confidence among investors and consumers. As financial systems evolve and interconnect globally, adherence to these principles remains essential for maintaining market stability, protecting stakeholders, and promoting equitable economic development. A comprehensive understanding of these principles is indispensable for legal professionals, policymakers, and market participants navigating the complexities of financial law in a dynamic and interconnected world.

27.2 Contractual Issues in Finance

Contractual issues in finance encompass a wide range of considerations that shape financial transactions and relationships between parties.

Key Aspects:

1. **Formation and Terms**: Financial contracts are governed by principles of offer, acceptance, and consideration. Clear and precise terms regarding financial obligations, payment schedules, interest rates, and conditions of performance are essential for contractual clarity and enforceability.
2. **Contractual Freedom**: Parties in financial transactions have the freedom to negotiate and agree upon terms that define their rights, duties, and liabilities. This principle allows for flexibility in structuring transactions to meet the parties' specific needs and objectives.
3. **Standard Form Contracts**: In financial markets, standard form contracts are prevalent, such as loan

agreements, derivatives contracts, and investment agreements. These contracts often incorporate industry-standard terms and conditions, balancing the need for efficiency with the requirement for fairness and transparency.

4. **Risk Allocation**: Financial contracts allocate risks between parties, specifying responsibilities for market fluctuations, default scenarios, force majeure events, and other contingencies. Effective risk allocation mechanisms are crucial for managing uncertainties and protecting parties' interests.
5. **Breach and Remedies**: Contractual disputes in finance may arise from breaches of contract, such as non-payment, non-performance, or violations of contractual terms. Remedies available to aggrieved parties include damages, specific performance, or termination of the contract, depending on the nature of the breach and applicable legal principles.
6. **Regulatory Compliance**: Financial contracts must comply with relevant regulatory requirements, including securities laws, banking regulations, and consumer protection statutes. Compliance ensures that contracts are enforceable and that parties operate within legal boundaries.

27.3 Regulatory Framework for Financial Markets

The regulatory framework for financial markets establishes rules and standards to ensure market integrity, investor protection, and systemic stability.

Components:

1. **Securities Regulations**: Regulations governing the issuance, trading, and disclosure of securities ensure transparency, fairness, and investor confidence in

capital markets. Key regulations include registration requirements, insider trading prohibitions, and disclosure obligations.
2. **Banking Regulations**: Regulations governing banks and financial institutions aim to safeguard depositor funds, maintain financial stability, and prevent systemic risks. These regulations cover capital adequacy, liquidity requirements, lending practices, and risk management standards.
3. **Consumer Protection Laws**: Laws protecting consumers in financial transactions ensure fair treatment, disclosure of terms, and prevention of predatory practices. These laws promote trust in financial services and products, enhancing consumer confidence and market participation.
4. **International Standards and Cooperation**: Global financial markets operate under international standards and agreements, such as the Basel Accords for banking regulation and IOSCO principles for securities regulation. International cooperation facilitates the harmonization of regulatory practices, cross-border supervision, and resolution of legal conflicts.

27.4 Case Studies in Financial Law

Case studies illustrate the application of legal principles and regulatory frameworks in resolving complex issues in financial markets.

Example 1: Derivatives Mis-selling Case: A financial institution is sued for mis-selling complex derivatives products to a corporate client. The case highlights issues of contractual misrepresentation, suitability of financial products, and regulatory obligations to provide fair and clear information to clients.

Example 2: Insider Trading Investigation: Regulators investigate allegations of insider trading involving senior executives of a publicly traded company. The case examines securities laws on insider trading, fiduciary duties of corporate officers, and regulatory enforcement measures to maintain market integrity.

Example 3: Bankruptcy and Debt Restructuring: A multinational corporation undergoes bankruptcy proceedings, requiring cross-border coordination of creditors, debt restructuring negotiations, and compliance with international insolvency laws. The case underscores the importance of legal frameworks in managing financial distress and protecting stakeholders' interests.

Conclusion

Private law aspects of finance encompass contractual issues, regulatory frameworks, and practical applications through case studies that illustrate the complexities and challenges in global financial markets. By adhering to legal principles, navigating regulatory requirements, and learning from real-world scenarios, stakeholders can promote financial stability, protect investor interests, and foster sustainable economic growth. A robust understanding of financial law is essential for legal professionals, regulators, and market participants to navigate the evolving landscape of global finance responsibly and effectively.

Chapter 28: Project Finance

28.1 Fundamentals of Project Finance

Project finance is a specialized method of financing large-scale infrastructure and industrial projects where the project's assets and cash flows serve as collateral for loans. This form of financing is distinct from traditional corporate finance because it relies primarily on the project's projected cash flows for repayment, rather than the creditworthiness of the project sponsors. It is commonly used for projects such as infrastructure development (e.g., highways, airports, power plants), natural resource extraction (e.g., mining, oil, and gas), and large-scale industrial projects (e.g., manufacturing facilities).

Key Elements and Principles:

1. **Structure and Participants**: Project finance involves a structured financial arrangement typically led by a consortium of lenders (banks, financial institutions) and investors. These parties provide debt and equity financing based on the project's financial projections, with a special purpose vehicle (SPV) often established to ring-fence the project from the sponsors' other assets.

2. **Project Cash Flow**: The viability of project finance hinges on the project's ability to generate predictable and sufficient cash flows to service debt obligations and provide returns to equity investors. Cash flow projections are crucial in assessing project feasibility and determining financing terms.

3. **Risk Allocation**: Project finance requires meticulous risk assessment and allocation among stakeholders. Risks commonly considered include construction risks (e.g., delays, cost overruns), operational risks (e.g., performance of technology, market demand), and

financial risks (e.g., interest rate fluctuations, currency risks). Contracts and legal agreements, such as construction contracts, supply agreements, and off-take agreements, often include risk mitigation provisions to protect investors and lenders.

4. **Security and Collateral**: Lenders in project finance rely on the project's assets, cash flows, and contractual rights as primary collateral. This may include mortgage over project assets, pledges of shares in the SPV, and guarantees from sponsors or other credit enhancements to mitigate risks.
5. **Long-Term Financing**: Projects financed through project finance often require long-term financing structures that match the project's economic life. Loan tenures can extend over decades, reflecting the long payback periods associated with infrastructure and industrial projects.
6. **Non-Recourse or Limited Recourse Financing**: Project finance structures often involve non-recourse or limited recourse financing, where lenders have limited or no recourse to the sponsors' other assets in case of project default. This shifts the risk to lenders and enhances the project's creditworthiness based on its standalone performance.
7. **Legal and Regulatory Considerations**: Project finance requires navigating complex legal and regulatory environments. This includes compliance with local laws, permits, environmental regulations, and contractual obligations that impact project execution and financing.
8. **Role of Advisors and Consultants**: Given the complexity of project finance transactions, advisors and consultants play a crucial role in structuring deals,

conducting due diligence, negotiating contracts, and managing risks on behalf of project sponsors, lenders, and investors.

Importance and Application:

Project finance plays a vital role in financing large-scale projects that contribute to economic development, infrastructure improvement, and industrial growth. By leveraging the project's assets and cash flows, project finance facilitates investment in projects with substantial capital requirements and long payback periods that traditional financing methods may not adequately support. It promotes private sector participation in public infrastructure projects and fosters collaboration between public entities, private investors, and financial institutions to achieve mutually beneficial outcomes.

Conclusion:

Fundamentals of project finance underscore its structured approach to financing complex projects based on cash flow predictability, risk management, and legal frameworks. This financing method supports infrastructure development, industrial expansion, and natural resource extraction by aligning investor interests with project performance. As global demand for infrastructure and energy grows, project finance remains a pivotal tool for mobilizing capital and expertise to address societal needs and promote sustainable economic growth. Understanding the principles and dynamics of project finance is essential for stakeholders seeking to navigate the complexities of financing large-scale projects effectively and responsibly in a dynamic global economy.

28.2 Risk Allocation in Project Finance

Risk allocation is a critical aspect of project finance, involving the identification, assessment, and mitigation of risks among project stakeholders.

Key Elements of Risk Allocation:

1. **Construction Risks**: Project finance addresses risks associated with construction, including delays, cost overruns, and contractor performance. Contracts typically define responsibilities, timelines, and penalties for non-compliance to manage these risks effectively.
2. **Operational Risks**: Once operational, projects face risks related to performance, maintenance, and technological obsolescence. Mitigation strategies include maintenance agreements, technology warranties, and contingency plans to ensure uninterrupted operations.
3. **Market Risks**: Projects are exposed to market risks such as demand fluctuations, commodity price volatility, and regulatory changes affecting revenue streams. Off-take agreements, price hedging mechanisms, and diversification strategies help manage these risks and stabilize cash flows.
4. **Financial Risks**: Financial risks encompass interest rate fluctuations, currency exchange risks (for international projects), and capital structure risks. Hedging instruments, debt structuring techniques, and financial covenants mitigate exposure to financial volatility.
5. **Environmental and Social Risks**: Compliance with environmental regulations and social responsibilities is crucial. Environmental impact assessments, community engagement programs, and adherence to

international standards (e.g., IFC Performance Standards) mitigate reputational risks and legal liabilities.
6. **Legal and Regulatory Risks**: Projects must navigate complex legal and regulatory environments, including permitting requirements, land acquisition, tax implications, and government approvals. Legal advisors ensure compliance and mitigate legal risks through comprehensive due diligence and contract negotiations.

28.3 Legal and Regulatory Framework

The legal and regulatory framework in project finance provides the foundation for structuring, executing, and operating projects while ensuring compliance and protecting stakeholders' interests.

Components of the Legal and Regulatory Framework:
1. **Project Structuring**: Legal advisors assist in structuring projects to optimize tax efficiency, mitigate risks, and enhance project bankability. This involves choosing appropriate legal entities (e.g., SPVs), drafting project documents, and negotiating agreements with stakeholders.
2. **Contractual Agreements**: Key contracts include construction contracts, supply agreements, off-take agreements, and financing agreements. These contracts define the rights, obligations, and responsibilities of parties, ensuring clarity and enforceability throughout project phases.
3. **Permitting and Approvals**: Projects require permits and approvals from regulatory authorities, environmental agencies, and local governments. Legal advisors facilitate compliance with regulatory

requirements, navigate permitting processes, and mitigate risks associated with regulatory changes.
4. **Financial Regulations**: Financial regulations govern project financing, securities issuance, and investor protection. Compliance with banking regulations, securities laws, anti-money laundering rules, and tax regulations ensures transparency, accountability, and legal certainty in financial transactions.
5. **Dispute Resolution**: Legal frameworks provide mechanisms for resolving disputes arising from project contracts, regulatory issues, or stakeholder conflicts. Arbitration clauses, mediation processes, and judicial recourse mechanisms safeguard parties' rights and minimize litigation risks.

28.4 Case Studies in Project Finance

Case studies offer practical insights into successful and challenging project finance transactions, highlighting strategies, risks, and outcomes.

Example 1: Infrastructure Development Project: A consortium of investors and lenders finances a toll road project in Southeast Asia. The case study examines risk allocation strategies, including construction delays, traffic projections, and revenue volatility, mitigated through robust contractual agreements and financial hedging mechanisms.

Example 2: Renewable Energy Project: Financing a wind farm in Europe involves navigating regulatory approvals, grid connectivity issues, and power purchase agreements. The case study showcases innovative financing structures, environmental compliance measures, and stakeholder engagement strategies critical for project success.

Example 3: Mining Project: Financing a mining project in Africa involves managing political risks, community relations, and commodity price fluctuations. The case study evaluates legal frameworks for land acquisition, environmental permitting, and social responsibility initiatives to mitigate operational risks and enhance project sustainability.

Conclusion

Project finance relies on effective risk allocation, adherence to legal and regulatory frameworks, and lessons learned from case studies to finance and execute complex infrastructure and industrial projects globally. By leveraging legal expertise, regulatory compliance, and practical insights from successful projects, stakeholders can optimize project outcomes, manage risks effectively, and contribute to sustainable economic development. A comprehensive understanding of project finance dynamics is essential for legal professionals, financiers, and project developers navigating the evolving landscape of global infrastructure investment and development.

Chapter 29: Public International Law

29.1 Principles of Public International Law

Public International Law (PIL) governs the relations between states, international organizations, and other entities in the international community. It is a complex and evolving legal framework that shapes interactions on a global scale, addressing issues ranging from diplomatic relations to human rights, environmental protection, and the use of force. The principles of PIL are derived from treaties, customary practices, judicial decisions, and scholarly writings, reflecting consensus among states and evolving norms of international behaviour.

Key Principles:

1. **Sovereignty**: Sovereignty is a fundamental principle of PIL, affirming the equality and independence of states in the international system. It entails the right of states to govern their internal affairs without external interference, subject to obligations under international law.
2. **State Responsibility**: States are responsible for their conduct under international law, encompassing actions of state organs, state officials, and entities exercising governmental authority. State responsibility includes obligations to respect and ensure human rights, uphold treaty commitments, and refrain from actions that violate international norms.
3. **Sources of International Law**: The sources of international law include treaties, customary international law, general principles of law recognized by civilized nations, and judicial decisions. Treaties are formal agreements between states, while customary law evolves from state practices accepted as binding by the international community.

4. **International Organizations**: International organizations, such as the United Nations (UN) and the World Trade Organization (WTO), play significant roles in PIL. They are governed by their constitutive treaties and operate within the framework of international law to promote peace, security, cooperation, and sustainable development.
5. **Human Rights**: Human rights are universal, inherent rights recognized under international law, protecting individuals' dignity, equality, and freedom from abuse. International human rights treaties and customary law establish standards for state conduct and accountability for human rights violations.
6. **Use of Force and Conflict Resolution**: PIL regulates the use of force between states, emphasizing peaceful dispute resolution through negotiation, mediation, arbitration, and judicial settlement. The United Nations Charter prohibits the use of force except in self-defense or with Security Council authorization, promoting collective security and preventing armed conflicts.
7. **Environmental Protection**: Environmental principles in PIL address global challenges such as climate change, biodiversity conservation, and sustainable development. Treaties like the Paris Agreement establish obligations for states to mitigate greenhouse gas emissions and cooperate in environmental conservation efforts.
8. **State Immunity**: State immunity protects states from foreign jurisdiction and enforcement, safeguarding sovereignty and promoting diplomatic relations. Exceptions exist for commercial activities, human rights violations, and other specified matters under international law.

Importance and Application:
Public International Law is indispensable for promoting global peace, cooperation, and respect for fundamental rights and principles. It provides a framework for states to interact, resolve disputes, and collaborate on shared challenges in a rules-based international order. PIL governs diverse areas of international relations, including trade, humanitarian law, state succession, and the protection of vulnerable populations, reflecting evolving norms and collective aspirations for a just and peaceful world.

Conclusion:
The principles of Public International Law underscore the importance of mutual respect, cooperation, and adherence to legal obligations in global affairs. By upholding principles of sovereignty, state responsibility, human rights, and environmental stewardship, PIL fosters stability, justice, and sustainable development across borders. As the international community faces complex challenges and opportunities, a robust understanding and application of PIL are essential for navigating global issues, promoting multilateral cooperation, and advancing shared goals of peace, security, and prosperity for all nations and peoples.

29.2 Sources of International Law

Sources of international law are diverse and include treaties, customary practices, general principles recognized by nations, judicial decisions, and writings of legal scholars. Treaties are formal agreements between states or international organizations, codifying rights, and obligations. Customary international law arises from consistent state practices accepted as binding, while general principles of law are common to legal systems worldwide. Judicial decisions from international courts and tribunals interpret and develop international law, influencing state conduct and establishing precedents. Legal scholars contribute through academic writings and opinions, shaping interpretations and applications of international legal norms.

29.3 International Organizations and Institutions

International organizations and institutions play pivotal roles in shaping and implementing public international law. Organizations like the United Nations (UN), the International Court of Justice (ICJ), and the World Trade Organization (WTO) provide frameworks for cooperation, conflict resolution, and governance. The UN promotes peace, security, and human rights through its Charter and specialized agencies, fostering multilateral diplomacy and collective action on global issues. The ICJ settles disputes between states based on international law, while the WTO regulates international trade and resolves trade disputes. These institutions facilitate international cooperation, uphold legal standards, and address transnational challenges, reflecting the evolving dynamics of global governance.

29.4 Case Studies in Public International Law

Case studies illustrate the practical application and impact of public international law in resolving complex international disputes and promoting global cooperation.

Example 1: Nicaragua v. United States (ICJ): The ICJ case addressed Nicaragua's allegations of unlawful military intervention and support for contras by the United States in the 1980s. The court ruled on violations of sovereignty and non-interference principles under international law, establishing precedents on state responsibility and the use of force.

Example 2: Gabcikovo-Nagymaros Project (ICJ): Hungary and Slovakia disputed the construction of a dam on the Danube

River, leading to environmental concerns and allegations of treaty violations. The ICJ decision highlighted principles of environmental protection, equitable utilization of shared resources, and peaceful resolution of transboundary water disputes.

Example 3: South China Sea Arbitration (PCA): The Permanent Court of Arbitration (PCA) ruled on maritime claims in the South China Sea, addressing conflicting territorial claims and China's assertion of historical rights. The arbitration decision clarified international maritime law, including rights under the UN Convention on the Law of the Sea (UNCLOS), influencing regional security and maritime governance.

Conclusion

Public international law draws from diverse sources, institutional frameworks, and case studies to regulate state conduct, promote global cooperation, and resolve disputes peacefully. By upholding legal standards, facilitating international dialogue, and addressing global challenges, international organizations and institutions contribute to a rules-based international order that advances justice, human rights, and sustainable development worldwide. Case studies exemplify the practical application of international law principles, demonstrating their role in shaping international relations and promoting stability in an interconnected world.

Chapter 30: Regulation and Infrastructure of International Commercial Arbitration

30.1 Legal Framework for International Arbitration

The legal framework for international commercial arbitration provides a structured mechanism for resolving disputes outside traditional court systems, tailored to meet the needs of global business transactions. Arbitration offers flexibility, confidentiality, and enforceability of awards across international borders, governed by national laws and international conventions.

Key Elements:

1. **Arbitration Agreements**: Parties agree to resolve disputes through arbitration, stipulating procedural rules, arbitral tribunal composition, and governing law. Arbitration agreements are enforceable under national laws and recognized internationally under the New York Convention on the Recognition and Enforcement of Foreign Arbitral Awards.

2. **Arbitral Institutions**: Institutions like the International Chamber of Commerce (ICC), the London Court of International Arbitration (LCIA), and the Singapore International Arbitration Centre (SIAC) administer arbitration proceedings. They provide rules, appoint arbitrators, and facilitate efficient dispute resolution under institutional guidelines.

3. **Arbitral Tribunals**: Arbitral tribunals consist of impartial arbitrators appointed by parties or arbitral institutions based on expertise in legal, technical, or industry-specific matters. Tribunals conduct hearings, assess evidence, and render binding decisions (awards) that resolve disputes effectively.

4. **Procedural Flexibility**: Arbitration allows parties to customize procedures, choose arbitrators, and determine hearing schedules and locations, accommodating diverse cultural and legal backgrounds in international disputes.
5. **Enforcement of Awards**: Arbitral awards are enforceable globally through the New York Convention, promoting certainty and finality in dispute resolution outcomes. Courts in over 160 countries uphold arbitral awards, subject to limited grounds for refusal, ensuring the efficacy of arbitration as a preferred method for resolving cross-border disputes.
6. **Legal Support and Compliance**: National laws and procedural rules govern arbitration proceedings, ensuring compliance with due process, fairness, and transparency. Legal frameworks regulate arbitrator conduct, procedural fairness, and enforcement of interim measures to safeguard parties' rights throughout arbitration.

Importance and Application:
The legal framework for international arbitration facilitates efficient, impartial, and enforceable resolution of cross-border disputes, enhancing predictability and reducing litigation costs for businesses worldwide. Arbitration promotes party autonomy, respects cultural diversity, and supports international trade and investment by providing a neutral forum for resolving complex commercial conflicts.

Conclusion:
The legal framework for international commercial arbitration underscores its role in promoting global commerce, fostering trust among parties, and advancing legal certainty in cross-border transactions. By upholding principles of fairness, enforceability, and procedural flexibility, international

arbitration contributes to a harmonized and efficient dispute resolution mechanism that supports economic growth and stability in an interconnected global economy. Understanding and navigating the regulations and infrastructure of international arbitration are essential for legal practitioners, businesses, and stakeholders seeking effective resolution of international commercial disputes in a dynamic and competitive business environment.

30.2 Arbitration Agreements and Clauses

Arbitration agreements and clauses are foundational elements of international commercial arbitration, defining the terms under which parties agree to resolve disputes outside traditional court systems.

Key Aspects:

1. **Formation and Contents**: Arbitration agreements are contractual provisions where parties agree to submit disputes arising from their commercial relationship to arbitration. They outline procedural rules, the number and qualifications of arbitrators, the seat of arbitration, governing law, and the language of proceedings.

2. **Enforceability**: Arbitration agreements are enforceable under national laws and international conventions, such as the New York Convention. Courts generally uphold arbitration agreements, respecting party autonomy in choosing dispute resolution mechanisms.

3. **Scope and Validity**: Clarity in drafting arbitration clauses is crucial to defining the scope of disputes subject to arbitration. Validity considerations include consent of parties, compliance with formalities under applicable law, and exclusion of disputes not intended for arbitration.

4. **Multi-Party and Multi-Contract Arbitration**: Arbitration agreements can accommodate multiple parties or contracts through the joinder of additional parties or consolidation of related arbitration proceedings. These mechanisms promote efficiency and consistency in resolving complex disputes involving multiple stakeholders.
5. **Adaptability**: Arbitration clauses can be tailored to suit the specific needs of parties and the characteristics of their commercial relationships. Flexibility in procedural rules, choice of arbitrators, and venue selection enhances the efficiency and effectiveness of arbitration as a dispute resolution mechanism.

30.3 Institutional vs. Ad Hoc Arbitration

Arbitration proceedings may be administered by institutions (institutional arbitration) or conducted without institutional support (ad hoc arbitration), each offering distinct advantages and procedural frameworks.

Institutional Arbitration:
1. **Administration and Rules**: Institutional arbitration is administered by specialized arbitral institutions (e.g., ICC, LCIA, SIAC), which provide procedural rules, appoint arbitrators, and administer fees. Institutional rules offer predictability, administrative support, and a framework for resolving disputes under established guidelines.
2. **Arbitrator Appointment**: Institutions facilitate the appointment of arbitrators, often from their panels of qualified professionals with expertise in specific industries or legal disciplines. This ensures arbitrator impartiality, competence, and efficiency in handling complex disputes.

3. **Enforcement of Awards**: Institutional arbitration benefits from the institutional reputation and compliance with international standards, facilitating enforcement of arbitral awards globally under the New York Convention. Institutions oversee procedural fairness, award scrutiny, and transparency in dispute resolution.

Ad Hoc Arbitration:

1. **Flexibility and Autonomy**: Ad hoc arbitration allows parties to tailor procedures, select arbitrators directly, and negotiate terms without institutional intervention. This flexibility accommodates unique case dynamics, cultural preferences, and cost considerations, fostering party autonomy in dispute resolution.
2. **Procedural Challenges**: Ad hoc arbitration requires parties to manage administrative tasks, procedural complexities, and logistical arrangements independently. Clear arbitration clauses and agreements are essential to defining procedures, arbitrator selection, and dispute resolution mechanisms effectively.
3. **Enforcement and Credibility**: Ad hoc awards may face challenges in enforcement due to procedural irregularities or a perceived lack of institutional oversight. However, ad hoc arbitration benefits from confidentiality, procedural flexibility, and direct party control over dispute resolution outcomes.

30.4 Case Studies in International Arbitration

Case studies illustrate the practical application and outcomes of international arbitration in resolving complex commercial disputes across diverse industries and jurisdictions.

Example 1: ICC Arbitration in Construction Dispute: A multinational construction project in Asia involves disputes over contract performance and payment delays. ICC arbitration administered under ICC rules facilitates expedited proceedings, expert determination of technical issues, and enforcement of awards, ensuring project continuity and financial accountability.

Example 2: Ad Hoc Arbitration in Technology Licensing Dispute: Parties in a technology licensing agreement dispute intellectual property rights and royalty payments. Ad hoc arbitration allows customization of procedural rules, expert determination of licensing terms, and confidential resolution without public scrutiny, preserving business relationships and proprietary information.

Example 3: SIAC Arbitration in Cross-Border Commercial Contract: Cross-border commercial contracts between European and Asian companies face disputes over breach of contract and supply chain disruptions. SIAC arbitration administered under SIAC rules ensures procedural fairness, expedited resolution, and enforceability of awards, fostering international trade relations and regulatory compliance.

Conclusion

International commercial arbitration offers a structured and effective mechanism for resolving cross-border disputes, supported by arbitration agreements, institutional frameworks, and case studies that demonstrate its adaptability and enforceability in global business environments. Whether through institutional administration or ad hoc procedures, arbitration accommodates diverse commercial relationships, promotes procedural fairness, and upholds party autonomy in achieving equitable and enforceable dispute resolution outcomes. Understanding the regulations and infrastructure of international arbitration is essential for legal practitioners, businesses, and stakeholders navigating complex international disputes and safeguarding commercial interests in a globalized economy.

Chapter 31: Research Methodology in Law

31.1 Fundamentals of Legal Research

Fundamentals of legal research encompass systematic methods and techniques used to identify, analyze, and interpret legal sources and principles essential for resolving legal issues and supporting legal arguments. Legal research in law involves comprehensive exploration of primary sources (e.g., statutes, regulations, case law) and secondary sources (e.g., legal commentary, scholarly articles, treatises) to understand legal doctrines, precedents, and evolving interpretations.

Key Components:

1. **Primary Sources**: Legal research begins with primary sources such as legislative enactments (statutes), judicial decisions (case law), and administrative regulations. These sources establish binding legal norms, rules, and precedents that govern legal rights, duties, and procedures.

2. **Case Law Analysis**: Analyzing judicial decisions involves identifying relevant cases, understanding court reasoning, and assessing precedential value in shaping legal principles. Case law research explores how courts interpret statutes, apply legal doctrines, and resolve disputes in specific factual contexts.

3. **Statutory Interpretation**: Interpreting statutes requires identifying legislative intent, and analyzing text, legislative history, and context to determine the scope and application of statutory provisions. Statutory research involves accessing current and historical versions of statutes, amendments, and legislative debates.

4. **Secondary Sources**: Legal researchers consult secondary sources like legal encyclopedias, annotated codes, law reviews, and treatises to gain insights into legal concepts, trends, and scholarly interpretations. Secondary sources provide critical analysis, commentary, and references to primary authorities, aiding in understanding complex legal issues.
5. **Legal Databases and Tools**: Access to online legal databases (e.g., Westlaw, LexisNexis) and research tools enhances efficiency in legal research. These platforms offer comprehensive search capabilities, case citators, legislative histories, and cross-referencing features to locate relevant authorities and verify legal citations.
6. **Citation and Validation**: Effective legal research involves accurate citation of authorities and validation of sources to ensure the reliability and credibility of legal arguments. Citation formats (e.g., Bluebook, APA) adhere to standardized conventions for referencing statutes, cases, and scholarly works in legal writing.
7. **Practical Application**: Legal research methodologies support various legal tasks, including drafting legal memoranda, preparing briefs, advising clients, and supporting litigation strategies. Research findings contribute to informed decision-making, persuasive advocacy, and compliance with legal standards and ethical obligations.

Importance and Application:
Fundamentals of legal research are indispensable for legal professionals, scholars, and students in navigating complex legal landscapes, interpreting legal principles, and advancing legal knowledge. Effective research methodologies promote accuracy, thoroughness, and clarity in legal analysis, facilitating

reasoned arguments and informed legal opinions across diverse practice areas and jurisdictions.

Conclusion:

Legal research methodology forms the cornerstone of legal scholarship and practice, empowering stakeholders to access, interpret, and apply legal principles effectively. By mastering fundamental research techniques, legal professionals enhance their ability to uphold justice, advocate for client interests, and contribute to the evolution of law in a dynamic and evolving societal context. Embracing rigorous research methodologies fosters excellence in legal education, scholarship, and professional development, promoting ethical conduct and adherence to principles of justice in the pursuit of legal expertise and service.

31.2 Research Design and Methods

Research design and methods in legal research encompass systematic approaches and frameworks for conducting inquiries, gathering evidence, and analyzing legal issues to develop comprehensive and substantiated conclusions.

Key Aspects:
1. **Research Framework**: Establishing a research framework involves defining research objectives, selecting methodologies, and outlining procedures for conducting legal inquiries. Research designs may include doctrinal (legal analysis based on statutes, case law) or empirical (data-driven analysis, surveys, interviews) approaches, depending on research goals and subject matter.
2. **Methodological Approaches**: Legal research methods range from qualitative (interpretative analysis, case studies) to quantitative (statistical analysis, empirical

data collection), adapting methodologies to address specific legal questions and theoretical frameworks. Methods include comparative analysis, doctrinal scrutiny, case studies, and interdisciplinary approaches integrating law with social sciences or humanities.
3. **Literature Review**: Conducting a literature review involves evaluating existing legal scholarship, case law, and regulatory frameworks relevant to the research topic. Literature reviews inform research methodology, identify gaps in knowledge, and validate research hypotheses through critical analysis of primary and secondary sources.
4. **Legal Analysis Techniques**: Legal research employs analytical techniques such as doctrinal analysis (interpretation of statutes, case law), legal reasoning (deductive and inductive reasoning), and synthesis of legal principles to construct coherent arguments and substantiate research findings. Methods also include legal taxonomy, classification of legal concepts, and application of theoretical frameworks to legal issues.
5. **Ethical Considerations**: Research design in law emphasizes ethical principles, confidentiality, informed consent (for empirical research involving human subjects), and compliance with legal and regulatory standards. Ethical guidelines ensure integrity, fairness, and respect for the rights of research participants and stakeholders.

31.3 Data Collection and Analysis

Data collection and analysis in legal research involve systematic gathering, validation, and interpretation of empirical evidence, legal precedents, and factual information to support research hypotheses and conclusions.

Key Processes:
1. **Data Sources**: Legal researchers collect data from primary sources (e.g., statutes, case law, contracts), secondary sources (e.g., legal commentary, scholarly articles), and empirical sources (e.g., surveys, interviews, case studies). Data sources vary based on research objectives, jurisdictional context, and availability of information.
2. **Empirical Research Methods**: Empirical legal research employs qualitative (interviews, focus groups) and quantitative (surveys, statistical analysis) methods to gather data on legal phenomena, behaviours, and outcomes. Methodological rigour ensures the validity, reliability, and relevance of empirical findings in legal analysis.
3. **Legal Database Analysis**: Utilizing legal databases (e.g., Westlaw, LexisNexis) and research tools facilitates comprehensive data retrieval, case citation analysis, and cross-referencing of legal authorities. Database analysis supports doctrinal research, legal precedent identification, and comparative legal analysis across jurisdictions.
4. **Data Validation and Interpretation**: Validating data involves assessing the accuracy, completeness, and relevance of information obtained from diverse sources. Legal researchers interpret data through thematic analysis, case narrative synthesis, and comparative assessment to derive meaningful insights and conclusions relevant to research objectives.
5. **Statistical Analysis**: Quantitative legal research employs statistical techniques (e.g., regression analysis, and hypothesis testing) to analyze empirical data, measure relationships between variables, and

assess the significance of findings in legal contexts. Statistical analysis enhances empirical research validity, supports evidence-based conclusions, and informs policy or legal reform recommendations.

31.4 Presenting Legal Research

Presenting legal research involves effectively communicating findings, analysis, and conclusions to diverse audiences, including legal professionals, policymakers, academics, and stakeholders.

Key Considerations:

1. **Research Structure**: Structuring legal research involves organizing content logically with a clear introduction, methodology description, findings presentation, and a conclusion summarizing key insights and implications. A structured format enhances the readability, comprehension, and accessibility of research outcomes.

2. **Writing Style and Clarity**: Legal research employs precise, concise, and jargon-free language to convey complex legal concepts, arguments, and analysis. Writing style emphasizes clarity, coherence, and adherence to academic or professional writing conventions (e.g., citation formats, and legal terminology).

3. **Visual Presentation**: Incorporating visual aids (e.g., tables, charts, diagrams) enhances presentation clarity, facilitates data visualization, and supports the interpretation of complex legal data or statistical findings. Visual elements supplement textual analysis, improve audience engagement, and reinforce research findings effectively.

4. **Legal Argumentation**: Legal research presents arguments based on rigorous analysis of legal

principles, precedents, and empirical evidence. Structuring arguments logically, addressing counterarguments, and substantiating claims with credible sources strengthen the persuasive impact and academic rigour of research presentations.
5. **Audience Engagement**: Tailoring research presentations to audience needs, interests, and knowledge levels fosters engagement and understanding. Effective communication techniques include oral presentations, conference papers, policy briefs, and multimedia formats that resonate with diverse stakeholders and promote discourse on legal issues.

Conclusion

Research methodology in law encompasses rigorous approaches to designing, conducting, and presenting legal inquiries, emphasizing methodological diversity, ethical standards, and evidence-based analysis. By integrating theoretical frameworks with empirical research methods, legal scholars and practitioners contribute to knowledge advancement, policy development, and legal reform initiatives in addressing contemporary challenges and promoting justice, fairness, and the rule of law in society. Mastering research design, data collection, analysis techniques, and presentation skills enhances the impact and relevance of legal research in informing legal practice, policy decisions, and scholarly discourse in a dynamic and evolving global legal landscape.

Chapter 32: Research Methods in Business, Commercial, and Corporate Law

32.1 Legal Research in Business Law

Legal research in business law involves systematic exploration and analysis of legal principles, regulations, and case law relevant to commercial transactions, corporate governance, and regulatory compliance within business contexts.

Key Aspects:

1. **Transactional Analysis**: Business law research focuses on the legal aspects of commercial transactions, including contract formation, negotiation, and enforcement. Researchers analyze statutory provisions, case precedents, and industry standards to assess legal risks, rights, and obligations affecting business agreements.

2. **Corporate Governance**: Research in corporate law examines legal frameworks governing corporate entities, board governance, shareholder rights, and fiduciary duties. Scholars explore corporate statutes, regulatory guidelines (e.g., SEC regulations), and judicial decisions shaping corporate governance practices and compliance standards.

3. **Regulatory Compliance**: Legal researchers investigate regulatory frameworks impacting business operations, including antitrust laws, consumer protection regulations, securities laws, and international trade regulations. Compliance research involves interpreting regulatory requirements, assessing legal liabilities, and advising businesses on risk management strategies.

4. **Emerging Issues**: Research in business law addresses emerging legal issues in digital commerce, intellectual

property rights, data privacy, and sustainability practices. Scholars analyze evolving legal doctrines, regulatory developments, and case law trends influencing business strategies and corporate decision-making in a globalized economy.
5. **Interdisciplinary Perspectives**: Integrating interdisciplinary perspectives (e.g., economics, finance, ethics) enhances legal research in business law, examining broader implications of legal principles on economic efficiency, corporate social responsibility, and ethical business conduct.

Importance and Application:
Legal research in business, commercial, and corporate law is essential for informing business practices, promoting legal compliance, and mitigating legal risks in dynamic business environments. By analyzing legal frameworks, interpreting judicial decisions, and anticipating regulatory changes, researchers contribute to informed decision-making, strategic planning, and sustainable business operations in a competitive marketplace.

Conclusion:
Effective legal research methods in business law empower legal scholars, practitioners, and corporate stakeholders to navigate complex legal challenges, uphold corporate governance standards, and foster innovation and responsible business practices. By integrating rigorous research methodologies with practical insights, legal professionals enhance legal compliance, corporate governance effectiveness, and ethical conduct in business operations, advancing principles of accountability, transparency, and legal certainty in commercial transactions and corporate governance frameworks.

32.2 Comparative Legal Analysis

Comparative legal analysis in business, commercial, and corporate law involves examining similarities and differences in legal systems, regulations, and judicial decisions across jurisdictions to identify best practices, regulatory trends, and implications for global business operations. Researchers conduct comparative studies to assess legal frameworks governing commercial transactions, corporate governance structures, and regulatory compliance in diverse national and international contexts. By analyzing how different legal systems address similar legal issues or regulatory challenges, comparative legal analysis informs business strategies, legal reforms, and cross-border transactions, enhancing legal certainty and compliance in global markets.

32.3 Empirical Research Methods

Empirical research methods in business, commercial, and corporate law involve gathering and analyzing quantitative or qualitative data to investigate legal phenomena, behaviours, and outcomes within business contexts. Researchers employ surveys, interviews, case studies, and statistical analysis to explore empirical questions related to corporate governance practices, regulatory compliance, consumer behaviour, and business strategies. Empirical research contributes empirical evidence to legal scholarship, informing policy decisions, regulatory reforms, and corporate strategies based on data-driven insights into legal practices, market behaviours, and business operations.

32.4 Case Studies in Legal Research

Case studies in legal research provide in-depth examinations of specific legal issues, disputes, or regulatory challenges within business, commercial, and corporate law. Researchers analyze real-world cases, court decisions, or corporate controversies to explore legal precedents, doctrinal principles, and practical implications for legal practice and business operations. Case studies illustrate the application of legal theories, strategic decision-making, and consequences of legal disputes or regulatory non-compliance, offering valuable insights into legal strategies, risk management practices, and ethical considerations in business environments.

Conclusion

Research methods in business, commercial, and corporate law encompass diverse approaches including comparative legal analysis, empirical research methods, and case studies. These methodologies contribute to understanding legal frameworks, regulatory compliance, and business practices in a globalized economy. By applying rigorous research techniques, legal scholars, practitioners, and corporate stakeholders enhance legal compliance, strategic decision-making, and ethical conduct in business operations, fostering sustainable growth and legal certainty in commercial transactions and corporate governance frameworks.

Chapter 33: Research Skills and Methods in Law

33.1 Advanced Legal Research Techniques

Advanced legal research techniques in law encompass sophisticated methodologies and skills employed by legal scholars, practitioners, and researchers to explore complex legal issues, interpret legal sources, and contribute to legal scholarship and practice.

Key Aspects:

1. **Electronic Legal Databases**: Utilizing advanced features of electronic legal databases (e.g., Westlaw, LexisNexis) enhances research efficiency and accuracy. Researchers leverage Boolean operators, advanced search algorithms, and citation analysis tools to locate relevant statutes, case law, and scholarly articles, facilitating comprehensive legal analysis.

2. **Legal Analytics**: Legal analytics tools offer data-driven insights into judicial decision-making, case outcomes, and litigation trends. Researchers apply statistical analysis, predictive modelling, and data visualization techniques to analyze legal data, identify patterns, and forecast legal outcomes, supporting strategic litigation strategies and legal research methodologies.

3. **Artificial Intelligence in Legal Research**: Integrating artificial intelligence (AI) technologies (e.g., natural language processing, machine learning) enhances legal research capabilities. AI-powered legal research platforms automate document review, legal citation analysis, and contract analysis tasks, improving research accuracy, efficiency, and decision support in complex legal matters.

4. **Interdisciplinary Research**: Conducting interdisciplinary research integrates legal analysis with

insights from other disciplines (e.g., economics, sociology, political science). Researchers apply interdisciplinary methodologies to explore multifaceted legal issues, assess societal impacts, and propose holistic solutions to legal challenges in diverse contexts.
5. **Advanced Citation and Validation Techniques**: Advanced legal research incorporates rigorous citation management and validation techniques to ensure the accuracy and reliability of legal sources. Researchers verify legal citations, assess the credibility of authorities, and adhere to citation norms (e.g., Bluebook, APA) in legal writing, enhancing transparency and scholarly rigour in legal research publications.

Importance and Application:
Advanced legal research techniques are crucial for legal professionals and scholars to navigate complex legal landscapes, address emerging legal issues, and contribute to knowledge advancement in law. By adopting innovative research methodologies, leveraging technological tools, and embracing interdisciplinary approaches, researchers enhance legal scholarship, inform policy development, and support evidence-based decision-making in legal practice and academia.

Conclusion:
Advanced legal research techniques empower legal scholars, practitioners, and researchers to navigate intricate legal challenges, promote legal innovation, and uphold principles of justice and fairness in legal systems worldwide. By mastering advanced research methodologies, integrating technological advancements, and fostering interdisciplinary collaboration, legal professionals contribute to legal reform, policy advocacy,

and ethical governance, promoting societal welfare and legal excellence in a dynamic and evolving global legal landscape.

33.2 Legal Writing and Drafting

Legal writing and drafting are essential skills in law, enabling effective communication of legal analysis, arguments, and conclusions to diverse audiences, including judges, clients, and stakeholders.

Key Aspects:

1. **Clarity and Precision**: Legal writing emphasizes clarity, precision, and conciseness in conveying complex legal concepts, statutes, case law, and regulatory provisions. Clear writing enhances comprehension, minimizes ambiguity, and facilitates effective communication of legal arguments and interpretations.

2. **Structure and Organization**: Structuring legal documents (e.g., memoranda, briefs, contracts) involves logical organization of issues, facts, legal analysis, and conclusions. Document structure enhances readability, coherence, and persuasive impact, guiding readers through reasoned arguments and supporting evidence.

3. **Legal Citations and Authorities**: Legal writing incorporates accurate citation of statutes, case law, and scholarly sources following standardized citation formats (e.g., Bluebook, APA). Proper citation supports legal arguments, validates legal reasoning, and enhances the credibility of legal research and analysis.

4. **Drafting Skills**: Drafting legal documents (e.g., contracts, and pleadings) requires attention to detail, language precision, and adherence to legal norms and conventions. Effective drafting anticipates legal implications, defines rights and obligations clearly, and

mitigates risks through precise contractual language and legal drafting techniques.
5. **Plain Language and Audience Considerations**: Communicating legal concepts in plain language improves accessibility and comprehension for non-legal audiences (e.g., clients, and policymakers). Tailoring language to audience knowledge levels, needs, and expectations enhances communication effectiveness and facilitates informed decision-making.

33.3 Analytical and Critical Thinking Skills

Analytical and critical thinking skills are fundamental in legal research and practice, enabling rigorous analysis, evaluation of legal issues, and development of reasoned arguments and solutions.

Key Aspects:
1. **Issue Identification and Analysis**: Analytical skills involve identifying legal issues, dissecting complex factual scenarios, and applying relevant legal principles, statutes, and case law to formulate legal arguments and strategies. Thorough issue analysis ensures a comprehensive examination of legal complexities and implications.
2. **Legal Reasoning**: Critical thinking in law involves logical reasoning, evaluation of evidence, and synthesis of legal doctrines to support persuasive arguments and legal conclusions. Analytical rigour strengthens legal analysis, identifies precedents, and anticipates counterarguments in constructing robust legal positions.
3. **Problem-Solving Abilities**: Legal professionals apply analytical and critical thinking skills to analyze legal problems, assess risks, and develop innovative

solutions. Problem-solving skills navigate legal challenges, address client needs, and achieve favourable outcomes through strategic legal advice and advocacy.
4. **Research Integration**: Integrating research findings with analytical thinking enhances legal scholarship and practice. Critical evaluation of legal sources, empirical data, and interdisciplinary insights informs evidence-based legal arguments, policy recommendations, and judicial decision-making in complex legal disputes.
5. **Ethical and Professional Judgment**: Critical thinking in law incorporates ethical considerations, professional ethics, and principles of justice in legal analysis and decision-making. Ethical reasoning guides ethical dilemmas, promotes integrity, and upholds ethical standards in legal practice and advocacy.

33.4 Presentation and Communication of Legal Research

Presentation and communication of legal research involve effectively conveying research findings, analysis, and conclusions to diverse audiences through oral advocacy, written reports, and multimedia formats.

Key Considerations:
1. **Oral Advocacy Skills**: Presenting legal arguments in oral hearings, client meetings, or academic forums requires persuasive communication, clarity, and confidence in articulating legal positions, addressing questions, and engaging with stakeholders.
2. **Written Communication**: Communicating legal research in written formats (e.g., briefs, articles, reports) demands clarity, structure, and adherence to legal writing conventions. Effective writing conveys

complex legal concepts, analysis, and recommendations succinctly and persuasively.
3. **Visual and Multimedia Tools**: Incorporating visual aids (e.g., slides, diagrams, charts) enhances presentation clarity, supports data visualization, and reinforces key legal arguments in oral presentations and academic seminars.
4. **Audience Engagement**: Tailoring communication to audience knowledge levels, interests, and expectations fosters engagement and understanding. Effective communication techniques include storytelling, case studies, and interactive discussions that resonate with diverse stakeholders and promote dialogue on legal issues.
5. **Professionalism and Ethical Communication**: Presenting legal research with professionalism, integrity, and respect for diverse perspectives promotes ethical communication practices. Ethical considerations include confidentiality, transparency, and adherence to professional standards in disseminating legal information and analysis.

Conclusion

Research skills and methods in law encompass legal writing and drafting, analytical and critical thinking skills, and presentation and communication of legal research. By mastering these skills, legal professionals enhance their ability to conduct rigorous legal research, formulate persuasive arguments, and communicate findings effectively to support informed decision-making, advance legal scholarship, and uphold principles of justice and fairness in legal practice and academia. Embracing continuous skill development and ethical practices strengthens legal professionalism, promotes public

Chapter 34: Securities Law

34.1 Principles of Securities Regulation

Securities law encompasses the regulatory framework governing the issuance, trading, and regulation of securities, including stocks, bonds, and derivatives, to protect investors, ensure market integrity, and promote transparency in financial markets.

Key Aspects:

1. **Regulatory Objectives**: Securities regulation aims to safeguard investor interests by enforcing disclosure requirements, preventing fraud, and maintaining fair and orderly markets. Regulatory bodies (e.g., SEC in the United States, and FCA in the UK) oversee compliance with securities laws to promote market stability and investor confidence.

2. **Disclosure Requirements**: Issuers of securities must disclose material information relevant to investment decisions, including financial performance, risks, and corporate governance practices. Disclosure obligations ensure transparency, enable informed investment decisions, and deter fraudulent practices in securities offerings and trading activities.

3. **Market Manipulation and Insider Trading**: Securities laws prohibit market manipulation, insider trading, and other fraudulent practices that distort market prices and undermine investor trust. Regulations impose strict penalties for unauthorized disclosure of non-public information and unauthorized trading based on insider knowledge.

4. **Investor Protection**: Securities regulation prioritizes investor protection through the enforcement of fiduciary duties, disclosure standards, and investor

education initiatives. Regulatory agencies monitor market conduct, investigate complaints, and prosecute securities violations to uphold investor rights and maintain market integrity.
5. **International Standards**: Securities laws harmonize with international standards (e.g., IOSCO principles) to facilitate cross-border securities offerings and trading activities. Harmonization promotes regulatory consistency, reduces compliance costs for multinational firms, and enhances global market integration while respecting jurisdictional differences.

Importance and Application:
Principles of securities regulation are critical for fostering investor confidence, maintaining market efficiency, and facilitating capital formation in domestic and global financial markets. By enforcing regulatory standards, promoting transparency, and mitigating systemic risks, securities laws uphold financial stability and support economic growth.

Conclusion:
Understanding the principles of securities regulation is essential for legal professionals, financial institutions, and policymakers navigating complex regulatory landscapes. By adhering to regulatory requirements, promoting market integrity, and advancing investor protection, securities laws contribute to sustainable financial markets, informed investment decisions, and ethical conduct in securities transactions globally. The continued evolution of securities regulation addresses emerging challenges, promotes innovation, and reinforces public trust in financial markets, reinforcing principles of fairness, transparency, and accountability in securities law enforcement and compliance efforts.

34.2 Legal Framework for Securities Markets

The legal framework for securities markets establishes rules and regulations governing the issuance, trading, and oversight of securities to ensure market integrity, investor protection, and transparency.

Key Aspects:

1. **Regulatory Authorities**: Securities markets operate under the supervision of regulatory authorities (e.g., SEC in the United States, FCA in the UK) responsible for enforcing securities laws, setting regulatory standards, and overseeing market participants to maintain fair and orderly markets.
2. **Securities Offerings**: Issuers must comply with regulatory requirements for securities offerings, including registration statements, prospectus disclosures, and compliance with disclosure standards to provide investors with accurate and timely information for investment decisions.
3. **Market Conduct Rules**: Securities regulations include market conduct rules governing trading practices, price transparency, and fair dealing obligations among market participants. Rules aim to prevent market manipulation, insider trading, and abusive practices that undermine market integrity and investor trust.
4. **Investor Protection**: Legal protections for investors encompass fiduciary duties, disclosure obligations, and safeguards against fraudulent schemes. Securities laws mandate the disclosure of material information, prohibit misrepresentation, and enforce penalties for violations to safeguard investor interests and promote market confidence.

International Coordination: Securities regulation often aligns with international standards (e.g., IOSCO principles) to facilitate cross-border securities offerings and regulatory cooperation. Harmonization promotes regulatory consistency, enhances market efficiency, and facilitates global capital flows while respecting jurisdictional differences in regulatory enforcement.

34.3 Insider Trading and Market Manipulation

Insider trading and market manipulation are prohibited practices under securities laws aimed at preserving market fairness, preventing unfair advantages, and protecting investors from deceptive practices.

Key Aspects:

1. **Insider Trading**: Securities laws prohibit insiders (e.g., corporate officers, directors, major shareholders) from trading securities based on non-public material information. Legal prohibitions ensure equal access to market information, prevent unfair trading advantages, and uphold investor confidence in market transparency.
2. **Market Manipulation**: Market manipulation involves deliberate actions to artificially influence securities prices, trading volumes, or market conditions for personal gain or to deceive investors. Regulations prohibit manipulative activities (e.g., wash sales, price rigging) to maintain market integrity, ensure price discovery, and deter fraudulent schemes.
3. **Regulatory Enforcement**: Regulatory authorities monitor market activities, investigate suspicious trading patterns, and enforce penalties for insider trading and market manipulation violations. Enforcement actions include civil sanctions, disgorgement of illegal profits, and criminal prosecution to deter unlawful conduct and protect market participants.

4. **Compliance and Surveillance**: Securities exchanges and regulatory agencies implement compliance programs and surveillance systems to detect and prevent insider trading and market manipulation. Monitoring trading activities, conducting investigations, and promoting whistleblower protections enhance market oversight and regulatory effectiveness.
5. **Legal Precedents and Case Law**: Legal precedents and case law establish judicial interpretations and enforcement standards for insider trading and market manipulation offences. Court decisions guide legal definitions, evidentiary requirements, and penalties for violations to ensure consistent application of securities laws.

34.4 Case Studies in Securities Law

Case studies in securities law provide practical illustrations of legal principles, regulatory enforcement actions, and judicial decisions shaping securities markets, investor rights, and corporate governance practices.

Key Considerations:
1. **Landmark Cases**: Case studies examine landmark court decisions (e.g., SEC v. XYZ Corporation) addressing securities fraud, insider trading, or market manipulation allegations. Analysis of judicial rulings clarifies legal standards, liability determinations, and implications for regulatory enforcement and investor protection.
2. **Regulatory Actions**: Case studies highlight regulatory actions (e.g., SEC enforcement actions) against individuals or entities for securities law violations. Case analyses assess regulatory approaches, penalties

imposed, and compliance remediation efforts to deter misconduct and uphold market integrity.
3. **Corporate Governance Issues**: Securities law case studies explore corporate governance failures (e.g., governance lapses, executive misconduct) influencing securities market performance and investor confidence. Examination of governance practices and regulatory responses underscores the importance of ethical leadership and accountability in corporate stewardship.
4. **Market Impact**: Case studies examine market repercussions (e.g., stock price volatility, investor losses) resulting from securities law violations or regulatory enforcement actions. Analysis of market responses informs risk management strategies, investor relations practices, and corporate compliance measures to mitigate legal and reputational risks.
5. **Educational Value**: Case studies in securities law provide educational value for legal professionals, business executives, and students studying securities regulation, corporate law, and financial market ethics. Practical insights from real-world scenarios enhance understanding of legal complexities, regulatory challenges, and ethical considerations in securities markets.

Conclusion

Securities law encompasses a comprehensive legal framework governing securities markets, investor protections, and regulatory enforcement mechanisms. Understanding legal principles, regulatory requirements, and case law in securities regulation is essential for promoting market integrity, investor confidence, and sustainable financial markets. By enforcing transparency, preventing market abuse, and enhancing regulatory compliance, securities laws contribute to fair and efficient capital markets, safeguard investor interests, and uphold ethical standards in global financial systems. Continued vigilance, regulatory oversight, and adherence to legal standards are crucial in maintaining trust, resilience, and stability in securities markets amid evolving economic conditions and technological advancements shaping the future of financial regulation.

Chapter 35: Strategic Management and Leadership

35.1 Principles of Strategic Management

Strategic management involves the formulation, implementation, and evaluation of organizational goals and initiatives to achieve competitive advantage and long-term success in dynamic business environments. At its core, strategic management integrates organizational vision, mission, and values with proactive decision-making to align resources, capabilities, and actions towards achieving strategic objectives.

Key Aspects:

1. **Vision and Mission Alignment**: Strategic management begins with defining a clear vision and mission statement that articulate the organization's purpose, values, and strategic direction. Alignment of vision and mission guides strategic planning, decision-making, and resource allocation to support organizational growth and sustainability.
2. **Environmental Analysis**: Strategic management requires continuous assessment of external and internal factors impacting the organization's competitive landscape. Environmental analysis evaluates market trends, industry dynamics, competitor strategies, regulatory changes, and technological advancements to identify opportunities and threats that influence strategic decisions.
3. **Strategic Formulation**: Formulating strategy involves setting strategic goals, identifying strategic initiatives, and developing action plans to achieve organizational objectives. Strategic formulation integrates analysis of strengths, weaknesses, opportunities, and threats (SWOT analysis), competitive positioning strategies

(e.g., differentiation, cost leadership), and market segmentation to optimize resource allocation and enhance competitive advantage.
4. **Implementation Planning**: Strategic management emphasizes effective implementation planning to translate strategic plans into operational actions and outcomes. Implementation planning involves setting clear objectives, allocating resources, defining roles and responsibilities, establishing performance metrics, and monitoring progress to ensure alignment with strategic goals and timelines.
5. **Performance Evaluation**: Strategic management includes ongoing evaluation and adjustment of organizational performance against strategic objectives and key performance indicators (KPIs). Performance evaluation measures progress, identifies deviations from plans, and facilitates corrective actions or strategic pivots to adapt to changing market conditions and achieve desired outcomes.

Importance and Application:
Principles of strategic management are essential for guiding organizational growth, fostering innovation, and sustaining competitive advantage in a globalized economy. By promoting strategic alignment, proactive decision-making, and organizational agility, strategic management enables businesses to navigate uncertainty, capitalize on opportunities, and achieve long-term profitability and market leadership.

Conclusion:
Strategic management and leadership play pivotal roles in shaping organizational success, resilience, and sustainability in dynamic business environments. By applying principles of strategic management—visionary leadership, environmental scanning, strategic formulation, implementation planning, and

performance evaluation—organizations enhance strategic agility, foster innovation, and drive sustainable growth amidst evolving market complexities and competitive pressures. Embracing strategic management principles empowers leaders to navigate strategic challenges, capitalize on emerging opportunities, and cultivate a culture of continuous improvement and strategic foresight to achieve organizational excellence and strategic outcomes in a rapidly changing global marketplace.

35.2 Legal Aspects of Corporate Strategy

Legal aspects of corporate strategy encompass the integration of legal considerations into strategic decision-making processes to mitigate risks, ensure compliance with regulatory requirements, and enhance organizational resilience and sustainability.

Key Aspects:

1. **Compliance and Regulatory Frameworks**: Corporate strategies must align with legal and regulatory frameworks governing business operations, including corporate governance, environmental regulations, labour laws, and intellectual property rights. Legal compliance safeguards organizational reputation, minimizes legal liabilities, and fosters trust with stakeholders.
2. **Risk Management**: Legal aspects of corporate strategy involve identifying, assessing, and managing legal risks associated with business activities, transactions, and market operations. Legal risk management strategies mitigate potential liabilities, litigation risks, and regulatory penalties, safeguarding organizational assets and enhancing financial stability.

3. **Contractual Agreements and Negotiations**: Legal considerations in corporate strategy encompass drafting, negotiating, and enforcing contractual agreements (e.g., mergers and acquisitions, joint ventures, commercial contracts) to protect organizational interests, define rights and obligations, and mitigate contractual disputes through legal remedies and dispute resolution mechanisms.
4. **Corporate Governance and Ethics**: Legal aspects of corporate strategy emphasize adherence to ethical standards, corporate governance best practices, and fiduciary duties owed to stakeholders. Legal frameworks guide board oversight, executive accountability, shareholder rights, and transparency in corporate decision-making processes to promote integrity and sustainable business practices.
5. **Litigation and Dispute Resolution**: Corporate strategy includes proactive management of litigation risks and legal disputes through litigation avoidance strategies, alternative dispute resolution (ADR), and litigation management practices. Legal defence strategies safeguard organizational reputation, financial resources, and shareholder value amid legal challenges and adversarial proceedings.

35.3 Leadership in Legal Practice

Leadership in legal practice emphasizes visionary leadership, strategic decision-making, and ethical stewardship to navigate legal complexities, foster client trust, and promote excellence in legal services and advocacy.

Key Aspects:
1. **Strategic Vision and Direction**: Legal leaders provide strategic vision and direction by aligning legal practice

goals with organizational objectives, client needs, and industry trends. Strategic leadership promotes innovation, service differentiation, and competitive advantage in legal service delivery.

2. **Client Relationship Management**: Effective legal leadership prioritizes client relationship management by understanding client goals, anticipating legal needs, and delivering tailored solutions that add value and enhance client satisfaction. Client-focused leadership builds long-term partnerships, fosters loyalty, and sustains business growth through referrals and repeat engagements.
3. **Team Development and Mentorship**: Legal leaders cultivate a culture of excellence and professional growth by investing in talent development, mentorship programs, and continuing education initiatives for legal professionals. Leadership development enhances team cohesion, expertise, and performance, fostering a collaborative work environment and attracting top legal talent.
4. **Ethical Leadership and Professionalism**: Leadership in legal practice upholds ethical standards, integrity, and professional ethics in client representation, advocacy, and organizational stewardship. Ethical leadership promotes trust, transparency, and accountability in legal practice, guiding ethical decision-making and promoting public confidence in the legal profession.
5. **Innovation and Adaptability**: Legal leaders drive innovation and adaptability by embracing technological advancements, legal automation tools, and data analytics to enhance legal service delivery, efficiency, and client outcomes. Innovative leadership fosters

agility, resilience, and responsiveness to evolving legal landscapes and client expectations.

35.4 Case Studies in Strategic Management

Case studies in strategic management provide practical insights into strategic decision-making processes, organizational challenges, and successful strategies employed by businesses to achieve competitive advantage and sustainable growth.

Key Considerations:

1. **Strategic Planning and Implementation**: Case studies analyze strategic planning processes, including goal setting, environmental analysis, and strategy formulation to align organizational resources and capabilities with market opportunities and competitive threats.

2. **Change Management and Organizational Transformation**: Case studies examine organizational change initiatives, leadership roles, and change management strategies employed to navigate industry disruptions, enhance operational efficiency, and foster organizational resilience amid market uncertainties.

3. **Innovation and Market Leadership**: Strategic management case studies explore innovative business models, product development strategies, and market entry tactics that propel businesses to industry leadership and market differentiation through innovation-driven growth strategies.

4. **Risk Management and Crisis Response**: Case studies in strategic management evaluate risk management frameworks, crisis response strategies, and resilience planning efforts that mitigate operational risks, regulatory challenges, and external threats impacting organizational performance and reputation.

5. **Performance Evaluation and Continuous Improvement**: Strategic management case studies assess performance metrics, key performance indicators (KPIs), and performance evaluation techniques used to monitor strategic outcomes, measure success, and drive continuous improvement in organizational performance and strategic effectiveness.

Conclusion

Strategic management and leadership in legal practice integrate legal expertise, ethical leadership, and strategic decision-making to navigate legal complexities, achieve organizational goals, and promote sustainable business growth. By embracing legal aspects of corporate strategy, fostering leadership excellence, and analyzing strategic management case studies, legal professionals enhance their ability to drive innovation, mitigate risks, and deliver exceptional legal services that uphold legal standards, client expectations, and organizational success in a competitive global marketplace.

Chapter 36: Taxation Principles, Policy, and Law

36.1 Fundamentals of Taxation Law

Fundamentals of taxation law encompass the legal principles, policies, and regulations governing the imposition, assessment, and collection of taxes by governmental authorities to finance public expenditures and achieve economic objectives.

Key Aspects:

1. **Taxation Jurisdiction**: Taxation law establishes the authority of governments (federal, state, local) to levy and collect taxes on individuals, businesses, and transactions within their jurisdiction. Legal principles define tax bases, rates, and administrative procedures governing tax compliance and enforcement.

2. **Types of Taxes**: Taxation law encompasses several types of taxes, including income taxes, corporate taxes, sales taxes, property taxes, and excise taxes, each governed by specific legal frameworks and regulations. Different tax types serve diverse fiscal purposes, such as funding public services, redistributing wealth, and regulating economic behaviour.

3. **Taxpayer Rights and Obligations**: Taxation law delineates taxpayer rights, such as the right to appeal tax assessments, confidentiality of taxpayer information, and due process protections in tax disputes. Legal obligations include timely filing of tax returns, accurate reporting of income and deductions, and payment of taxes owed according to prescribed deadlines and requirements.

4. **Tax Planning and Compliance**: Taxation law guides tax planning strategies, including tax minimization through

legitimate deductions, credits, and exemptions permitted under tax laws. Compliance with tax regulations requires adherence to reporting requirements, record-keeping obligations, and disclosure of relevant financial information to tax authorities.
5. **Tax Policy and Economic Impact**: Taxation law influences economic behaviour, investment decisions, and market dynamics through tax incentives, disincentives, and regulatory measures aimed at promoting economic growth, equity, and fiscal sustainability. Tax policy debates often centre on balancing revenue generation with economic efficiency and social equity considerations.

Importance and Application:
Fundamentals of taxation law are essential for taxpayers, businesses, and policymakers to navigate legal obligations, optimize tax efficiency, and comply with regulatory requirements in domestic and international tax environments. Understanding taxation principles informs strategic financial planning, risk management, and compliance strategies to mitigate tax liabilities and support sustainable business practices.

Conclusion:
Fundamentals of taxation law encompass legal frameworks, policies, and principles governing tax imposition, compliance, and administration essential for promoting fiscal responsibility, economic stability, and public welfare. By upholding tax transparency, fairness, and administrative efficiency, taxation law fosters trust in governmental taxation systems, supports equitable distribution of tax burdens, and advances fiscal policies that align with societal objectives and economic development goals in a dynamic global economy.

36.2 Tax Policy and Administration

Tax policy and administration encompass the formulation, implementation, and evaluation of governmental strategies and practices governing tax systems to achieve fiscal objectives, promote economic growth, and ensure equitable distribution of tax burdens.

Key Aspects:

1. **Tax Policy Objectives**: Tax policy aims to generate government revenue to fund public expenditures, redistribute wealth, influence economic behaviour, and achieve social and economic objectives. Policy decisions address tax rates, bases, exemptions, incentives, and administrative reforms to enhance tax compliance and economic efficiency.

2. **Tax Administration Framework**: Tax administration involves government agencies responsible for enforcing tax laws, collecting taxes, and administering tax compliance programs. Administrative functions include tax assessment, taxpayer registration, audit procedures, dispute resolution, and taxpayer education initiatives to ensure fair and efficient tax administration.

3. **Tax Compliance and Enforcement**: Tax policy and administration promote voluntary compliance through taxpayer education, simplified tax filing processes, and enforcement measures targeting tax evasion, fraud, and non-compliance. Effective enforcement mechanisms deter tax avoidance schemes and promote fairness in tax collection.

4. **International Taxation**: Tax policy addresses international tax issues, including cross-border transactions, transfer pricing, double taxation treaties, and harmonization of tax rules to prevent tax evasion,

promote global tax transparency, and facilitate international trade and investment.
5. **Policy Evaluation and Reform**: Tax policy analysis evaluates the economic impact, distributional effects, and administrative efficiency of tax reforms to inform policy adjustments and legislative reforms. Policy reforms aim to simplify tax codes, reduce compliance costs, close loopholes, and enhance tax fairness and competitiveness in global markets.

36.3 Comparative Tax Systems

Comparative tax systems analyze differences and similarities in tax structures, policies, and administration practices across countries to understand global tax trends, regulatory frameworks, and implications for taxpayers and businesses operating in diverse economic environments.

Key Considerations:
1. **Tax System Structures**: Comparative tax analysis examines variations in tax system structures, including progressive vs. flat tax rates, direct vs. indirect taxes, and centralized vs. decentralized tax administration models. Variations reflect national priorities, economic conditions, and social policies influencing tax policy formulation and implementation.
2. **Taxation of Individuals and Businesses**: Comparative tax systems assess how countries tax individuals (e.g., personal income tax, wealth tax) and businesses (e.g., corporate income tax, value-added tax) based on income levels, deductions, credits, and incentives. Differences in tax treatment impact economic behaviour, investment decisions, and competitiveness in global markets.
3. **Tax Policy Implications**: Comparative tax analysis explores policy implications of tax reforms, including

revenue implications, distributional effects, economic growth impacts, and compliance costs for taxpayers and businesses. Policy insights inform strategic tax planning, risk management, and policy advocacy efforts in domestic and international tax environments.
4. **Global Tax Coordination**: Comparative tax systems highlight challenges and opportunities for global tax coordination, international tax competition, and efforts to combat tax evasion and base erosion. Coordination initiatives (e.g., OECD BEPS project) promote cooperation among tax authorities, harmonization of tax rules, and alignment with international tax standards to enhance tax fairness and transparency.
5. **Case Studies and Best Practices**: Comparative tax systems leverage case studies and best practices to benchmark tax reforms, administrative reforms, and policy innovations across countries. Comparative analysis informs policymakers, tax professionals, and stakeholders about effective tax policy measures, regulatory frameworks, and compliance strategies that promote economic efficiency and fiscal sustainability.

36.4 Case Studies in Tax Law

Case studies in tax law provide practical illustrations of legal principles, regulatory enforcement actions, and judicial decisions shaping tax policies, compliance strategies, and taxpayer rights and obligations in domestic and international tax environments.

Key Considerations:
1. **Taxation of Cross-Border Transactions**: Case studies examine the tax implications of cross-border transactions, including transfer pricing, tax treaties, and multinational corporate structures. Analysis of tax planning strategies and regulatory responses addresses

challenges in international tax compliance and enforcement.

2. **Taxation of Corporate Transactions**: Case studies analyze tax consequences of corporate mergers, acquisitions, reorganizations, and divestitures. Legal precedents and regulatory guidance inform tax structuring, due diligence processes, and tax implications for stakeholders involved in corporate transactions.

3. **Taxation of Individuals and Estates**: Case studies explore tax planning strategies for individuals, estates, and trusts, including income tax, estate tax, gift tax, and wealth transfer tax considerations. Legal insights and compliance best practices guide taxpayer decision-making and wealth preservation strategies.

4. **Tax Litigation and Dispute Resolution**: Case studies in tax law review judicial rulings, administrative decisions, and dispute resolution outcomes in tax controversies, tax audits, and litigation proceedings. Analysis of legal arguments, evidentiary standards, and procedural rules informs tax litigation strategies and taxpayer rights protections.

5. **Emerging Tax Issues and Policy Debates**: Case studies examine emerging tax issues (e.g., digital taxation, environmental taxes) and policy debates influencing tax reform agendas, legislative developments, and regulatory responses. Case analysis informs public policy discussions, advocacy efforts, and stakeholder engagements on evolving tax challenges and opportunities.

Conclusion

Taxation principles, policy, and law shape national revenue systems, economic incentives, and regulatory frameworks essential for fiscal governance, economic development, and social welfare. By understanding the fundamentals of taxation law, comparative tax systems, and case studies in tax law, policymakers, tax professionals, and stakeholders enhance their ability to navigate complex tax environments, promote tax compliance, and advance equitable and efficient tax policies that support sustainable economic growth and global competitiveness. Continued dialogue, collaboration, and innovation in tax policy and administration foster resilience, transparency, and responsiveness to evolving tax challenges in a dynamic global economy.

Chapter 37: Telecommunications Law

37.1 Principles of Telecommunications Regulation

Principles of telecommunications regulation encompass legal frameworks, policies, and regulatory practices governing the telecommunications industry to promote competition, protect consumer interests, ensure universal access to telecommunications services, and foster innovation in communication technologies.

Key Aspects:

1. **Regulatory Objectives**: Telecommunications regulation aims to achieve public policy goals, including promoting efficient use of spectrum, expanding broadband infrastructure, enhancing service quality, and safeguarding national security interests. Regulatory frameworks balance industry competitiveness with consumer protection and regulatory oversight.

2. **Licensing and Spectrum Management**: Telecommunications regulation includes licensing requirements and spectrum management policies governing the allocation, assignment, and use of radio frequencies for wireless communication services. Regulatory agencies (e.g., FCC in the US, and Ofcom in the UK) oversee spectrum auctions, licensing approvals, and compliance with technical standards to optimize spectrum utilization and prevent interference.

3. **Market Competition and Antitrust Regulation**: Telecommunications regulation promotes market competition through antitrust laws, merger reviews, and regulatory measures (e.g., price controls, and unbundling obligations) to prevent monopolistic practices, enhance consumer choice, and foster innovation in telecommunications services and technologies.

4. **Consumer Protection**: Telecommunications law safeguards consumer rights by enforcing transparency in service pricing, billing practices, and quality of service standards. Regulatory agencies address consumer complaints, enforce privacy protections, and mandate disclosure requirements to ensure fair treatment and service reliability for telecommunications subscribers.
5. **Emerging Technologies and Digital Transformation**: Telecommunications regulation adapts to technological advancements, including 5G deployment, Internet of Things (IoT), and digital services, by establishing regulatory frameworks that promote investment, innovation, and cybersecurity protections in digital communications infrastructure and technologies.

Importance and Application:

Principles of telecommunications regulation are essential for fostering competitive markets, expanding broadband access, and promoting digital inclusion in the digital economy. By enforcing regulatory compliance, protecting consumer interests, and stimulating investment in telecommunications infrastructure, regulation supports economic growth, technological innovation, and societal connectivity.

Conclusion:

Telecommunications law plays a critical role in shaping regulatory frameworks, policy initiatives, and industry practices that govern communication networks, services, and technologies essential for global connectivity, economic development, and societal well-being. By upholding principles of telecommunications regulation—competition, consumer protection, spectrum management, and technological innovation—regulatory agencies and stakeholders advance digital transformation, bridge digital divides, and ensure equitable access to reliable and secure telecommunications services in an interconnected world. Continued collaboration, regulatory reforms, and technological advancements are essential to address emerging challenges and opportunities in telecommunications law, reinforcing principles of regulatory effectiveness, industry resilience, and digital infrastructure development in a rapidly evolving telecommunications landscape.

37.2 Legal Framework for Telecom Services

The legal framework for telecommunications services establishes regulatory principles, statutory provisions, and administrative rules governing the provision, operation, and oversight of telecommunications networks, services, and technologies.

Key Aspects:
1. **Regulatory Authority**: The legal framework designates regulatory authorities responsible for licensing, supervision, and enforcement of telecommunications laws and policies. Regulatory agencies oversee compliance with service quality standards, technical specifications, and consumer protection measures to ensure fair competition and reliable service delivery.
2. **Licensing and Authorization**: Telecom laws define licensing requirements, application procedures, and conditions for operating telecommunications networks and services. Regulatory approvals include spectrum licenses for wireless communication, infrastructure deployment permits, and service provider registrations to promote market entry and investment in telecom infrastructure.

3. **Service Provision Obligations**: Legal frameworks impose obligations on telecom operators to provide universal access to essential services, ensure network reliability, and adhere to service quality benchmarks. Regulations address consumer rights, privacy protections, data security standards, and emergency communications requirements to safeguard public interests and promote user trust.
4. **Interconnection and Access**: Telecom laws mandate interconnection agreements among operators to facilitate seamless connectivity, interoperability, and efficient service delivery across networks. Regulatory oversight ensures fair access to network facilities, equitable cost-sharing arrangements, and dispute-resolution mechanisms to promote competitive markets and enhance consumer choice.
5. **Regulatory Compliance and Enforcement**: Telecom laws enforce regulatory compliance through monitoring, audits, and enforcement actions against violations of licensing conditions, anti-competitive practices, and consumer rights infringements. Regulatory sanctions include fines, license revocations, and corrective measures to deter non-compliance and protect public interests in telecommunications services.

37.3 Comparative Analysis of Telecom Laws

Comparative analysis of telecommunications laws evaluates regulatory frameworks, policy approaches, and legal principles across countries to assess differences, similarities, and implications for industry stakeholders, market dynamics, and technological innovation.

Key Considerations:

1. **Regulatory Models**: Comparative analysis compares regulatory models (e.g., regulatory independence, sector-specific vs. converged regulation) adopted by countries to oversee telecommunications markets, promote competition, and protect consumer interests. Variations in regulatory approaches impact market structure, investment incentives, and regulatory outcomes in telecom services.
2. **Spectrum Management**: Comparison of spectrum allocation policies, licensing regimes, and auction mechanisms examines strategies for optimizing spectrum utilization, promoting 5G deployment, and balancing public and commercial interests in spectrum management. Regulatory harmonization efforts enhance international cooperation and spectrum coordination to support global connectivity and digital innovation.
3. **Consumer Protection**: Comparative analysis assesses consumer protection frameworks, privacy regulations, and data security measures implemented by countries to safeguard consumer rights, mitigate risks of data breaches, and ensure transparency in telecom service offerings. Legal standards influence consumer trust, regulatory compliance costs, and cross-border data flows in global telecommunications markets.
4. **Technological Innovation**: Comparative studies explore regulatory responses to emerging technologies (e.g., IoT, artificial intelligence) and digital services (e.g., cloud computing, OTT applications) shaping telecom markets. Regulatory flexibility, innovation incentives, and policy adaptation strategies foster technological advancements, market competitiveness, and regulatory agility in digital transformation.

5. **Policy Convergence and Harmonization**: Comparative analysis identifies opportunities for policy convergence, regulatory harmonization, and best practice sharing among countries to address familiar challenges (e.g., cybersecurity threats, regulatory gaps) and promote regulatory coherence in global telecommunications governance. International cooperation initiatives (e.g., ITU, WTO agreements) facilitate the alignment of regulatory frameworks and mutual recognition of regulatory standards to enhance market integration and regulatory effectiveness.

37.4 Emerging Issues in Telecommunications Law

Emerging issues in telecommunications law encompass evolving challenges, regulatory trends, and policy debates influencing industry dynamics, digital transformation, and regulatory responses in global telecom markets.

Key Issues:

1. **5G Deployment and Spectrum Policy**: Regulatory frameworks for 5G deployment, spectrum management, and infrastructure investments address technical standards, spectrum availability, and deployment challenges to support next-generation mobile networks, IoT applications, and digital connectivity.
2. **Data Privacy and Cybersecurity**: Legal frameworks for data protection, privacy regulations (e.g., GDPR, CCPA), and cybersecurity measures address risks of data breaches, cyber threats, and regulatory compliance obligations impacting telecom operators, service providers, and consumer data management practices.
3. **Net Neutrality and Open Internet**: Policy debates on net neutrality principles, traffic management practices,

and regulatory safeguards examine implications for fair access, content delivery, and internet governance in promoting an open and competitive digital ecosystem.
4. **Regulatory Convergence**: Convergence of telecom, media, and technology sectors (e.g., OTT services, digital platforms) requires regulatory adaptation, competition policy reforms, and cross-sectoral collaboration to address market dynamics, consumer choice, and regulatory oversight in converged digital markets.
5. **Artificial Intelligence and IoT Regulation**: Regulatory frameworks for AI technologies, IoT devices, and smart infrastructure governance explore legal challenges, ethical considerations, and regulatory frameworks to ensure accountability, transparency, and responsible use of emerging technologies in telecom services.

Conclusion

Telecommunications law plays a pivotal role in shaping regulatory frameworks, promoting market competition, and fostering innovation in global telecom markets. By understanding legal frameworks for telecom services, conducting a comparative analysis of telecom laws, and addressing emerging issues in telecommunications law, policymakers, regulators, and industry stakeholders enhance regulatory effectiveness, promote digital connectivity, and advance consumer welfare in an evolving digital economy. Continued dialogue, regulatory reforms, and international cooperation are essential to address complex challenges, leverage technological opportunities, and achieve sustainable development goals in telecommunications governance and digital transformation initiatives worldwide.

Chapter 38: The Corporate Form and Its Issues

38.1 Legal Nature of Corporations

The legal nature of corporations defines their distinct identity as legal entities separate from their shareholders, with rights, responsibilities, and legal standing to conduct business operations, enter into contracts, and incur liabilities under corporate law.

Key Aspects:

1. **Corporate Personality**: Corporations possess legal personality separate from their owners, enabling them to own assets, incur debts, sue or be sued in their own name, and enter into contracts independently of shareholders. This legal concept shields shareholders from personal liability for corporate obligations, promoting risk-sharing and investor confidence in corporate investments.

2. **Limited Liability**: The principle of limited liability limits shareholders' fiscal responsibility to their investment in the corporation, protecting personal assets from corporate debts and liabilities. Limited liability encourages investment, entrepreneurship, and corporate growth by mitigating risks associated with business operations and financial obligations.

3. **Corporate Governance**: Corporate law establishes governance structures, including boards of directors, executive management, and shareholder rights, to oversee corporate affairs, decision-making processes, and accountability to stakeholders. Governance practices promote transparency, fiduciary duties, and ethical standards in corporate management to safeguard shareholder interests and ensure corporate sustainability.

4. **Formation and Registration**: Corporations are formed through incorporation processes governed by state or national laws, requiring registration, articles of incorporation, and compliance with regulatory requirements (e.g., capitalization, corporate governance disclosures). Legal formalities establish corporate existence, powers, and obligations to operate lawfully within regulatory frameworks.
5. **Corporate Rights and Obligations**: Corporations possess legal rights to own property, enter into contracts, borrow capital, and engage in business activities within statutory limits and regulatory compliance. Corporate obligations include adherence to corporate laws, tax obligations, regulatory filings, and fiduciary duties owed to shareholders, employees, and stakeholders affected by corporate decisions.

Importance and Application:
Understanding the legal nature of corporations is essential for stakeholders, including shareholders, directors, officers, and investors, to navigate corporate governance, liability risks, regulatory compliance, and corporate transactions. Legal principles governing corporate formation, operations, and governance ensure corporate accountability, investor protection, and business continuity in dynamic economic environments.

Conclusion:
The legal nature of corporations defines their distinctive attributes as autonomous legal entities capable of conducting business activities, managing assets, and assuming liabilities under corporate law. By upholding principles of corporate personality, limited liability, governance structures, and regulatory compliance, corporations promote economic growth, investor confidence, and corporate responsibility in

global markets. Continued adherence to corporate law principles, ethical business practices, and regulatory oversight reinforces corporate accountability, transparency, and stakeholder trust in sustaining long-term value creation and corporate resilience amid evolving legal, economic, and societal challenges.

38.2 Corporate Governance and Compliance

Corporate governance and compliance encompass principles, practices, and regulatory frameworks governing the internal management, decision-making processes, and accountability mechanisms within corporations to promote transparency, integrity, and shareholder value.

Key Aspects:

1. **Board of Directors**: Corporate governance establishes the role and responsibilities of the board of directors in overseeing corporate strategy, risk management, and executive performance. Governance practices emphasize board independence, diversity, competence, and ethical standards to enhance oversight effectiveness and shareholder representation.

2. **Executive Management**: Governance frameworks define the roles and responsibilities of executive officers (e.g., CEO, CFO) in operational management, financial stewardship, and strategic leadership aligned with corporate objectives and shareholder interests. Executive compensation practices link performance metrics to corporate goals and shareholder value creation.

3. **Shareholder Rights**: Corporate governance safeguards shareholder rights, including voting rights, proxy access, and information transparency, enabling shareholders to

participate in major corporate decisions, elect directors, and hold management accountable for corporate performance and governance practices.
4. **Compliance and Ethics**: Governance policies mandate compliance with legal requirements, regulatory standards (e.g., Sarbanes-Oxley Act, GDPR), and ethical guidelines governing corporate conduct, financial reporting, internal controls, and risk mitigation strategies. Corporate ethics programs promote integrity, corporate citizenship, and responsible business practices to build trust and mitigate reputational risks.
5. **Stakeholder Engagement**: Governance frameworks promote stakeholder engagement, including employees, customers, suppliers, and communities affected by corporate activities. Social responsibility initiatives, sustainability practices, and corporate disclosures enhance transparency, accountability, and stakeholder relations in corporate decision-making processes.

38.3 Liability and Responsibility of Corporate Actors

The liability and responsibility of corporate actors define legal obligations, fiduciary duties, and potential liabilities imposed on directors, officers, and shareholders under corporate law, regulatory standards, and judicial precedents.

Key Considerations:
1. **Fiduciary Duties**: Corporate directors and officers have fiduciary duties of loyalty and care to act in the best interests of the corporation and its shareholders. Duties include exercising reasonable care, diligence, and loyalty in decision-making, avoiding conflicts of interest, and disclosing material information affecting corporate governance and performance.

2. **Legal Liabilities**: Corporate actors may face legal liabilities for breaches of fiduciary duties, violations of corporate laws (e.g., insider trading, fraudulent activities), negligence in corporate management, or failure to comply with regulatory obligations. Liability risks extend to financial penalties, civil lawsuits, regulatory sanctions, and reputational harm impacting personal and corporate interests.
3. **Corporate Governance Failures**: Legal accountability for corporate governance failures, such as financial misconduct, executive misconduct, or compliance breaches, underscores the importance of robust governance frameworks, internal controls, and risk management practices to mitigate corporate liability risks and preserve shareholder value.
4. **Shareholder Derivative Actions**: Shareholders may initiate derivative actions on behalf of the corporation to recover damages or seek injunctive relief against corporate misconduct, breaches of fiduciary duties, or management failures compromising shareholder rights and corporate integrity.
5. **Risk Management and Insurance**: Corporate actors mitigate liability risks through risk management strategies, directors, and officers (D&O) liability insurance coverage, indemnification agreements, and legal defenses to protect against personal and corporate liabilities arising from corporate governance disputes or legal proceedings.

38.4 Case Studies in Corporate Law

Case studies in corporate law analyze judicial decisions, legal precedents, and corporate governance practices influencing corporate operations, shareholder rights, regulatory compliance, and liability management in diverse business contexts.

Key Considerations:
1. **Corporate Governance Reforms**: Case studies examine corporate governance reforms (e.g., Enron scandal, Sarbanes-Oxley Act) following governance failures, financial misconduct, or regulatory lapses affecting shareholder confidence and corporate accountability.
2. **Director and Officer Responsibilities**: Legal cases review director and officer responsibilities, fiduciary duties, and liability exposures in corporate decision-making, governance oversight, and compliance with regulatory standards shaping corporate governance practices and shareholder protections.
3. **Shareholder Rights and Activism**: Case analyses explore shareholder rights, proxy battles, activist investor campaigns, and corporate governance disputes influencing board composition, executive compensation, and strategic decisions aligning shareholder interests with corporate governance reforms.
4. **Legal Compliance and Regulatory Enforcement**: Case studies assess legal compliance challenges, regulatory enforcement actions, and corporate responses to regulatory scrutiny, enforcement investigations, and penalties affecting corporate reputation, financial stability, and governance integrity.
5. **Mergers and Acquisitions**: Corporate law cases examine legal frameworks, shareholder approvals, due diligence practices, and regulatory considerations in mergers, acquisitions, and corporate transactions

impacting shareholder value, corporate governance, and regulatory compliance obligations.

Conclusion

The corporate form and its legal issues encompass governance principles, liability considerations, and case studies shaping corporate behaviour, regulatory compliance, and stakeholder relations in dynamic business environments. By understanding corporate governance practices, legal responsibilities, and case law insights, stakeholders enhance corporate governance effectiveness, mitigate liability risks, and uphold ethical standards promoting shareholder trust, regulatory compliance, and sustainable corporate performance in global markets. Continued adherence to corporate governance best practices, regulatory reforms, and stakeholder engagement fosters transparency, accountability, and resilience in corporate governance frameworks supporting long-term value creation and corporate sustainability initiatives.

Chapter 39: The Law of Devolution in Wales

39.1 Principles of Devolution in Wales

Devolution in Wales refers to the legal framework and constitutional arrangements that delegate legislative powers, administrative responsibilities, and decision-making authority from the UK Parliament to the devolved government in Wales, known as the Senedd Cymru (Welsh Parliament).

Key Aspects:

1. **Legal Basis**: Devolution in Wales is based on statutory provisions, primarily the Government of Wales Act 1998 and subsequent amendments, which define the scope of devolved powers, institutional structures, and governance arrangements for Welsh devolution. The Senedd Cymru has legislative competence over specified policy areas, including health, education, transport, and environment, subject to reserved matters reserved for the UK Parliament.

2. **Principles of Autonomy**: Devolution principles uphold Wales' autonomy in legislative and executive functions within devolved areas, enabling the Senedd Cymru to enact laws, formulate policies, and administer public services tailored to Welsh priorities, societal needs, and regional interests.

3. **Competence and Legislation**: Legislative competence grants the Senedd Cymru authority to pass laws (Acts of Senedd Cymru) within devolved policy areas, adhering to legal constraints, constitutional frameworks, and statutory requirements governing legislative processes, parliamentary scrutiny, and legal validity of enacted legislation.

4. **Administrative Responsibilities**: Devolved administration assigns executive responsibilities to the Welsh Government, led by the First Minister, to implement policies, manage public services, and allocate resources within devolved sectors, ensuring accountability, transparency, and effective governance in delivering public services and policy outcomes.
5. **Intergovernmental Relations**: Devolution frameworks facilitate intergovernmental cooperation and collaboration between the UK Government and the Welsh Government through mechanisms (e.g., Joint Ministerial Committee) to address shared policy interests, funding arrangements, legislative consent procedures, and constitutional developments affecting Wales' governance and public policy priorities.

Importance and Application:

Understanding the principles of devolution in Wales is crucial for policymakers, legal professionals, stakeholders, and the public to navigate constitutional arrangements, legislative powers, and governance structures shaping Welsh autonomy, regional governance, and intergovernmental relations in a multi-level governance framework.

Conclusion:

The principles of devolution in Wales embody constitutional principles, legal frameworks, and governance arrangements underpinning Wales' autonomy, legislative competence, and administrative responsibilities within the UK constitutional framework. By upholding principles of devolution, statutory obligations, and democratic accountability, Wales enhances legislative scrutiny, policy responsiveness, and public service delivery tailored to Welsh needs, cultural diversity, and regional aspirations. Continued adherence to devolution principles, constitutional reforms, and intergovernmental cooperation promotes governance stability, policy innovation, and democratic governance in supporting Wales' socio-economic development, public welfare, and inclusive governance in a dynamic constitutional landscape.

39.2 Legal Framework for Welsh Devolution

The legal framework for Welsh devolution comprises constitutional statutes, legislative provisions, and institutional arrangements defining the scope, powers, and governance structures governing the devolved administration and legislative competence of the Senedd Cymru (Welsh Parliament).

Key Aspects:

1. **Government of Wales Acts**: The legal basis for Welsh devolution includes the Government of Wales Act 1998, Government of Wales Act 2006, and subsequent amendments, which delineate the distribution of legislative powers between the UK Parliament and the Senedd Cymru. These Acts establish the framework for devolved governance, executive authority, and legislative competence over specified policy areas, known as devolved powers.

2. **Legislative Competence**: The Senedd Cymru has legislative competence to enact laws (Acts of Senedd Cymru) within devolved areas, including health, education, environment, and transportation, subject to reserved matters reserved for the UK Parliament. Legislative processes adhere to statutory requirements, parliamentary procedures, and legal constraints ensuring the validity and enforceability of enacted legislation.

3. **Executive Powers**: The Welsh Government, led by the First Minister, exercises executive powers and

administrative responsibilities to implement policies, manage public services, and allocate resources within devolved sectors. Executive functions encompass policy formulation, budget management, public service delivery, and regulatory oversight, supporting Welsh governance objectives and public welfare priorities.
4. **Judicial Review and Accountability**: Legal frameworks include provisions for judicial review of Welsh devolution laws, administrative decisions, and compliance with constitutional principles, ensuring accountability, transparency, and adherence to legal standards in governance, public administration, and legislative scrutiny.
5. **Constitutional Developments**: Constitutional developments in Welsh devolution law involve statutory amendments, legislative reforms, and institutional arrangements (e.g., Senedd electoral system, intergovernmental relations) to enhance legislative scrutiny, governance effectiveness, and democratic accountability in addressing Welsh socio-economic challenges and regional disparities.

39.3 Comparative Analysis with Other UK Regions

Comparative analysis with other UK regions examines devolution arrangements, constitutional frameworks, and governance models across Scotland, Northern Ireland, and English regions to assess legislative powers, governance structures, and intergovernmental relations influencing regional autonomy, policy-making, and public service delivery.

Key Considerations:
1. **Devolution Models**: Comparative analysis evaluates devolution models (e.g., asymmetrical devolution, reserved powers, legislative competence) adopted in Scotland, Northern Ireland, and England's regions

compared to Welsh devolution arrangements, highlighting variations in constitutional frameworks, legislative powers, and administrative responsibilities governing regional governance and autonomy.
2. **Legal and Governance Structures**: Comparison of legal frameworks and governance structures assesses institutional frameworks (e.g., Scottish Parliament, Northern Ireland Assembly, English regional assemblies) establishing regional legislative competence, executive authority, and fiscal powers to manage public services, economic policies, and regional development initiatives.
3. **Intergovernmental Relations**: Comparative studies explore intergovernmental relations and cooperation mechanisms (e.g., Joint Ministerial Committee, interparliamentary dialogue) between the UK Government, devolved administrations, and regional authorities to address shared policy interests, funding arrangements, and constitutional reforms affecting regional governance and legislative harmonization.
4. **Policy Implications**: Analysis of policy implications examines legislative powers, policy competences (e.g., health, education, environment), and fiscal autonomy impacting regional policy-making, public service delivery, and socio-economic outcomes in addressing regional disparities, demographic challenges, and public welfare priorities across UK regions.

Constitutional Reforms: Comparative insights inform constitutional reforms, governance reforms, and legislative developments in enhancing regional autonomy, legislative scrutiny, and democratic governance across UK regions, promoting effective governance, public accountability, and policy responsiveness in a multi-level governance framework.

39.4 Case Studies in Welsh Devolution Law

Case studies in Welsh devolution law analyze judicial decisions, legislative enactments, and governance challenges influencing Welsh constitutional developments, legislative powers, and institutional reforms shaping regional governance, public policy, and legal accountability.

Key Considerations:

1. **Legislative Competence**: Case studies review legislative competences exercised by the Senedd Cymru in enacting laws within devolved areas, including health, education, and local government, addressing policy priorities, legislative scrutiny, and compliance with constitutional constraints under the Government of Wales Acts.
2. **Administrative Devolution**: Analysis of administrative devolution examines executive powers, policy implementation, and public service delivery managed by the Welsh Government, assessing governance effectiveness, regulatory oversight, and accountability mechanisms in achieving Welsh governance objectives and public welfare outcomes.
3. **Judicial Review and Legal Challenges**: Case analyses explore judicial review cases challenging Welsh devolution laws, administrative decisions, and constitutional compliance with legal standards, influencing governance accountability, legislative scrutiny, and judicial interpretations shaping Welsh constitutional law and governance reforms.
4. **Intergovernmental Relations**: Case studies investigate intergovernmental relations, collaborative initiatives, and policy coordination between the UK Government, Welsh Government, and local authorities to address shared policy interests, funding arrangements, and constitutional developments affecting Welsh regional governance and legislative harmonization.
5. **Public Policy Impact**: Case studies assess the impact of Welsh devolution laws on public policy outcomes, regional development initiatives, and socio-economic reforms in promoting Welsh autonomy, legislative

innovation, and democratic governance in addressing regional priorities and enhancing public service delivery across Wales.

Conclusion

The law of devolution in Wales encompasses legal frameworks, constitutional arrangements, and governance structures defining Welsh autonomy, legislative competence, and administrative responsibilities within the UK constitutional framework. By understanding the principles of Welsh devolution, conducting comparative analysis with other UK regions, and analyzing case studies in Welsh devolution law, stakeholders enhance governance effectiveness, legislative scrutiny, and regional accountability in promoting Welsh governance objectives, public welfare priorities, and democratic governance in a dynamic constitutional landscape. Continued adherence to devolution principles, intergovernmental cooperation, and constitutional reforms supports governance stability, policy innovation, and regional resilience in addressing Welsh socio-economic challenges and advancing inclusive governance in a multi-level governance framework.

Chapter 40: The Law of Maritime Security: 'Navies' and the Rule of Law at Sea

40.1 Principles of Maritime Security Law

Maritime security law encompasses legal principles, international conventions, and regulatory frameworks governing naval operations, maritime law enforcement, and safeguarding maritime interests to ensure safety, security, and rule of law at sea.

Key Aspects:
1. **International Legal Framework**: Maritime security law is governed by international treaties, conventions (e.g., United Nations Convention on the Law of the Sea - UNCLOS), and customary international law principles regulating maritime activities, territorial waters, exclusive economic zones (EEZs), and high seas governance to promote peaceful navigation, freedom of navigation, and maritime security cooperation among nations.
2. **Naval Operations and Sovereignty**: Principles of maritime security affirm naval operations' role in safeguarding national sovereignty, territorial integrity, and maritime boundaries against threats (e.g., piracy, terrorism, illicit activities) endangering maritime security, economic interests, and maritime environment protection under international law and regional agreements.
3. **Law Enforcement and Maritime Jurisdiction**: Maritime security law defines states' jurisdictional powers, law enforcement authorities (e.g., coast guards, navies), and legal mechanisms (e.g., hot pursuit, flag state jurisdiction) to combat maritime crimes, enforce regulatory compliance, and prosecute offenders violating international maritime laws, safety regulations, or environmental protections.

4. **Maritime Safety and Environmental Protection**: Legal frameworks promote maritime safety standards, vessel security measures (e.g., ISPS Code), and environmental protections (e.g., MARPOL Convention) to mitigate maritime risks, prevent marine pollution, and ensure sustainable maritime practices aligning with international maritime regulations, industry standards, and best practices.
5. **International Cooperation and Naval Diplomacy**: Principles of maritime security law emphasize international cooperation, naval diplomacy, and multilateral maritime security initiatives (e.g., maritime patrols, joint exercises) to foster maritime domain awareness, maritime interdiction operations, and cooperative maritime security frameworks enhancing regional stability, crisis response capabilities, and maritime governance effectiveness.

Importance and Application:
Understanding the principles of maritime security law is essential for naval officers, maritime stakeholders, policymakers, and legal professionals to navigate legal complexities, international obligations, and operational challenges in promoting maritime security, the rule of law at sea, and protecting global maritime interests.

Conclusion:
The principles of maritime security law underscore legal frameworks, international conventions, and cooperative measures shaping naval operations, law enforcement activities, and maritime governance strategies to uphold maritime security, the rule of law at sea, and safeguarding maritime interests worldwide. By adhering to international legal obligations, enhancing maritime safety measures, and promoting maritime security cooperation, nations strengthen maritime governance capacities, mitigate maritime threats, and advance sustainable maritime development goals in ensuring safe, secure, and resilient maritime environments for global trade, maritime commerce, and marine resource conservation in a dynamic maritime security landscape.

40.2 Legal Role of Navies

The legal role of navies in maritime security encompasses responsibilities, authorities, and operational mandates under international law and domestic legal frameworks to safeguard national maritime interests, ensure maritime safety, and uphold the rule of law at sea.

Key Aspects:

1. **Safeguarding National Sovereignty**: Navies play a crucial role in protecting national sovereignty, territorial waters, and exclusive economic zones (EEZs) against external threats, ensuring maritime security, and defending maritime boundaries under international legal principles and national laws.
2. **Combatting Maritime Threats**: Legal mandates empower navies to combat maritime threats, including piracy, armed robbery at sea, terrorism, illicit trafficking, and unauthorized maritime activities jeopardizing maritime security, economic interests, and environmental sustainability.
3. **Law Enforcement and Maritime Operations**: Navies enforce maritime laws, conduct law enforcement operations (e.g., maritime patrols, inspections), and apprehend offenders violating international maritime regulations, safety standards, or environmental protections, collaborating with coast guards, law enforcement agencies, and international partners to uphold maritime security and legal compliance.
4. **Search and Rescue Operations**: Navies perform search and rescue operations (SAR) under international humanitarian law (IHL), assisting distressed vessels, rescuing mariners in peril, ensuring prompt response to maritime emergencies, adhering to legal obligations, and humanitarian principles, and coordinating SAR protocols.
5. **Naval Diplomacy and Cooperative Security**: Navies engage in naval diplomacy, multilateral maritime exercises, and cooperative security initiatives (e.g., joint patrols, capacity-building programs) to enhance

regional stability, promote maritime domain awareness, and foster international cooperation in maritime security governance, crisis response, and rule of law enforcement at sea.

40.3 International Maritime Security Agreements

International maritime security agreements comprise multilateral treaties, regional arrangements, and cooperative frameworks establishing legal obligations, operational protocols, and mutual commitments among states to enhance maritime security cooperation, combat maritime threats, and promote the rule of law enforcement at sea.

Key Considerations:
1. **United Nations Conventions**: International maritime security agreements include United Nations Conventions (e.g., UNCLOS), regional maritime security frameworks (e.g., Djibouti Code of Conduct), and bilateral agreements facilitating maritime security cooperation, information sharing, and capacity-building initiatives to address common maritime challenges, strengthen maritime governance, and promote rule-based maritime order.
2. **Regional Maritime Initiatives**: Regional maritime security agreements (e.g., ASEAN Maritime Security Cooperation, Gulf of Guinea Commission) promote regional cooperation, joint patrols, and collaborative maritime security operations among neighbouring states, enhancing maritime domain awareness, maritime interdiction capabilities, and coordinated responses to maritime threats affecting regional stability and maritime commerce.
3. **Counter-Piracy Operations**: International maritime security agreements support counter-piracy operations, naval patrols (e.g., Combined Maritime Forces), and maritime task forces (e.g., EU Naval Force Operation Atalanta) to deter, disrupt, and prosecute piracy attacks, safeguard shipping lanes, and protect maritime trade routes vital to global commerce and economic prosperity.

4. **Maritime Law Enforcement**: Agreements facilitate maritime law enforcement cooperation, extradition treaties, and mutual legal assistance frameworks to combat transnational maritime crimes, prosecute offenders, and uphold legal standards in enforcing international maritime laws, safety regulations, and environmental protections across maritime jurisdictions.
5. **Humanitarian Assistance and Disaster Response**: International maritime security agreements promote humanitarian assistance, disaster response coordination, and joint maritime operations (e.g., Pacific Partnership) to provide humanitarian aid, medical assistance, and disaster relief in response to natural disasters, maritime emergencies, and humanitarian crises affecting coastal communities and maritime populations.

40.4 Case Studies in Maritime Security

Case studies in maritime security analyze operational challenges, legal complexities, and strategic responses in addressing maritime threats, enforcing maritime law, and enhancing maritime security cooperation through international agreements, naval operations, and regional maritime security initiatives.

Key Considerations:
1. **Counter-Piracy Operations in the Gulf of Aden**: Case studies examine multinational naval task forces (e.g., Combined Task Force 151) conducting counter-piracy operations, coordinating patrols, and interdicting pirate attacks to safeguard shipping lanes, protect maritime commerce, and prosecute piracy offenders under international legal frameworks and maritime security agreements.
2. **Maritime Interdiction Operations**: Case analyses assess maritime interdiction operations targeting illicit trafficking (e.g., narcotics, arms smuggling) and illegal fishing activities, enhancing maritime law enforcement,

border security, and regulatory compliance under international maritime security agreements, maritime law enforcement protocols, and cooperative maritime security initiatives.
3. **Regional Maritime Security Cooperation**: Case studies explore regional maritime security cooperation (e.g., Western Indian Ocean), joint naval exercises, and capacity-building programs to enhance maritime domain awareness, maritime interdiction capabilities, and cooperative responses to maritime threats, piracy incidents, and maritime terrorism affecting regional stability and maritime governance.
4. **Legal Challenges and Prosecution**: Case analyses review legal challenges, jurisdictional issues, and legal frameworks governing maritime law enforcement, prosecution of maritime offenders, and adherence to international legal standards in combating maritime crimes, enforcing maritime regulations, and upholding the rule of law at sea.
5. **Environmental Protection and Maritime Safety**: Case studies examine maritime incidents (e.g., oil spills, maritime accidents) affecting marine ecosystems, maritime safety, and environmental protection efforts under international conventions (e.g., MARPOL), regional agreements, and cooperative initiatives promoting sustainable maritime practices, pollution prevention measures, and environmental stewardship in maritime operations.

Conclusion

The law of maritime security underscores legal frameworks, international agreements, and cooperative measures shaping naval operations, maritime law enforcement, and maritime security governance to safeguard national interests, promote the rule of law at sea and ensure safe, secure, and resilient maritime environments. By adhering to international maritime security agreements, enhancing naval capabilities, and conducting cooperative maritime security initiatives, states strengthen maritime governance capacities, mitigate maritime threats, and advance sustainable maritime development goals in safeguarding global maritime interests and promoting maritime stability in a dynamic maritime security landscape.

Chapter 41: The Transportation of Cargo

41.1 Legal Framework for Cargo Transportation

The legal framework governing the transportation of cargo is a multifaceted domain that involves a complex interplay of international conventions, national laws, and industry regulations. At its core, this framework aims to standardize practices, ensure the safety and security of goods, and resolve disputes arising from cargo transportation across borders. One of the foundational pillars in this realm is the International Convention for the Unification of Certain Rules of Law relating to Bills of Lading, commonly known as the Hague Rules of 1924, which was subsequently updated by the Hague-Visby Rules in 1968. These rules established key responsibilities for carriers and shippers, particularly in maritime transport, setting forth liability limitations and mandatory obligations regarding the care of cargo.

In addition to the Hague-Visby Rules, the Hamburg Rules of 1978 were introduced to provide a more balanced legal regime by addressing some of the perceived shortcomings of the earlier conventions, such as the emphasis on carrier liability and shippers' rights. These rules, though less widely adopted, offer an alternative framework that some nations prefer due to their more equitable treatment of carriers and shippers. Further modernizing the legal landscape, the Rotterdam Rules of 2008 aim to unify and update the international maritime carriage of goods by sea, integrating electronic transport records and extending their application to multimodal transport.

Beyond maritime law, air cargo transport is primarily governed by the Warsaw Convention of 1929, which was later amended by the Montreal Convention of 1999. These conventions delineate the responsibilities and liabilities of carriers in international air transportation, addressing issues such as cargo damage, delay, and loss. The Montreal Convention modernized and consolidated the various amendments and supplementary protocols of the Warsaw system, reflecting the evolving needs of international air transport and providing a more cohesive regulatory framework.

On the national level, countries have their own specific laws and regulations that interact with these international conventions, creating a layered legal environment. For instance, the United States follows the Carriage of Goods by Sea Act (COGSA), which incorporates aspects of the Hague-Visby Rules, while the European Union's regulations often reflect the principles found in both the Hague-Visby and Hamburg Rules, tailored to suit the EU's legal landscape.

Moreover, industry-specific standards and guidelines play a crucial role in the transportation of cargo. Organizations such as the International Air Transport Association (IATA) and the International Maritime Organization (IMO) develop and enforce standards that ensure safety, security, and efficiency in cargo transport. These standards cover a wide range of issues, including packaging, documentation, and handling of hazardous materials.

The legal framework for cargo transportation also encompasses aspects of contract law, as contracts of carriage define the terms and conditions under which cargo is transported. These contracts are often subject to the laws of the jurisdiction in which they are executed, or the governing law specified by the parties involved. Dispute resolution mechanisms, including arbitration and litigation, are crucial components of this framework, providing avenues for resolving conflicts that arise during cargo transport.

In conclusion, the legal framework for cargo transportation is a dynamic and intricate system that reflects the global nature of trade and the need for harmonized regulations. By balancing international conventions, national laws, and industry standards, this framework seeks to facilitate the smooth, secure, and efficient movement of goods across the world, adapting to the continuous evolution of global commerce.

41.2 International Conventions on Cargo Transport

International conventions play a pivotal role in standardizing the legal frameworks governing cargo transport across borders, ensuring consistency and predictability in international trade. The most significant conventions include the Hague Rules of 1924 and their subsequent updates, the Hague-Visby Rules, which establish the responsibilities and liabilities of carriers in maritime transport. The Hamburg Rules of 1978 sought to address the limitations of the Hague-Visby Rules by offering a more balanced approach between carrier liability and shippers' rights. The Rotterdam Rules of 2008 further modernized the legal landscape, covering multimodal transport and incorporating provisions for electronic documentation. In air cargo transport, the Warsaw Convention of 1929, amended by the Montreal Convention of 1999, delineates carrier liabilities and shippers' rights, aiming to streamline air transport regulations. These conventions, collectively, create a cohesive international framework that facilitates the efficient and secure movement of goods, minimizing legal ambiguities and promoting global trade.

41.3 Liability and Risk in Cargo Transport

Liability and risk in cargo transport are critical aspects that dictate the allocation of responsibility between carriers and shippers for potential losses or damages to goods during transit. The legal principles governing these aspects vary across different modes of transport and are heavily influenced by international conventions, national laws, and contractual agreements. Maritime transport is primarily regulated by the Hague-Visby Rules and the Hamburg Rules, which specify the extent of a carrier's liability and the circumstances under which liability can be limited or excluded. In air transport, the Montreal Convention sets forth the liability limits for carriers and outlines the conditions under which shippers can claim compensation for lost or damaged cargo. The determination of liability often hinges on factors such as the nature of the goods, the adequacy of packaging, and the adherence to safety and handling protocols. Risk management strategies, including insurance and indemnity clauses in contracts of carriage, are essential for mitigating potential financial losses and ensuring the smooth resolution of disputes in cargo transport.

41.4 Case Studies in Cargo Transportation Law

Case studies in cargo transportation law provide practical insights into the application of legal principles and the resolution of disputes in real-world scenarios. One notable case is the "M/V Athos I" incident, where the oil tanker struck a submerged anchor in the Delaware River, leading to extensive environmental damage and cargo loss. The ensuing legal battle highlighted issues of carrier liability and the obligations of port authorities under the Hague-Visby Rules. Another significant case involved the "Air France Flight 4590" crash, where litigation centred on the liability of air carriers under the Montreal Convention for the loss of high-value cargo. These cases underscore the complexities of determining liability and the interplay between international conventions, national laws, and contractual terms. They also illustrate the importance of thorough documentation, adherence to safety standards, and effective risk management practices in mitigating legal disputes and ensuring fair compensation for affected parties in the cargo transport industry.

Chapter 42: Themes in Socio-Legal Studies

42.1 Interdisciplinary Approaches to Law

Interdisciplinary approaches to law encompass the integration of insights and methodologies from various academic disciplines to enrich the understanding and practice of legal systems. This approach recognizes that law does not operate in a vacuum but is deeply embedded in and influenced by social, economic, political, and cultural contexts. By drawing on disciplines such as sociology, anthropology, economics, political science, and psychology, socio-legal studies seek to explore how laws are created, interpreted, and enforced, and how they affect and are affected by societal forces.

One of the primary benefits of interdisciplinary approaches is the ability to analyze the law from multiple perspectives, providing a more comprehensive understanding of its implications. For example, incorporating sociological theories allows scholars to examine how laws influence and are influenced by social norms, behaviours, and institutions. This can shed light on issues such as inequality, discrimination, and social justice, highlighting the law's role in either perpetuating or challenging these phenomena.

Anthropological approaches contribute by focusing on the cultural dimensions of law, exploring how legal concepts and practices vary across different societies and cultures. This perspective can reveal the cultural underpinnings of legal systems and how cultural values shape legal norms and vice versa. It also helps in understanding the pluralistic nature of many legal systems, where multiple legal traditions coexist and interact.

Economic analyses of law, commonly known as law and economics, apply economic principles to evaluate the efficiency and effectiveness of legal rules and institutions. This approach often involves cost-benefit analysis and the assessment of legal rules based on their economic impact, such as how they influence behaviour, allocate resources, and affect market dynamics. It provides valuable insights into areas like property law, contract law, and regulatory policies. Political science offers tools to understand the law's relationship with power and governance. It examines how legal institutions and processes are shaped by political forces, how laws are used to achieve political objectives, and the role of law in the functioning of the state. This approach is particularly useful in studying constitutional law, administrative law, and human rights law, where legal principles are closely intertwined with political ideologies and power structures.

Psychological approaches to law, or legal psychology, investigate the cognitive and emotional aspects of legal decision-making and behaviour. This includes the study of how judges, jurors, and other legal actors make decisions, how legal processes affect individuals' mental states, and how psychological principles can improve legal procedures and outcomes. Insights from psychology can enhance the fairness and effectiveness of the legal system by addressing biases, improving jury instructions, and developing better interrogation techniques.

By integrating these diverse perspectives, interdisciplinary approaches to law enrich the understanding of legal phenomena and contribute to more nuanced and effective legal scholarship and practice. They enable legal professionals and scholars to address complex legal issues holistically, considering the broader social, economic, political, and cultural contexts in which the law operates. This not only enhances the theoretical foundations of legal studies but also improves the practical application of law in addressing real-world challenges.

42.2 Legal Pluralism and Social Justice

Legal pluralism refers to the existence and interaction of multiple legal systems within a single geographic area or society. This phenomenon is especially prevalent in post-colonial societies, Indigenous communities, and areas with significant ethnic or cultural diversity. Legal pluralism recognizes that state law is not the only source of legal norms and authority; customary law, religious law, and informal community norms often coexist with formal legal systems. This multiplicity of legal orders can both challenge and enhance social justice. On one hand, legal pluralism can provide marginalized communities with access to justice systems that align more closely with their cultural practices and values, potentially addressing issues that state law overlooks. On the other hand, it can also perpetuate inequality if certain groups are subject to discriminatory customary practices or if there is unequal recognition and enforcement of different legal systems. Balancing the coexistence of these systems requires a nuanced approach that respects cultural diversity while upholding fundamental human rights and ensuring equitable access to justice for all members of society.

42.3 Law and Society in Comparative Perspective

Comparative socio-legal studies examine how different legal systems and societies influence each other and how law functions across various cultural, political, and social contexts. This comparative perspective involves analyzing similarities and differences in legal institutions, practices, and outcomes between countries or regions. It provides insights into how laws are shaped by societal values and how they, in turn, shape social behaviour. For instance, studying the different approaches to family law in various countries can reveal how cultural attitudes toward marriage, gender roles, and child-rearing influence legal norms and vice versa. Comparative analysis also highlights the impact of historical and political factors on legal development, such as how colonial legacies affect contemporary legal systems in former colonies. By understanding these dynamics, scholars and policymakers can identify best practices, avoid pitfalls, and develop more effective and culturally sensitive legal reforms that address the specific needs of different societies.

42.4 Case Studies in Socio-Legal Research

Case studies in socio-legal research provide in-depth examinations of specific instances where law and society intersect, offering detailed insights into the practical application and impact of legal principles in real-world situations. These studies often focus on particular events, legal disputes, or institutional practices, using qualitative methods such as interviews, ethnography, and document analysis. For example, a case study might explore the implementation of transitional justice mechanisms in a post-conflict society, examining how legal processes like truth commissions and war crimes tribunals contribute to reconciliation and social healing. Another case study could investigate the role of community-based dispute resolution in rural areas, assessing its effectiveness in delivering justice compared to formal legal systems. By focusing on specific examples, case studies illuminate the complexities and nuances of how law operates in different contexts, highlighting how legal norms are interpreted, negotiated, and enforced on the ground. These insights are invaluable for developing a more comprehensive and context-sensitive understanding of law and its role in society, ultimately informing better policy and practice.

Chapter 43: Trademarks: Comparative and International Perspectives

43.1 Principles of Trademark Law

Trademark law serves to protect distinctive signs, logos, symbols, names, and other identifiers that distinguish the goods or services of one entity from those of others. The primary principles of trademark law include distinctiveness, non-deceptiveness, and the requirement of use in commerce. Distinctiveness is crucial as it ensures that a trademark is capable of identifying the source of goods or services and distinguishing them from others in the marketplace. Trademarks can be inherently distinctive (such as fanciful or arbitrary marks) or acquire distinctiveness through extensive use.

Non-deceptiveness is another fundamental principle, ensuring that trademarks do not mislead consumers about the nature, quality, or origin of the goods or services they represent. This principle protects consumer interests and maintains market integrity by preventing confusion and fraud.

The requirement of use in commerce underscores the principle that trademarks are not merely theoretical rights but are intended to be actively used in trade. This principle is integral to the legal protection of trademarks, as it ensures that trademark rights are based on actual use and reputation in the marketplace.

Internationally, the protection of trademarks is guided by agreements such as the Paris Convention for the Protection of Industrial Property and the Agreement on Trade-Related Aspects of Intellectual Property Rights (TRIPS). The Paris Convention, established in 1883, allows for the national treatment of trademarks, meaning that signatories must grant the same protection to foreign trademarks as they do to domestic ones. It also introduces the right of priority, enabling trademark owners to seek protection in multiple countries within a specified period after filing in one member country.

TRIPS, part of the World Trade Organization (WTO) agreements, establishes minimum standards for trademark protection that member countries must adhere to. These standards include the recognition of service marks, protection of well-known trademarks, and the requirement that trademarks must be renewed every ten years.

In addition to these international frameworks, regional systems such as the European Union Trademark (EUTM) and the African Intellectual Property Organization (OAPI) provide unified registration and protection mechanisms within their respective regions. The EUTM, for instance, allows for a single trademark registration that grants protection across all EU member states, streamlining the process and reducing costs for trademark owners.

Comparative perspectives in trademark law reveal significant variations in how different jurisdictions approach trademark protection. For instance, the United States follows the first-to-use principle, granting trademark rights based on the actual use of the mark in commerce. In contrast, many other countries, including those in the European Union, follow the first-to-file principle, where rights are granted based on the first registration of the mark.

These differences highlight the importance of understanding the specific legal frameworks and practices of each jurisdiction when seeking trademark protection internationally. The principles of trademark law, while rooted in common goals of protecting business interests and consumer trust, are thus implemented in diverse ways across the globe, reflecting the varying legal traditions and commercial priorities of different regions.

43.2 International Trademark Treaties

International trademark treaties play a crucial role in harmonizing trademark laws across different jurisdictions, facilitating the protection and enforcement of trademark rights globally. Key treaties include the Paris Convention for the

Protection of Industrial Property, the Madrid System for the International Registration of Marks, and the Agreement on Trade-Related Aspects of Intellectual Property Rights (TRIPS). The Paris Convention, one of the earliest treaties in this field, establishes the principles of national treatment and right of priority, ensuring that foreign trademark owners receive the same protection as domestic ones and can claim priority in member countries within a specified period. The Madrid System, managed by the World Intellectual Property Organization (WIPO), simplifies the process of registering trademarks internationally by allowing applicants to file a single application that covers multiple countries. TRIPS, administered by the World Trade Organization (WTO), sets comprehensive minimum standards for the protection and enforcement of trademark rights, ensuring that member countries provide robust legal frameworks for trademarks. These treaties collectively enhance global cooperation in trademark protection, reducing legal barriers and fostering international trade.

43.3 Comparative Analysis of Trademark Laws

A comparative analysis of trademark laws reveals significant differences and similarities in how various jurisdictions approach the registration, protection, and enforcement of trademarks. In the United States, trademark rights are primarily established through the actual use of the mark in commerce, following the first-to-use principle. This contrasts with the first-to-file principle prevalent in many other countries, including those in the European Union, where the rights are granted based on the first registration of the mark. The European Union Trademark (EUTM) system allows for a single trademark registration that protects all EU member states, streamlining the process for businesses operating in multiple countries. Japan, while also following the first-to-file principle, emphasizes the importance of distinctiveness and requires a thorough examination process to ensure that the trademark is not similar to existing ones. In India, trademark law is influenced by both common law and statutory principles, recognizing rights through use as well as registration. These variations necessitate a strategic approach for businesses seeking international trademark protection, considering the specific legal requirements and practices of each jurisdiction to effectively safeguard their brands.

43.4 Case Studies in Trademark Law

Case studies in trademark law offer valuable insights into the practical application and implications of trademark principles in real-world scenarios. One notable case is the "Apple Inc. v. Samsung Electronics Co." dispute, where Apple sued Samsung for trademark and design patent infringement related to the iPhone. This case highlighted the importance of protecting trade dress and the distinctiveness of product design in addition to traditional trademarks. Another significant case is the "Louboutin v. Yves Saint Laurent" dispute over the use of red soles on high-heeled shoes. The court's decision to protect Louboutin's trademarked red soles underscored the recognition of colour as a distinctive and protectable feature under trademark law. In the context of international trademark disputes, the "Budweiser" case involving Anheuser-Busch and the Czech brewery Budějovický Budvar demonstrated the complexities of trademark rights across different jurisdictions, with both companies holding rights to the name "Budweiser" in various regions. These case studies illustrate the diverse challenges and considerations in trademark law, including the protection of non-traditional trademarks, the interplay between diverse types of intellectual property, and the impact of international legal frameworks on trademark disputes.

Chapter 44: Transfer of Technology Law

44.1 Legal Framework for Technology Transfer
The legal framework for technology transfer encompasses a variety of laws, regulations, and international agreements designed to facilitate the movement of technology between entities, regions, and countries. Technology transfer involves the sharing of technological knowledge, expertise, and innovations through mechanisms such as licensing, joint ventures, partnerships, and research collaborations. This process is crucial for fostering innovation, economic development, and competitive advantage across different sectors.

At the international level, agreements such as the Agreement on Trade-Related Aspects of Intellectual Property Rights (TRIPS) and the Paris Convention for the Protection of Industrial Property set foundational standards for intellectual property (IP) protection, which is integral to technology transfer. TRIPS, administered by the World Trade Organization (WTO), establishes minimum standards for IP rights enforcement, ensuring that member countries provide robust legal frameworks that protect IP, thereby encouraging technology transfer by safeguarding inventors' and innovators' interests.

National laws play a pivotal role in regulating technology transfer by providing the legal basis for the protection and commercialization of intellectual property. In the United States, for instance, the Bayh-Dole Act of 1980 significantly impacted technology transfer by allowing universities and other research institutions to retain ownership of inventions developed with federal funding. This law facilitated the commercialization of research by enabling institutions to license their technologies to private enterprises. Similarly, the European Union has implemented regulations that encourage technology transfer, such as the EU's Horizon Europe program, which funds research and innovation projects and promotes collaboration between academia and industry.

Contract law is another critical component of the legal framework for technology transfer. Licensing agreements, which are the most common means of technology transfer, are governed by contract law principles. These agreements outline the terms and conditions under which technology is transferred, including the scope of use, duration, financial arrangements (such as royalties), confidentiality provisions, and dispute resolution mechanisms. Ensuring that these contracts are well-drafted and enforceable is essential for protecting the interests of both the technology provider and the recipient.

Intellectual property law, particularly patent law, is fundamental to technology transfer. Patents protect technological innovations by granting inventors exclusive rights to their inventions, preventing others from making, using, or selling the patented technology without permission. This exclusivity incentivizes innovation by allowing inventors to recoup their investments through licensing or direct commercialization. Patent law also facilitates technology transfer by enabling inventors to license their technologies to others, thereby disseminating modern technologies and promoting further innovation.

Competition law (antitrust law) also affects technology transfer, ensuring that licensing agreements and other transfer arrangements do not lead to anti-competitive practices. For example, competition authorities may scrutinize licensing agreements to prevent monopolistic practices that could stifle innovation or restrict access to technology. The European Commission and the United States Federal Trade Commission (FTC) both enforce competition laws that oversee technology transfer transactions to maintain fair competition in the market. Additionally, national policies and strategies can significantly influence technology transfer. Many countries have established technology transfer offices (TTOs) and innovation agencies to support the commercialization of research and facilitate partnerships between academia and industry. These entities often provide resources, funding, and expertise to assist in the negotiation of technology transfer agreements and the management of intellectual property.

In summary, the legal framework for technology transfer is a multifaceted system that involves international agreements, national laws, contract law, intellectual property law, and competition law. This framework aims to promote innovation, protect intellectual property rights, ensure fair competition, and facilitate the effective dissemination of technology. By providing clear legal guidelines and protections, the framework encourages entities to engage in technology transfer, fostering economic growth and technological advancement globally.

44.2 Intellectual Property and Technology Transfer

Intellectual property (IP) is a cornerstone of technology transfer, serving as the primary mechanism through which technological innovations are protected, managed, and exchanged. The primary forms of IP relevant to technology transfer include patents, trademarks, copyrights, and trade secrets. Patents are particularly crucial, as they grant inventors exclusive rights to their inventions, preventing unauthorized use and allowing them to license their technologies. This exclusivity incentivizes innovation by enabling inventors to monetize their inventions through licensing agreements or direct commercialization. Trademarks protect brand names and logos, which are essential for establishing market identity and trust. Copyrights safeguard original works of authorship, including software and technical documentation, ensuring creators can control and benefit from their creations. Trade secrets protect confidential business information and technological know-how, offering competitive advantages. Effective IP management is critical for successful technology transfer, as it ensures that the rights of inventors and innovators are protected while facilitating the dissemination of modern technologies through licensing, joint ventures, and partnerships.

44.3 Regulatory Issues in Technology Transfer

Regulatory issues play a significant role in the technology transfer process, impacting the ease and legality of transferring technologies across borders and between entities. One major regulatory concern is compliance with export control laws, which govern the transfer of certain technologies that have potential military applications or are considered critical to national security. Countries like the United States have stringent export control regulations, such as the International Traffic in Arms Regulations (ITAR) and the Export Administration Regulations (EAR), which require licenses for the export of specific technologies. Another critical regulatory issue is adherence to antitrust laws, which prevent anti-competitive practices that could arise from technology licensing agreements. Authorities like the European Commission and the U.S. Federal Trade Commission review these agreements to ensure they do not stifle competition or create monopolies. Additionally, environmental regulations can influence technology transfer, especially when technologies involve hazardous materials or processes that may impact the environment. Regulatory compliance is essential to mitigate legal risks and ensure that technology transfers are conducted lawfully and ethically, promoting innovation while safeguarding public interests.

44.4 Case Studies in Technology Transfer Law

Case studies in technology transfer law provide practical insights into the application of legal principles and the complexities involved in transferring technologies. One notable example is the transfer of CRISPR-Cas9 technology, a revolutionary gene-editing tool. The technology, developed by researchers at the University of California, Berkeley, and the Broad Institute, has been the subject of intense patent litigation and licensing negotiations. The disputes over patent rights and licensing agreements highlight the importance of clear IP management and the challenges of navigating overlapping claims in innovative technologies. Another significant case is the collaboration between pharmaceutical companies and universities for the development of COVID-19 vaccines. The partnerships involved complex agreements covering IP rights, profit-sharing, and regulatory compliance, illustrating the critical role of legal frameworks in facilitating rapid technology transfer during a global health crisis. Additionally, the transfer of green technologies, such as renewable energy solutions, often involves navigating international treaties, national regulations, and funding mechanisms. These case studies underscore the multifaceted nature of technology transfer law and the necessity for robust legal frameworks to address the diverse challenges and opportunities in the field.

Chapter 45: Transitional Justice

45.1 Principles of Transitional Justice

Transitional justice refers to the set of judicial and non-judicial measures implemented by societies to address the legacies of human rights abuses and achieve accountability, reconciliation, and justice. These measures are applied in the context of transitioning from conflict or authoritarian rule to peace and democracy. The core principles of transitional justice encompass truth, justice, reparation, and guarantees of non-recurrence.

1. Truth: The principle of truth involves uncovering and acknowledging the facts about past human rights violations. Truth-seeking mechanisms, such as truth commissions, are established to investigate and document the nature, causes, and consequences of these abuses. The goal is to provide a comprehensive historical record that recognizes the suffering of victims and restores their dignity. By revealing the truth, societies aim to promote collective understanding, foster reconciliation, and prevent denial or distortion of past events.

2. Justice: Justice in transitional contexts emphasizes holding perpetrators accountable for their actions. This principle encompasses both retributive justice, which seeks to punish those responsible for serious crimes, and restorative justice, which aims to repair the harm caused by these violations. Judicial processes, including national and international courts, play a crucial role in ensuring that perpetrators are prosecuted and that victims receive a measure of justice. Additionally, traditional, and community-based justice mechanisms may be employed to address crimes and foster reconciliation at the local level.

3. Reparation: Reparation involves providing compensation, restitution, and rehabilitation to victims of human rights abuses. This principle recognizes the need to address the material and psychological harm suffered by individuals and communities. Reparation measures can include financial compensation, the return of property, medical and psychological care, and public apologies. Effective reparation programs aim to restore victims' dignity, rebuild their lives, and acknowledge the wrongs they endured, contributing to their sense of justice and societal healing.

4. Guarantees of Non-Recurrence: Preventing the recurrence of human rights violations is a fundamental principle of transitional justice. This involves implementing institutional reforms to strengthen the rule of law, promote good governance, and ensure respect for human rights. Reforms may include vetting and reforming security forces, judiciary, and other state institutions implicated in past abuses. Additionally, promoting human rights education, fostering a culture of accountability, and supporting civil society is crucial for building resilient and just societies. By addressing the root causes of conflict and authoritarianism, guarantees of non-recurrence aim to create conditions for sustainable peace and democracy.

Transitional justice is inherently context-specific, and tailored to the unique needs and circumstances of each society. It often requires a combination of measures to address the multifaceted nature of past abuses and their impact on individuals and communities. Successful transitional justice initiatives engage a wide range of stakeholders, including victims, civil society, government institutions, and the international community, ensuring that the processes are inclusive, participatory, and reflective of diverse perspectives. In summary, the principles of transitional justice—truth, justice, reparation, and guarantees of non-recurrence—provide a comprehensive framework for addressing past human rights abuses and fostering a just and peaceful future. By embracing these principles, societies transitioning from conflict or authoritarianism can confront their past, promote healing and reconciliation, and build a foundation for lasting peace and democracy.

45.2 Legal Framework for Transitional Justice Mechanisms

The legal framework for transitional justice mechanisms comprises a blend of international law, national legislation, and customary practices designed to address human rights abuses and foster societal reconciliation in post-conflict or post-authoritarian contexts. Key elements of this framework include international human rights treaties, national laws and policies, and hybrid legal mechanisms.

1. International Human Rights Treaties: International treaties and conventions provide a foundational legal basis for transitional justice. Notable instruments include the Universal Declaration of Human Rights (UDHR), the International Covenant on Civil and Political Rights (ICCPR), and the Rome Statute of the International Criminal Court (ICC). These treaties establish norms and standards for human rights protection, accountability, and justice that transitional justice mechanisms must adhere to. For example, the Rome Statute empowers the ICC to prosecute individuals for genocide, war crimes, and crimes against humanity, thereby reinforcing global standards for accountability.

2. National Laws and Policies: Countries undergoing transitions often enact specific laws and policies to implement transitional justice measures. These legal instruments might establish truth commissions, special tribunals, or reparations programs. For instance, South Africa's Promotion of National Unity and Reconciliation Act of 1995 created the Truth and Reconciliation Commission (TRC), which was mandated to investigate apartheid-era human rights violations and recommend reparations. National laws can also address amnesty provisions, ensuring they align with international obligations to prosecute serious crimes.

3. Hybrid Legal Mechanisms: Hybrid legal mechanisms combine elements of both national and international law to address complex transitional justice needs. These mechanisms often involve mixed national and international personnel and apply a combination of domestic and international legal standards. The Special Court for Sierra Leone (SCSL) is a prime example, established to prosecute those bearing the greatest responsibility for serious violations of international humanitarian law during Sierra Leone's civil war. Such hybrid models aim to enhance local ownership while benefiting from international expertise and legitimacy.

4. Customary Practices: In addition to formal legal frameworks, customary and Indigenous practices play a significant role in transitional justice, particularly in regions where formal legal systems may be weak or distrusted. Traditional justice mechanisms, such as Rwanda's Gacaca courts, have been used to handle large-scale human rights abuses at the community level. These mechanisms emphasize restorative justice and reconciliation, integrating cultural norms and practices into the transitional justice process.

5. Institutional Reforms: Legal frameworks for transitional justice often mandate institutional reforms to prevent the recurrence of abuses. This includes vetting and reforming the judiciary, security forces, and other state institutions implicated in past violations. Institutional reforms are essential for rebuilding public trust and ensuring that state structures support, rather than undermine, human rights and the rule of law.

6. Victim Participation: A critical aspect of the legal framework for transitional justice is ensuring victim participation and inclusion. Legal mechanisms should provide avenues for victims to voice their experiences, participate in proceedings, and receive reparations. This principle is fundamental for the legitimacy and effectiveness of transitional justice processes, as it addresses victims' needs and rights and contributes to societal healing.

In summary, the legal framework for transitional justice mechanisms is a complex interplay of international standards, national laws, hybrid models, and customary practices. These elements collectively aim to provide comprehensive and effective responses to past human rights abuses, ensuring accountability, reparation, and reconciliation while promoting long-term peace and stability.

45.3 Comparative Analysis of Transitional Justice Models

A comparative analysis of transitional justice models reveals diverse approaches to addressing past human rights abuses, reflecting the unique contexts and needs of different societies. Key models include truth commissions, special courts and tribunals, amnesty programs, and reparations schemes. Each model has its strengths and challenges, and their effectiveness often depends on the specific historical, cultural, and political context.

1. Truth Commissions: Truth commissions are non-judicial bodies established to investigate and document human rights violations. Notable examples include South Africa's Truth and Reconciliation Commission (TRC) and the Truth Commission for El Salvador. Truth commissions typically focus on uncovering the truth about past abuses, recognizing victims' suffering, and promoting reconciliation. They often recommend reforms and reparations but do not prosecute perpetrators. The South African TRC is widely praised for its comprehensive approach and emphasis on restorative justice, while the El Salvador commission faced criticism for the limited implementation of its recommendations.

2. Special Courts and Tribunals: Special courts and tribunals are judicial bodies created to prosecute those responsible for serious human rights violations. The International Criminal Tribunal for Rwanda (ICTR) and the Special Court for Sierra Leone (SCSL) are prominent examples. These courts aim to provide accountability and deter future abuses by delivering justice for victims. The ICTR successfully prosecuted key figures responsible for the Rwandan genocide, while the SCSL addressed crimes committed during Sierra Leone's civil war. However, these tribunals are often costly and time-consuming, and their impact on local justice systems and communities can be mixed.

3. Amnesty Programs: Amnesty programs grant immunity from prosecution to individuals in exchange for truth-telling, demobilization, or other forms of cooperation. These programs can facilitate peace negotiations and encourage perpetrators to come forward. However, they are controversial as they may undermine accountability and justice for victims. South Africa's TRC included an amnesty provision that required perpetrators to fully disclose their actions in exchange for immunity. This approach aimed to balance the need for truth and reconciliation with the practicalities of transitioning from apartheid.

4. Reparations Schemes: Reparations schemes provide compensation, restitution, and rehabilitation to victims of human rights abuses. These programs recognize the harm suffered by victims and aim to restore their dignity and well-being. Argentina's reparations program for victims of the "Dirty War" and Chile's reparations for victims of Pinochet's regime are notable examples. Effective reparations schemes require substantial resources and political commitment to address the diverse needs of victims comprehensively.

5. Hybrid Models: Hybrid models integrate elements of different transitional justice mechanisms to address complex contexts. The hybrid court system in Cambodia, the Extraordinary Chambers in the Courts of Cambodia (ECCC), combines national and international judges and laws to prosecute Khmer Rouge leaders. This approach aims to balance international standards of justice with local ownership and participation.

6. Community-Based Approaches: Community-based approaches, such as Rwanda's Gacaca courts, involve local communities in the justice process. These mechanisms emphasize restorative justice and reconciliation, focusing on reintegrating offenders and repairing community relationships. While Gacaca courts addressed a vast number of genocide cases, they faced challenges related to due process and consistency.

In summary, transitional justice models vary widely, each offering unique benefits and facing distinct challenges. Comparative analysis underscores the importance of tailoring transitional justice mechanisms to the specific needs and contexts of societies in transition, ensuring a holistic approach that balances truth, justice, reparation, and non-recurrence.

45.4 Case Studies in Transitional Justice

Case studies in transitional justice provide valuable insights into the implementation and impact of various mechanisms in different contexts. These studies illustrate the successes, challenges, and lessons learned from diverse experiences in addressing past human rights abuses.

1. South Africa's Truth and Reconciliation Commission (TRC): South Africa's TRC is one of the most well-known transitional justice initiatives. Established in 1995, the TRC aimed to uncover the truth about human rights violations during apartheid, promote reconciliation, and recommend reparations. The TRC held public hearings, giving victims a platform to share their experiences and perpetrators an opportunity to confess their crimes in exchange for amnesty. The TRC's emphasis on restorative justice and its detailed final report significantly contributed to national healing and the acknowledgement of apartheid-era atrocities. However, the TRC also faced criticism for not sufficiently addressing socio-economic disparities and for granting amnesty to some high-profile perpetrators.

2. The International Criminal Tribunal for Rwanda (ICTR): The ICTR was established by the United Nations in 1994 to prosecute those responsible for the Rwandan genocide. Located in Arusha, Tanzania, the ICTR aimed to deliver justice for the victims of the genocide and contribute to the restoration of peace in Rwanda. The tribunal successfully prosecuted several high-ranking officials and played a crucial role in developing international criminal law, particularly concerning genocide and crimes against humanity. However, the ICTR faced challenges, including lengthy trial processes, prohibitive costs, and limited impact on national reconciliation efforts.

3. Argentina's Reparations Program: Following the end of the military dictatorship in 1983, Argentina implemented a comprehensive reparations program for victims of state terrorism during the "Dirty War." The program provided financial compensation, health care, and educational benefits to victims and their families. Argentina's approach to reparations has been lauded for its thoroughness and the significant resources allocated to support victims. This case highlights the importance of political will and societal support in implementing effective reparations programs.

4. Sierra Leone's Special Court: The Special Court for Sierra Leone (SCSL) was established to prosecute those bearing the greatest responsibility for serious violations of international humanitarian law during the country's civil war. The court, a hybrid institution combining national and international elements, successfully tried key figures, including former Liberian President Charles Taylor. The SCSL's work contributed to accountability and set important precedents in international criminal justice. However, it also faced criticism regarding its outreach and engagement with local communities.

5. Cambodia's Extraordinary Chambers in the Courts of Cambodia (ECCC): The ECCC, a hybrid court established to prosecute senior leaders of the Khmer Rouge for crimes committed between 1975 and 1979, blends national and international law and personnel. The ECCC has achieved notable convictions, including those of high-ranking Khmer Rouge officials. The court's approach emphasizes both legal accountability and historical documentation. Despite its achievements, the ECCC has faced criticism for its slow pace, prohibitive costs, and perceived political interference.

Chapter 46: Transnational Business Instruments

46.1 Legal Instruments for Transnational Business
Transnational business, characterized by the global movement of goods, services, capital, and technology, relies on a variety of legal instruments to facilitate and regulate cross-border transactions. These instruments encompass international agreements, conventions, treaties, and frameworks that harmonize legal standards, protect investments, and resolve disputes in the global marketplace.

1. International Trade Agreements: International trade agreements play a crucial role in regulating transnational business activities by establishing rules and reducing trade barriers. Examples include the World Trade Organization (WTO) agreements, such as the General Agreement on Tariffs and Trade (GATT) and the Agreement on Trade-Related Aspects of Intellectual Property Rights (TRIPS). These agreements govern the conduct of trade in goods and services, establish dispute settlement mechanisms, and promote fair competition among member states.

2. Bilateral Investment Treaties (BITs) and Multilateral Investment Treaties: BITs are agreements between two countries that promote and protect investments made by investors from one country in the territory of the other. These treaties typically include provisions for the protection of property rights, guarantees against expropriation without compensation, and mechanisms for resolving investment disputes. Multilateral investment treaties, such as the Energy Charter Treaty (ECT), extend similar protections across multiple countries, encouraging foreign direct investment (FDI) by providing legal certainty and safeguards for investors.

3. International Commercial Contracts: International commercial contracts are essential legal instruments governing agreements between businesses across borders. These contracts outline the terms and conditions of transactions, including sales of goods, services, licensing agreements, joint ventures, and distribution agreements. Standard contract terms often incorporate internationally recognized principles such as those found in the United Nations Convention on Contracts for the International Sale of Goods (CISG), which harmonizes rules governing international sales contracts and promotes certainty in commercial transactions.

4. Arbitration and Alternative Dispute Resolution (ADR) Mechanisms: Arbitration and ADR mechanisms provide flexible and efficient means for resolving disputes arising from transnational business transactions. International commercial arbitration, governed by conventions such as the New York Convention, enables parties to resolve disputes outside national courts in a neutral forum chosen by mutual agreement. ADR methods, including mediation and conciliation, offer collaborative approaches to dispute resolution, preserving business relationships and avoiding the costs and complexities of litigation in multiple jurisdictions.

5. Cross-Border Insolvency Frameworks: Cross-border insolvency frameworks facilitate the efficient administration of insolvent entities with assets or creditors in multiple jurisdictions. Instruments such as the UNCITRAL Model Law on Cross-Border Insolvency provide a framework for cooperation and coordination between national insolvency proceedings, ensuring fair treatment of creditors and maximizing asset recovery in global insolvency cases. These frameworks promote predictability and efficiency in resolving cross-border financial distress, supporting the orderly conduct of transnational business operations.

6. Corporate Social Responsibility (CSR) Standards: While not strictly legal instruments, CSR standards and guidelines influence transnational business practices by promoting ethical conduct, sustainability, and respect for human rights and the environment. Initiatives such as the UN Global Compact and OECD Guidelines for Multinational Enterprises encourage businesses to adopt responsible practices in their operations worldwide. Adherence to CSR principles enhances corporate reputation, mitigates risks, and fosters trust among stakeholders, contributing to sustainable development and positive social impact.

In conclusion, legal instruments for transnational business form a comprehensive framework that addresses the complexities and challenges of global commerce. By promoting legal certainty, protecting investments, facilitating trade, and resolving disputes effectively, these instruments support economic growth, foster international cooperation, and uphold the rule of law in the interconnected global economy.

46.2 International Trade Agreements and Instruments

International trade agreements and instruments are pivotal in shaping the regulatory framework for transnational business activities. These agreements aim to facilitate trade, reduce barriers, harmonize standards, and provide mechanisms for dispute resolution. Key international trade agreements and instruments include:

1. World Trade Organization (WTO): The WTO is the global organization that sets rules for international trade. Its agreements cover goods, services, intellectual property, and dispute settlement. The WTO agreements, such as the General Agreement on Tariffs and Trade (GATT) and the Agreement on Trade-Related Aspects of Intellectual Property Rights (TRIPS), establish principles of non-discrimination, transparency, and predictability in international trade relations.

2. Free Trade Agreements (FTAs): FTAs are agreements between two or more countries that reduce or eliminate tariffs, quotas, and other trade barriers on goods and services traded among them. Examples include the North American Free Trade Agreement (NAFTA, now USMCA), the Comprehensive and Progressive Agreement for Trans-Pacific Partnership (CPTPP), and the European Union's numerous bilateral and regional trade agreements. FTAs aim to enhance economic integration and promote trade liberalization among member states.

3. Bilateral Investment Treaties (BITs) and Multilateral Investment Treaties: BITs protect investments made by investors from one country in another country's territory. These treaties typically include provisions for investor protection, dispute resolution mechanisms, and guarantees against expropriation without compensation. Multilateral investment treaties, such as the Energy Charter Treaty (ECT), extend similar protections across multiple countries, promoting cross-border investments.

4. Regional Trade Agreements (RTAs): RTAs are agreements among countries within a specific region to reduce trade barriers and promote economic cooperation. Examples include the European Union's Single Market, the Association of Southeast Asian Nations (ASEAN) Free Trade Area, and the Mercosur agreement in South America. RTAs facilitate regional integration, harmonize regulations, and create larger markets for goods and services.

5. International Commercial Contracts: International commercial contracts govern agreements between businesses across borders. These contracts typically incorporate internationally recognized principles, such as those found in the United Nations Convention on Contracts for the International Sale of Goods (CISG). CISG provides uniform rules governing contracts for the sale of goods, promoting legal certainty, and facilitating international trade.

6. Trade Facilitation Agreements: Trade facilitation agreements aim to streamline customs procedures, reduce red tape, and enhance transparency in cross-border trade. The WTO Trade Facilitation Agreement (TFA) is a landmark agreement that sets out measures for expediting the movement, release, and clearance of goods, thereby reducing trade costs, and improving efficiency in global supply chains.

46.3 Regulatory Challenges in Transnational Business

Transnational business operations face various regulatory challenges that arise from differences in national laws, regulatory frameworks, and cultural practices. These challenges include:

1. Legal and Regulatory Divergence: Differences in legal systems and regulatory regimes across countries can create compliance burdens for transnational businesses. Companies must navigate diverse requirements related to taxation, labour laws, environmental standards, and intellectual property rights, leading to increased costs and complexity in operations.

2. Compliance with International Standards: While international trade agreements harmonize certain rules and standards, compliance with diverse international standards remains a challenge. Businesses must adhere to varying regulatory requirements across markets, impacting product development, manufacturing processes, and market entry strategies.

3. Political and Economic Instability: Political instability, changes in government policies, and economic crises in host countries can disrupt business operations and investment plans. Uncertainty surrounding regulatory changes and policy shifts may deter foreign investment and affect market stability.

4. Corruption and Bribery Risks: Corruption and bribery pose significant risks in transnational business transactions, particularly in countries with weak governance structures. Compliance with anti-corruption laws, such as the U.S. Foreign Corrupt Practices Act (FCPA) and the OECD Anti-Bribery Convention, is crucial for mitigating legal and reputational risks.

5. Intellectual Property Protection: Protecting intellectual property (IP) rights across multiple jurisdictions is challenging due to differences in IP laws and enforcement mechanisms. Transnational businesses must develop robust IP strategies to safeguard innovations, trademarks, and proprietary technology from infringement and misappropriation.

6. Cross-Border Dispute Resolution: Resolving disputes that arise from transnational business transactions can be complex and costly. Arbitration and alternative dispute resolution (ADR) mechanisms offer efficient alternatives to litigation in national courts but require careful consideration of jurisdictional issues and enforcement of arbitration awards.

46.4 Case Studies in Transnational Business Law

Case studies in transnational business law provide insights into real-world challenges and strategies employed by businesses and legal practitioners. Examples include:

1. Boeing-Airbus WTO Dispute: The Boeing-Airbus dispute before the WTO involved allegations of illegal subsidies and unfair competition between the two aerospace giants, Boeing (U.S.) and Airbus (EU). The case highlighted complexities in international trade rules, subsidy regimes, and dispute settlement mechanisms under the WTO agreements.

2. Volkswagen Emissions Scandal: The Volkswagen emissions scandal revealed regulatory compliance failures and ethical lapses in the automotive industry. Volkswagen admitted to using illegal software to manipulate emissions tests, leading to legal actions, regulatory fines, and reputational damage across multiple jurisdictions.

3. Microsoft Antitrust Case in the EU: The EU's antitrust case against Microsoft involved allegations of anti-competitive practices related to its Windows operating system and internet browser. The case underscored challenges in reconciling national competition laws with EU competition rules and highlighted the role of regulatory authorities in enforcing fair competition in digital markets.

4. Nestlé's Supply Chain Challenges: Nestlé faced legal and ethical challenges in its global supply chain, including allegations of child labour in cocoa production and environmental sustainability concerns. The case exemplifies the complexities of corporate responsibility across international operations and the importance of due diligence in supply chain management.

5. Uber's Regulatory Battles: Uber has encountered regulatory challenges in numerous countries regarding its business model, employment practices, and compliance with local transportation regulations. The case highlights the tensions between disruptive technologies and traditional regulatory frameworks in the sharing economy.

6. GlaxoSmithKline's Bribery Scandal: GlaxoSmithKline (GSK) faced allegations of bribery and corruption in China, leading to legal investigations, regulatory sanctions, and reputational damage. The case underscores the importance of compliance with anti-corruption laws and ethical standards in global business operations.

In conclusion, case studies in transnational business law illustrate the complexities, risks, and legal strategies involved in conducting business across borders. By examining these cases, policymakers, businesses, and legal professionals can better understand regulatory challenges, anticipate potential pitfalls, and develop effective compliance and risk management strategies in global markets.

Chapter 47: Transnational Corporate Law and Practice

47.1 Principles of Transnational Corporate Law

Transnational corporate law encompasses legal principles and practices that govern the activities, operations, and interactions of corporations operating across national boundaries. These principles address the complexities arising from globalization, cross-border investments, regulatory frameworks, and corporate governance. Key principles of transnational corporate law include:

1. Corporate Formation and Structure: Transnational corporate law governs the formation, registration, and organizational structure of multinational corporations (MNCs). It includes rules on corporate governance, shareholder rights, board responsibilities, and the establishment of subsidiaries, branches, or joint ventures in multiple jurisdictions.

2. Cross-Border Investments and Mergers: Legal frameworks for transnational corporations facilitate cross-border investments, mergers, acquisitions, and strategic alliances. These frameworks address regulatory approvals, antitrust considerations, tax implications, and compliance with foreign investment laws and international trade agreements.

3. Corporate Governance Standards: Transnational corporate law establishes standards of corporate governance to ensure transparency, accountability, and ethical conduct within multinational corporations. Principles of good governance include board independence, shareholder rights, disclosure requirements, and the adoption of international best practices such as those outlined in the OECD Principles of Corporate Governance.

4. Compliance with International Regulations: Multinational corporations must comply with diverse regulatory frameworks, including international trade agreements, environmental regulations, labour laws, and anti-corruption statutes such as the U.S. Foreign Corrupt Practices Act (FCPA) and the UK Bribery Act. Transnational corporate law guides compliance efforts to mitigate legal risks and uphold corporate responsibility.

5. Dispute Resolution Mechanisms: Legal mechanisms for resolving disputes involving transnational corporations include international arbitration, litigation in national courts, and alternative dispute resolution (ADR) methods. These mechanisms address contractual disputes, intellectual property rights, competition law violations, and investor-state disputes under bilateral investment treaties (BITs) or international trade agreements.

6. Corporate Social Responsibility (CSR) and Sustainability: Transnational corporate law increasingly emphasizes CSR principles and sustainability practices. MNCs are encouraged to adopt policies that promote environmental stewardship, respect human rights, support local communities, and adhere to global standards such as the UN Guiding Principles on Business and Human Rights.

7. Cross-Border Taxation and Transfer Pricing: Taxation is a significant consideration for transnational corporations, involving compliance with national tax laws, double taxation treaties, and transfer pricing regulations. Legal frameworks address tax planning strategies, tax incentives, and the prevention of tax evasion and avoidance practices.

8. Technology and Data Protection: In the digital age, transnational corporate law addresses legal issues related to technology, data protection, cybersecurity, and privacy. MNCs must navigate regulatory requirements, data transfer restrictions, consumer rights, and compliance with international standards such as the GDPR (General Data Protection Regulation) in the EU.

9. Corporate Risk Management and Compliance Programs: Effective corporate risk management entails developing robust compliance programs that align with transnational legal requirements and industry standards. These programs aim to identify, assess, mitigate, and monitor legal and operational risks across global operations.

10. Crisis Management and Reputation Protection: Transnational corporate law guides crisis management strategies to address emergencies, regulatory investigations, product recalls, and reputational risks. Legal frameworks emphasize proactive communication, stakeholder engagement, and ethical decision-making during crises.

In summary, principles of transnational corporate law provide a comprehensive framework for navigating the legal complexities and regulatory challenges faced by multinational corporations operating in a globalized economy. By adhering to these principles, MNCs can enhance legal compliance, promote sustainable business practices, and uphold corporate governance standards across diverse jurisdictions.

47.2 Legal Framework for Cross-Border Corporations

The legal framework for cross-border corporations encompasses a set of rules, agreements, and regulatory principles that govern the establishment, operation, and governance of multinational corporations (MNCs) across different jurisdictions. This framework addresses various aspects crucial to transnational corporate activities:

1. Corporate Formation and Registration: Cross-border corporations must comply with legal requirements for corporate formation and registration in each jurisdiction where they operate. This includes establishing subsidiaries, branches, or joint ventures, adhering to local corporate laws, and obtaining necessary permits or licenses.

2. Corporate Governance Standards: Legal frameworks prescribe corporate governance standards to ensure transparency, accountability, and ethical conduct within MNCs. These standards typically include rules on board composition, director responsibilities, shareholder rights, disclosure requirements, and the adoption of best practices in corporate governance.

3. Compliance with International and National Laws: Transnational corporate law mandates compliance with international treaties, conventions, and national laws governing areas such as trade, competition, taxation, intellectual property, labour rights, environmental protection, and anti-corruption. MNCs must navigate diverse legal landscapes and regulatory regimes across jurisdictions.

4. Cross-Border Investments and Mergers: Legal provisions facilitate cross-border investments, mergers, acquisitions, and divestitures by outlining procedures for regulatory approvals, antitrust reviews, shareholder consent, due diligence, and compliance with foreign investment regulations and international trade agreements.

5. Intellectual Property Protection: Legal frameworks address intellectual property (IP) rights protection and enforcement across borders, including patents, trademarks, copyrights, and trade secrets. MNCs must adhere to international IP treaties and national laws to safeguard their innovations, brands, and proprietary technology from infringement.

6. Dispute Resolution Mechanisms: Legal mechanisms for resolving disputes involving cross-border corporations include international arbitration, litigation in national courts, and alternative dispute resolution (ADR) methods such as mediation and conciliation. These mechanisms handle contractual disputes, IP disputes, commercial disputes, and investor-state disputes under BITs.

47.3 Regulatory Issues in Transnational Corporate Practice

Transnational corporate practice faces a range of regulatory challenges that impact operations, compliance, and strategic decision-making:

1. Legal and Regulatory Divergence: Differences in legal systems, regulatory frameworks, and cultural norms across countries create compliance complexities for MNCs. Companies must navigate varying requirements related to corporate governance, taxation, labour laws, environmental standards, and data protection.

2. Compliance with Anti-Corruption Laws: MNCs operating internationally must comply with stringent anti-corruption laws such as the U.S. Foreign Corrupt Practices Act (FCPA) and the UK Bribery Act. These laws prohibit bribery of foreign officials and require robust compliance programs to prevent corruption risks.

3. Data Privacy and Cybersecurity Regulations: Global data privacy laws, such as the GDPR in the EU and the CCPA in California, impose strict requirements on the collection, processing, and transfer of personal data. MNCs must implement data protection measures and ensure compliance with jurisdiction-specific regulations to mitigate cybersecurity risks.

4. Environmental and Sustainability Regulations: Environmental regulations vary widely across jurisdictions, requiring MNCs to comply with standards for emissions, waste management, resource conservation, and sustainable business practices. Non-compliance can lead to legal liabilities, reputational damage, and operational disruptions.

5. Taxation and Transfer Pricing Compliance: Cross-border taxation presents challenges related to tax planning, transfer pricing, double taxation treaties, and compliance with national tax laws. MNCs must navigate complex tax regimes and regulatory changes to optimize tax efficiency while ensuring compliance with regulatory requirements.

6. Trade Compliance and Tariffs: International trade regulations, including tariffs, export controls, sanctions, and trade agreements, impact MNCs engaged in global trade and supply chains. Compliance with trade laws and customs regulations is essential to avoid penalties, trade disputes, and disruptions in cross-border operations.

47.4 Case Studies in Transnational Corporate Law

Case studies in transnational corporate law illustrate real-world challenges, legal strategies, and lessons learned by multinational corporations:

1. Apple Inc. and EU Competition Law: Apple faced scrutiny by the European Commission over alleged antitrust violations related to its App Store policies and practices. The case highlighted the complexities of compliance with EU competition rules, digital market regulation, and the enforcement of fines for non-compliance.

2. Shell Nigeria and Corporate Social Responsibility (CSR): Shell encountered legal and ethical challenges in Nigeria, including allegations of environmental pollution, human rights abuses, and community relations issues. The case underscored the importance of CSR practices, stakeholder engagement, and sustainable development in mitigating legal risks and enhancing corporate reputation.

3. Volkswagen Diesel Emissions Scandal: Volkswagen faced legal repercussions worldwide for installing illegal software in diesel vehicles to cheat emissions tests. The case involved regulatory investigations, legal settlements, and reputational damage, highlighting the implications of corporate misconduct and regulatory compliance failures in global markets.

4. GlaxoSmithKline (GSK) and Anti-Corruption Compliance: GSK faced investigations and legal actions for bribery and corruption allegations in China. The case demonstrated the importance of implementing effective anti-corruption compliance programs, conducting due diligence, and adhering to global anti-corruption laws to mitigate legal and reputational risks.

5. Amazon and Cross-Border E-commerce: Amazon navigates regulatory challenges in multiple jurisdictions regarding e-commerce operations, data protection, consumer rights, and taxation. The case illustrates the complexities of cross-border trade compliance, regulatory changes, and the impact on business strategies and market expansion.

6. ExxonMobil and International Arbitration: ExxonMobil engaged in international arbitration to resolve disputes with foreign governments over oil and gas exploration contracts and regulatory issues. The case highlights the use of arbitration as a dispute resolution mechanism in complex international disputes involving resource extraction and investment protection.

In conclusion, case studies in transnational corporate law provide valuable insights into the legal complexities, regulatory challenges, and strategic considerations faced by multinational corporations operating in a globalized economy. By examining these cases, stakeholders can gain a deeper understanding of legal frameworks, compliance requirements, and effective risk management strategies in transnational corporate practice.

Chapter 48: Transnational Corporate Restructuring

48.1 Principles of Corporate Restructuring

Corporate restructuring refers to strategic initiatives undertaken by companies to reorganize their operations, finances, ownership structure, or legal entities. When conducted on a transnational scale, corporate restructuring involves navigating complex legal, regulatory, and operational challenges across multiple jurisdictions. Key principles of transnational corporate restructuring include:

1. **Strategic Planning and Objectives:** Corporate restructuring aims to achieve strategic objectives such as enhancing profitability, improving operational efficiency, reducing costs, optimizing capital structure, accessing new markets, or responding to competitive pressures. Transnational restructuring strategies must align with corporate goals while considering regulatory and legal implications in different countries.

2. **Legal Framework and Regulatory Compliance:** Transnational corporate restructuring requires compliance with diverse legal frameworks, including corporate laws, tax regulations, employment laws, competition laws, and securities regulations across the jurisdictions involved. Companies must navigate regulatory requirements and obtain necessary approvals to ensure restructuring activities are legally valid and enforceable.

3. **Cross-Border Mergers and Acquisitions (M&A):** M&A transactions are common forms of corporate restructuring involving the acquisition, merger, or divestiture of business entities across borders. Legal considerations include due diligence, valuation, negotiation of transaction terms, compliance with antitrust laws, shareholder approvals, and post-merger integration planning.

4. **Financial and Capital Restructuring:** Financial restructuring involves changes to a company's capital structure, debt obligations, financing arrangements, or asset ownership to

improve financial stability and liquidity. Transnational financial restructuring may involve debt restructuring, refinancing, issuing new securities, or accessing international capital markets while adhering to cross-border financial regulations.

5. Operational Restructuring and Business Reorganization: Operational restructuring aims to streamline business operations, improve efficiency, and enhance competitiveness. This may involve restructuring supply chains, relocating production facilities, outsourcing functions, or rationalizing the workforce across multiple jurisdictions while complying with employment laws and labour regulations.

6. Corporate Governance and Stakeholder Management: Effective corporate governance is critical during restructuring to ensure transparency, accountability, and protection of stakeholder interests. Principles of good governance guide decision-making processes, disclosure requirements, shareholder communications, and board oversight throughout the restructuring process.

7. Cross-Border Taxation and Transfer Pricing: Tax considerations play a crucial role in transnational corporate restructuring, including tax implications of mergers, acquisitions, asset transfers, and restructuring transactions. Companies must navigate international tax laws, transfer pricing regulations, double taxation treaties, and tax planning strategies to optimize tax efficiency and minimize risks.

8. Legal Protections and Risk Management: Transnational corporate restructuring involves managing legal risks and protecting shareholder rights, creditor interests, and other stakeholders. Legal protections may include contractual agreements, indemnities, warranties, dispute resolution clauses, and compliance with international arbitration or litigation procedures in case of disputes.

9. Employee Relations and Employment Laws: Restructuring initiatives impact employees across borders, requiring compliance with employment laws, labour regulations, collective bargaining agreements, and employee consultation requirements. Companies must manage workforce transitions, employee relocations, redundancy processes, and retention strategies while fostering positive employee relations.

10. Cultural and Integration Challenges: Cross-border corporate restructuring poses cultural and integration challenges stemming from differences in business practices, organizational cultures, management styles, and employee expectations across diverse geographical locations. Effective communication, cultural sensitivity, and change management strategies are essential to facilitate post-restructuring integration and alignment of organizational cultures.

In summary, principles of transnational corporate restructuring guide companies through strategic transformations while addressing legal complexities, regulatory compliance, financial considerations, stakeholder interests, and operational challenges across global markets. By adhering to these principles, companies can enhance organizational resilience, achieve sustainable growth, and capitalize on opportunities in a dynamic global business environment.

48.2 Legal Framework for Cross-Border Restructuring

Cross-border corporate restructuring involves navigating a complex legal framework that governs mergers, acquisitions, divestitures, and other restructuring activities across multiple jurisdictions. Key aspects of the legal framework include:

1. Corporate and Commercial Laws: Corporate restructuring must comply with the corporate laws of each jurisdiction involved, which govern company formation, governance structure, shareholder rights, and corporate governance practices. These laws vary significantly across countries and influence the legal requirements for restructuring transactions.

2. Cross-Border Mergers and Acquisitions (M&A): Legal frameworks for M&A transactions encompass regulatory approvals, antitrust regulations, competition laws, and shareholder rights protection. Companies must conduct due diligence, negotiate transaction terms, obtain regulatory clearances, and comply with disclosure requirements in accordance with local and international M&A laws.

3. Securities Regulations and Capital Markets: Restructuring activities involving securities, such as stock exchanges or bond offerings, are subject to securities regulations and capital market laws. Companies must adhere to disclosure obligations, market abuse regulations, insider trading rules, and regulatory oversight by securities regulators in each jurisdiction where securities are traded or offered.

4. Cross-Border Taxation and Transfer Pricing: Tax considerations play a critical role in cross-border restructuring, including tax implications of asset transfers, mergers, dividend distributions, and international tax planning strategies. Companies must navigate transfer pricing rules, double taxation treaties, withholding taxes, and tax-efficient restructuring options while complying with international tax laws.

5. Employment Laws and Workforce Considerations: Corporate restructuring impacts employees across borders, necessitating compliance with employment laws, labour regulations, collective bargaining agreements, and employee consultation requirements. Companies must manage workforce transitions, employee relocations, redundancy processes, and legal obligations related to employee rights and protections.

6. Insolvency and Bankruptcy Laws: In cases of financial distress or insolvency, restructuring may involve restructuring debt, bankruptcy proceedings, liquidation, or reorganization under insolvency laws. Companies must understand and comply with insolvency procedures, creditor rights, cross-border insolvency frameworks, and legal protections available under national and international bankruptcy laws.

48.3 Comparative Analysis of Restructuring Laws

A comparative analysis of restructuring laws across jurisdictions provides insights into legal frameworks, procedural requirements, and regulatory environments for corporate restructuring:

1. United States (U.S.) Bankruptcy Code: The U.S. Bankruptcy Code governs corporate bankruptcies, reorganizations, and liquidations, offering Chapter 11 reorganization for businesses to restructure debts and continue operations under court supervision. It provides mechanisms for creditor protection, debtor-in-possession financing, and restructuring plan approval.

2. European Union (EU) Cross-Border Insolvency Regulations: EU regulations on cross-border insolvency facilitate the recognition and enforcement of insolvency proceedings across EU member states. The EU Insolvency Regulation (recast) harmonizes rules on jurisdiction, recognition of judgments, and cooperation between insolvency practitioners in cross-border cases involving multinational corporations.

3. China's Corporate Restructuring Framework: China's legal framework for corporate restructuring includes laws on mergers, acquisitions, bankruptcy, and reorganization procedures. The Enterprise Bankruptcy Law and Company Law provide mechanisms for debt restructuring, asset acquisitions, and corporate governance reforms under judicial supervision.

4. Comparative Analysis of Employment Laws: Comparison of employment laws across jurisdictions assesses differences in labour regulations, collective bargaining rights, employee consultation requirements, redundancy procedures, and workforce protections during corporate restructuring. Legal considerations include employee rights, severance pay, and reemployment obligations post-restructuring.

5. Taxation and Transfer Pricing Regulations: Comparative analysis of taxation and transfer pricing regulations evaluates differences in corporate tax rates, deductions, credits, and incentives across jurisdictions. Companies assess the tax implications of restructuring transactions, asset transfers, profit repatriation, and compliance with international tax treaties to optimize tax efficiency.

48.4 Case Studies in Corporate Restructuring

Case studies in corporate restructuring provide practical insights into challenges, strategies, and outcomes of significant restructuring initiatives by multinational corporations:

1. Fiat Chrysler Automobiles (FCA) and Renault Merger Proposal: The proposed merger between FCA and Renault aimed to create a global automotive giant but faced regulatory hurdles, shareholder concerns, and government approvals in multiple jurisdictions. The case highlighted challenges in cross-border M&A, competition law compliance, and strategic alignment of corporate cultures.

2. Tata Steel and Thyssenkrupp Joint Venture: The joint venture between Tata Steel and Thyssenkrupp aimed to consolidate steel production in Europe, addressing overcapacity and competitive pressures in the global steel industry. The case involved negotiations, regulatory approvals, restructuring of operations, and workforce integration across borders.

3. General Electric (GE) Divestiture and Business Restructuring: GE's divestiture strategy involved restructuring its business portfolio by selling non-core assets, focusing on core industrial segments, and streamlining operations globally. The case examined strategic divestitures, asset sales, regulatory approvals, and financial restructuring to enhance profitability and shareholder value.

4. Airline Industry Restructuring Post-COVID-19 Pandemic: Global airlines faced financial distress and operational challenges due to the COVID-19 pandemic, leading to restructuring efforts involving government bailouts, debt renegotiations, fleet rationalization, workforce reductions, and compliance with aviation regulations and travel restrictions.

5. Sony Corporation's Corporate Reorganization: Sony's corporate reorganization aimed to streamline its electronics, entertainment, and gaming divisions to enhance profitability and innovation. The case involved restructuring plans, workforce adjustments, intellectual property management, and compliance with corporate governance standards in Japan and global markets.

6. Nokia and Microsoft Acquisition Integration: Nokia's acquisition by Microsoft involved integrating mobile device and services divisions to enhance Microsoft's smartphone capabilities. The case focused on cross-border M&A, intellectual property transfers, regulatory approvals, cultural integration, and strategic alignment of corporate strategies and technology platforms.

In conclusion, case studies and comparative analysis in transnational corporate restructuring offer valuable insights into legal complexities, regulatory challenges, strategic considerations, and operational implications for multinational corporations undertaking restructuring initiatives in a globalized economy. By examining these cases, stakeholders can learn from successful strategies, anticipate regulatory risks, and navigate legal frameworks effectively to achieve sustainable growth and competitive advantage.

Chapter 49: UN International Laws

49.1 Overview of United Nations Law

United Nations (UN) international law comprises a body of legal principles, treaties, conventions, resolutions, and practices established under the auspices of the United Nations. These laws govern relations between member states, international organizations, non-state actors, and individuals, aiming to promote peace, security, human rights, sustainable development, and international cooperation. Key aspects of UN international law include:

1. Charter of the United Nations (UN Charter): The UN Charter, adopted in 1945, is the foundational document of international law and the framework for the organization's principles and purposes. It establishes the structure of the UN, defines its organs (such as the General Assembly and Security Council), outlines principles of sovereignty, non-intervention, and peaceful settlement of disputes, and delineates the responsibilities of member states to uphold international peace and security.

2. International Treaties and Conventions: The UN facilitates the negotiation, adoption, and implementation of international treaties and conventions addressing various global challenges. Examples include the Universal Declaration of Human Rights (UDHR), International Covenant on Civil and Political Rights (ICCPR), International Covenant on Economic, Social and Cultural Rights (ICESCR), Convention on the Elimination of All Forms of Racial Discrimination (CERD), and Convention on the Rights of the Child (CRC).

3. International Humanitarian Law (IHL): Also known as the laws of war or the law of armed conflict, IHL governs the conduct of armed conflict and seeks to protect civilians, prisoners of war, and other non-combatants. The Geneva Conventions of 1949 and their Additional Protocols form the core of IHL, establishing rules on the treatment of wounded, sick, and shipwrecked persons, protection of civilians, and prohibition of certain weapons in warfare.

4. International Criminal Law: UN international law includes mechanisms for prosecuting individuals responsible for genocide, war crimes, crimes against humanity, and aggression. The International Criminal Court (ICC), established by the Rome Statute of 1998, prosecutes these crimes when national courts are unwilling or unable to do so, promoting accountability and justice at the international level.

5. Peacekeeping Operations and Security Council Resolutions: The UN Security Council authorizes peacekeeping missions to maintain international peace and security in conflict zones. Security Council resolutions enforce sanctions, arms embargoes, and measures to prevent and resolve disputes, addressing threats to peace and stability worldwide.

6. Sustainable Development Goals (SDGs): Agenda 2030, adopted by the UN General Assembly in 2015, sets forth 17 SDGs aimed at eradicating poverty, promoting education, achieving gender equality, ensuring environmental sustainability, and fostering inclusive economic growth. The SDGs guide international cooperation and national policies to address global challenges and promote sustainable development.

7. Environmental Law and Climate Change Agreements: UN frameworks such as the United Nations Framework Convention on Climate Change (UNFCCC) and the Paris Agreement establish commitments to combat climate change, reduce greenhouse gas emissions, adapt to climate impacts, and promote sustainable development practices globally.

8. Refugee Law and Human Rights Protection: UN agencies, including the Office of the United Nations High Commissioner for Refugees (UNHCR) and the Office of the High Commissioner for Human Rights (OHCHR), work to protect refugees, asylum seekers, and migrants, uphold human rights standards, and promote legal frameworks to address displacement, statelessness, and discrimination.

9. International Economic Law and Trade: UN bodies such as the United Nations Conference on Trade and Development (UNCTAD) promote international trade, investment, economic development, and cooperation through conventions, guidelines, and capacity-building initiatives aimed at enhancing global economic governance and reducing inequality.

10. International Peace and Security: The UN Security Council addresses threats to international peace and security through preventive diplomacy, peacebuilding efforts, sanctions, peacekeeping operations, and conflict resolution mechanisms, promoting collective security and multilateral cooperation among member states.

In summary, UN international law encompasses a comprehensive framework of legal norms, institutions, and mechanisms aimed at fostering global cooperation, protecting human rights, promoting sustainable development, maintaining international peace and security, and addressing transnational challenges in a rapidly evolving globalized world. By upholding these principles and commitments, the UN contributes to a rules-based international order and the realization of shared aspirations for a more just, peaceful, and sustainable future.

49.2 Key UN Conventions and Treaties

The United Nations (UN) plays a pivotal role in developing and promoting international law through a series of key conventions and treaties addressing global challenges and issues. These instruments cover a wide range of areas aimed at fostering cooperation, protecting human rights, promoting sustainable development, and ensuring international peace and security. Some of the key UN conventions and treaties include:

1. Universal Declaration of Human Rights (UDHR): Adopted in 1948, the UDHR sets out fundamental human rights and freedoms that all individuals are entitled to, regardless of nationality, ethnicity, religion, or other status. It serves as a foundational document for international human rights law.

2. International Covenant on Civil and Political Rights (ICCPR): The ICCPR, adopted in 1966, guarantees civil and political rights such as freedom of speech, assembly, and religion. It establishes obligations for state parties to respect and protect these rights, with oversight by the UN Human Rights Committee.

3. International Covenant on Economic, Social and Cultural Rights (ICESCR): Also adopted in 1966, the ICESCR recognizes economic, social, and cultural rights, including the rights to work, education, healthcare, and an adequate standard of living. States parties commit to progressively realizing these rights through national and international efforts.

4. Convention on the Elimination of All Forms of Racial Discrimination (CERD): Adopted in 1965, CERD prohibits racial discrimination and requires state parties to take effective measures to eliminate discrimination in all its forms and promote understanding among racial and ethnic groups.

5. Convention on the Elimination of All Forms of Discrimination Against Women (CEDAW): CEDAW, adopted in 1979, aims to eliminate discrimination against women and ensure their full participation in political, economic, social, and cultural life. States parties commit to taking measures to protect and promote women's rights.

6. Convention on the Rights of the Child (CRC): Adopted in 1989, the CRC outlines the rights of children to survival, development, protection, and participation. It sets standards for children's rights in health, education, family environment, juvenile justice, and protection from violence and exploitation.

7. Vienna Convention on Diplomatic Relations: Established in 1961, the Vienna Convention regulates diplomatic relations between states, defining the privileges and immunities of diplomatic missions and personnel, ensuring smooth diplomatic communication, and protecting diplomatic premises.

8. United Nations Framework Convention on Climate Change (UNFCCC): Adopted in 1992, the UNFCCC is the primary international treaty addressing climate change. It sets out obligations for countries to reduce greenhouse gas emissions, adapt to climate impacts, and cooperate on climate finance and technology transfer.

9. Paris Agreement: Agreed upon in 2015 under the UNFCCC, the Paris Agreement aims to limit global warming to well below 2 degrees Celsius above pre-industrial levels, with efforts to limit it to 1.5 degrees Celsius. It includes commitments by countries to submit nationally determined contributions (NDCs) and enhance climate resilience.

10. Convention on Biological Diversity (CBD): Adopted in 1992, the CBD promotes conservation, sustainable use, and equitable sharing of benefits from biodiversity. It sets targets for biodiversity conservation, ecosystem restoration, and sustainable development, with a focus on preserving biological resources.

49.3 Enforcement of UN Laws

Enforcement of UN laws involves mechanisms to ensure compliance and accountability among member states and other stakeholders. Key aspects of enforcement include:

1. Monitoring and Reporting Mechanisms: UN bodies, specialized agencies, and human rights mechanisms monitor compliance with international treaties and conventions through reporting, review processes, and country visits. They assess implementation efforts and identify areas for improvement.

2. Treaty Bodies and Committees: Treaty bodies, such as the Committee on the Rights of the Child or the Committee on the Elimination of Racial Discrimination, review state parties' reports, issue recommendations, and engage in dialogue to promote compliance with treaty obligations.

3. International Courts and Tribunals: International courts and tribunals, including the International Court of Justice (ICJ) and the International Criminal Court (ICC), adjudicate disputes between states, prosecute individuals for international crimes, and uphold principles of international law under UN auspices.

4. Peacekeeping Operations and Security Council Resolutions: The UN Security Council authorizes peacekeeping missions to maintain peace and security, enforce ceasefires, protect civilians, and facilitate political transitions. Security Council resolutions impose sanctions, arms embargoes, and other measures to address threats to international peace and security.

5. Economic Sanctions and Measures: The UN imposes economic sanctions and measures through Security Council resolutions to address threats to international peace, such as the proliferation of weapons of mass destruction or violations of human rights, aiming to compel compliance and modify the behaviour of targeted entities or states.

49.4 Case Studies in UN Law

Case studies illustrate the application and impact of UN laws in addressing global challenges and promoting international cooperation:

1. Rohingya Crisis and Genocide Allegations: The UN has condemned Myanmar for human rights abuses and genocide against Rohingya Muslims, calling for accountability and justice under international law. The case highlights UN efforts to address humanitarian crises, protect refugees, and uphold human rights standards.

2. Implementation of the Paris Agreement: Countries are working to implement their commitments under the Paris Agreement, submitting NDCs and enhancing climate actions to mitigate greenhouse gas emissions and adapt to climate impacts. The UN facilitates global cooperation and monitoring to achieve climate targets.

3. International Criminal Court and War Crimes Prosecutions: The ICC prosecutes individuals responsible for war crimes, crimes against humanity, genocide, and aggression, promoting accountability and justice for victims of international crimes. Cases before the ICC demonstrate the UN's efforts to uphold international humanitarian law and deter impunity.

4. Refugee Protection and UNHCR Mandate: The UNHCR provides protection and assistance to refugees, asylum seekers, and displaced persons worldwide, advocating for their rights under international law. Case studies illustrate UN efforts to address refugee crises, provide humanitarian aid, and seek durable solutions for displaced populations.

5. Peacekeeping Operations in Conflict Zones: UN peacekeeping missions, such as in South Sudan or Mali, support political processes, protect civilians, and stabilize conflict zones. Case studies examine UN efforts to prevent violence, facilitate peace negotiations, and rebuild societies affected by armed conflict.

6. Human Rights Monitoring and Country Reports: UN human rights mechanisms monitor and report on human rights situations globally, issuing recommendations to states and engaging in dialogue to improve human rights protections. Case studies highlight UN efforts to promote accountability, combat discrimination, and empower vulnerable populations.

In conclusion, UN international laws and mechanisms play a crucial role in addressing global challenges, promoting international cooperation, protecting human rights, and maintaining peace and security. Case studies and enforcement mechanisms illustrate the impact of UN laws in advancing collective efforts toward a more just, equitable, and sustainable world.

Chapter 50: World Trade Law

50.1 Principles of World Trade Law
World trade law governs international trade relations, agreements, and disputes among nations, aiming to facilitate global commerce while addressing economic, social, and developmental objectives. Key principles of world trade law include:

1. **Most-Favored-Nation (MFN) Principle:** Under the MFN principle, countries must extend equal trade advantages, such as lower tariffs or preferential treatment, to all WTO members, ensuring non-discriminatory trade relations and promoting fair competition.
2. **National Treatment Principle:** The national treatment principle requires countries to treat foreign goods, services, and nationals no less favourably than their own, once they have entered the domestic market, promoting equality and transparency in trade practices.
3. **Free Trade:** The promotion of free trade involves reducing barriers to international commerce, such as tariffs, quotas, and non-tariff barriers, to foster economic growth, enhance efficiency, and increase consumer choice.
4. **Trade Liberalization:** Trade liberalization entails the removal or reduction of trade barriers through negotiations and agreements, facilitating smoother international trade flows and benefiting economies through expanded market access and competitive pricing.
5. **Dispute Settlement Mechanisms:** Effective dispute settlement mechanisms, such as those provided by the World Trade Organization (WTO), resolve trade disputes between member states impartially, ensuring compliance with trade rules and promoting stability in global trade relations.
6. **Protection of Intellectual Property Rights (IPRs):** World trade law includes provisions protecting intellectual property rights (IPRs) such as patents, copyrights, trademarks, and trade secrets, fostering innovation, creativity, and fair competition in global markets.

7. Special and Differential Treatment: Recognizing differences in economic development and capacity among countries, special and differential treatment provisions allow developing countries flexibility in meeting trade obligations and accessing technical assistance to enhance their participation in international trade.

8. Trade Remedies: Trade remedies, including anti-dumping measures, countervailing duties, and safeguards, protect domestic industries from unfair trade practices such as dumping of subsidized goods or sudden surges in imports that threaten domestic producers.

9. Transparency and Predictability: Transparency in trade policies, regulations, and procedures ensures predictability for businesses and governments, reducing uncertainty and facilitating compliance with international trade rules and commitments.

10. Sustainable Development and Trade: Integration of sustainable development goals (SDGs) into trade policies promotes environmental protection, social inclusion, and economic growth, ensuring that trade contributes positively to global development objectives.

In summary, principles of world trade law provide a framework for promoting open, fair, and rules-based international trade relations, addressing economic disparities, fostering development, and resolving disputes to ensure global prosperity and sustainable economic growth. By upholding these principles, countries collaborate to create a conducive environment for trade that benefits all stakeholders and contributes to global economic stability.

50.2 Legal Framework for Global Trade

The legal framework for global trade encompasses a complex network of agreements, treaties, regulations, and institutions that govern international trade relations among nations. Key elements of the legal framework include:

1. World Trade Organization (WTO): The WTO establishes rules for international trade through multilateral agreements negotiated and ratified by member states. The WTO agreements cover trade in goods (GATT), services (GATS), intellectual property (TRIPS), and dispute settlement mechanisms (DSU), providing a legal framework for trade liberalization, market access, and fair competition.

2. Regional Trade Agreements (RTAs): RTAs, such as free trade agreements (FTAs) and customs unions, establish preferential trade terms between member countries, reducing tariffs and non-tariff barriers to promote regional economic integration and facilitate cross-border trade.

3. Bilateral Trade Agreements: Bilateral trade agreements between two countries regulate trade relations, tariffs, investment rules, and intellectual property protection, enhancing market access and promoting economic cooperation based on mutual interests and benefits.

4. Trade Facilitation Agreements: Trade facilitation agreements aim to simplify and harmonize customs procedures, reduce administrative barriers, and streamline trade documentation to expedite the movement of goods across borders and enhance efficiency in global supply chains.

5. National Trade Laws and Regulations: Countries maintain national trade laws and regulations governing import/export controls, customs procedures, product standards, sanitary and phytosanitary measures, and trade-related intellectual property rights (IPRs) to ensure compliance with international trade obligations and protect domestic industries.

6. Trade Remedies and Safeguards: Trade remedies, including anti-dumping duties, countervailing measures, and safeguards, protect domestic industries from unfair trade practices, such as dumping of subsidized goods or sudden surges in imports that threaten market stability or harm domestic producers.

7. Investment Protection Treaties: Bilateral and multilateral investment treaties (BITs and MITs) provide legal protections for foreign investments, including guarantees of fair and equitable treatment, protection against expropriation without compensation, and access to international arbitration for investor-state disputes.

8. International Standards and Technical Regulations: Countries adhere to international standards (e.g., ISO standards) and technical regulations (e.g., product safety and quality standards) established by international organizations to facilitate trade, ensure product interoperability, and protect consumer health and safety.

9. Trade-related Intellectual Property Rights (TRIPs): TRIPs agreements under the WTO regulate intellectual property protection in international trade, setting minimum standards for patents, copyrights, trademarks, trade secrets, and geographical indications to foster innovation, creativity, and fair competition in global markets.

10. Trade and Sustainable Development Goals (SDGs): Integration of SDGs into trade policies promotes sustainable development objectives, including environmental protection, social inclusion, and economic growth, ensuring that trade contributes positively to global development while addressing challenges such as climate change and poverty alleviation.

50.3 Dispute Resolution in World Trade

Dispute resolution mechanisms in world trade ensure impartial adjudication of trade disputes between countries, safeguarding the rules-based international trading system and promoting compliance with trade agreements. Key aspects of dispute resolution include:

1. WTO Dispute Settlement Understanding (DSU): The DSU provides procedures for settling disputes between WTO members, including consultations, panel hearings, and Appellate Body reviews. It ensures timely resolution of trade disputes, enforcement of WTO agreements, and compliance with rulings by member states.

2. Panel Hearings and Appellate Review: Dispute settlement panels examine legal arguments and factual evidence presented by disputing parties, issuing reports with findings and recommendations. The Appellate Body reviews panel reports, ensuring consistency in the interpretation and application of WTO rules and agreements.

3. Implementation of Dispute Settlement Rulings: WTO members are obligated to implement dispute settlement rulings promptly and effectively. Failure to comply may lead to authorization of retaliatory measures by the prevailing party, promoting enforcement of trade obligations and deterrence of non-compliance.

4. Arbitration and Mediation: Countries may resolve trade disputes through arbitration or mediation outside the WTO framework, using alternative dispute resolution mechanisms to negotiate settlements, resolve conflicts amicably, and maintain trade relations based on mutual interests.

5. Compliance and Monitoring: WTO oversees compliance with dispute settlement rulings and monitors implementation by member states, ensuring adherence to trade obligations and fostering a transparent, predictable, and rules-based international trading environment.

50.4 Case Studies in World Trade Law

Case studies in world trade law illustrate practical applications, challenges, and outcomes of trade disputes, agreements, and regulatory frameworks shaping global commerce:

1. Boeing-Airbus Subsidy Dispute: The long-standing dispute between the United States and the European Union over subsidies to Boeing and Airbus aircraft manufacturers involved multiple WTO rulings and retaliatory tariffs, highlighting complex issues in trade remedies, industrial subsidies, and compliance with WTO rules.

2. US-China Trade War and Tariff Escalation: The trade conflict between the United States and China escalated with tariffs imposed on billions of dollars' worth of goods, illustrating disputes over intellectual property rights, technology transfer, market access, and trade imbalances, impacting global supply chains and economic stability.

3. NAFTA (North American Free Trade Agreement) Renegotiation: The renegotiation of NAFTA between Canada, Mexico, and the United States addressed trade rules, investment protections, labour rights, and environmental standards, demonstrating regional trade integration, dispute resolution mechanisms, and economic cooperation.

4. Australia-Plain Packaging of Tobacco Products Dispute: Australia's implementation of plain packaging laws for tobacco products faced challenges under WTO rules from tobacco-producing countries, highlighting conflicts between public health measures, intellectual property rights, and trade obligations under TRIPs agreements.

5. Japan-South Korea Trade Dispute over Semiconductor Materials: The trade dispute between Japan and South Korea over restrictions on exports of semiconductor materials highlighted tensions over national security, economic interdependence, supply chain disruptions, and WTO dispute settlement mechanisms.

6. Brexit and Trade Relations: The United Kingdom's withdrawal from the European Union (Brexit) involved negotiations on trade agreements, customs arrangements, regulatory alignment, and dispute resolution mechanisms, impacting trade relations, market access, and economic integration in Europe and globally.

In conclusion, world trade law provides a comprehensive framework for regulating international trade relations, resolving disputes, and promoting economic cooperation and development. Case studies offer insights into the dynamic interactions, challenges, and implications of trade rules, agreements, and enforcement mechanisms on global markets, industries, and geopolitical relations.

Chapter 51: Key Principles of the Asian Countries Legal Systems

51.1 Overview of Asian Countries Legal Systems
Asia encompasses diverse legal systems shaped by historical, cultural, political, and economic factors, influencing legal principles, institutions, and practices across countries. Key Asian countries such as Japan, Singapore, South Korea, Taiwan, Malaysia, and Thailand each have unique legal systems characterized by:

1. Japan: Japan's legal system combines elements of civil law (derived from German and French legal systems) with Indigenous legal traditions. The Constitution of Japan, promulgated in 1947, establishes fundamental rights, separation of powers, and rule of law principles. The judiciary plays a significant role in interpreting laws and resolving disputes through a hierarchical court system.

2. Singapore: Singapore's legal system is based on common law principles inherited from British colonial rule. The Constitution of Singapore provides for the separation of powers between the judiciary, legislature, and executive. The Supreme Court serves as the highest court, overseeing a judiciary known for efficiency, independence, and adherence to the rule of law.

3. South Korea: South Korea's legal system combines elements of civil law (influenced by German and French legal traditions) and customary law. The Constitution of South Korea, adopted in 1987, establishes democratic governance, fundamental rights, and a three-tiered court system. The Constitutional Court interprets the constitutionality of laws, while specialized courts handle administrative and intellectual property disputes.

4. Taiwan: Taiwan's legal system integrates civil law principles (influenced by Japanese legal traditions) with elements of customary law. The Constitution of the Republic of China (Taiwan), promulgated in 1947, establishes democratic governance, fundamental rights, and separation of powers. The judiciary upholds the rule of law through a hierarchical court system, with the Judicial Yuan as the highest judicial authority.

5. Malaysia: Malaysia's legal system is dualistic, comprising elements of common law (inherited from British colonial rule) and Islamic law (Sharia). The Federal Constitution of Malaysia, enacted in 1957, delineates federal-state relations, fundamental rights, and the role of Islamic courts in family law matters. The judiciary includes civil courts, Sharia courts, and the Federal Court as the highest appellate authority.

6. Thailand: Thailand's legal system blends elements of civil law (derived from continental European legal traditions) with customary law and influences from Thai legal traditions. The Constitution of Thailand, most recently amended in 2017, provides for constitutional monarchy, fundamental rights, and a hierarchical court system. The judiciary interprets laws, resolves disputes, and upholds rule of law principles.

Comparative Analysis:
Common Features:
- **Rule of Law:** Across these countries, adherence to rule of law principles is fundamental, ensuring legal certainty, accountability, and fairness in judicial proceedings.
- **Judicial Independence:** Independent judiciaries uphold the constitutionality of laws, protect fundamental rights, and resolve disputes impartially.
- **Legal Pluralism:** Many Asian legal systems integrate diverse legal traditions, such as civil law, common law, and customary law, accommodating cultural and religious diversity.

Unique Characteristics:
- **Legal Origins:** Each country's legal system reflects historical influences and legal traditions, contributing to distinctive legal frameworks and practices.
- **Constitutional Foundations:** Constitutions define governance structures, powers of government branches, and fundamental rights, shaping legal institutions and principles.

- **Judicial Systems:** Varied court structures and specialized courts address specific legal matters, enhancing access to justice and legal remedies tailored to local contexts.

In conclusion, understanding the key principles of Asian countries' legal systems requires consideration of historical, cultural, and institutional contexts that shape legal norms, practices, and jurisprudence. Comparative analysis highlights similarities and differences, emphasizing the role of law in promoting societal order, economic development, and protection of individual rights within diverse Asian legal frameworks.

51.2 Comparative Constitutional Structures

The constitutional structures of Asian countries vary significantly, reflecting diverse historical, cultural, and political contexts. Here is a comparative overview:

1. Japan: Japan's Constitution, adopted in 1947, establishes a parliamentary democracy with a constitutional monarchy. It emphasizes fundamental human rights, the separation of powers among the executive, legislative, and judicial branches, and the role of the Emperor as a symbol of the state.

2. Singapore: Singapore's Constitution, enacted in 1959 and amended over time, establishes a parliamentary system with a unicameral legislature. It delineates fundamental liberties, separation of powers, and the President's role as a ceremonial head of state with custodial powers.

3. South Korea: South Korea's Constitution, promulgated in 1987 and amended several times, outlines a presidential system with separation of powers among the executive, legislative, and judicial branches. It guarantees fundamental rights and establishes a system of checks and balances, including a Constitutional Court to adjudicate constitutional disputes.

4. Taiwan: Taiwan's Constitution, adopted in 1947, originally governed all of China but now applies to Taiwan. It defines a democratic system with a separation of powers among the executive, legislative, and judicial branches. The Constitution has been amended to reflect Taiwan's evolving political and legal landscape.

5. Malaysia: Malaysia's Constitution, enacted in 1957 and amended subsequently, establishes a federal constitutional monarchy with a parliamentary democracy. It delineates the powers and functions of federal and state governments, protects fundamental liberties, and incorporates provisions for Islamic law (Sharia) in personal and family matters.

6. Thailand: Thailand's Constitution, most recently amended in 2017, defines a constitutional monarchy with a parliamentary system. It outlines the roles of the monarchy, executive, legislative, and judicial branches, guarantees fundamental rights, and includes provisions for electoral processes and checks on governmental power.

51.3 Key Legal Institutions in Asian Countries

Key legal institutions in Asian countries play crucial roles in upholding the rule of law, administering justice, and safeguarding legal rights. Common institutions include:

1. Judiciary: Independent judicial systems interpret laws, adjudicate disputes, and ensure impartiality in legal proceedings. Supreme and appellate courts uphold constitutional rights and provide final adjudication on legal matters.

2. Constitutional Courts: Constitutional courts review the constitutionality of laws and government actions, safeguarding fundamental rights and maintaining the separation of powers.

3. Bar Associations: Bar associations regulate legal professionals, uphold ethical standards, and promote legal education and professional development.

4. Legislative Bodies: Parliaments or legislative assemblies enact laws, oversee government actions, and represent public interests through legislative processes.

5. Executive Agencies: Government agencies implement laws, regulations, and policies, ensuring administrative efficiency and compliance with legal standards.

6. Specialized Courts: Specialized courts, such as commercial courts or administrative courts, handle specific legal matters, including commercial disputes, administrative appeals, and specialized legal issues.

51.4 Business and Corporate Law in Asian Countries

Business and corporate law frameworks in Asian countries facilitate economic development, regulate business activities, and protect investor interests. Key aspects include:

1. Company Formation and Regulation: Laws govern the establishment, registration, and governance of companies, specifying requirements for incorporation, shareholder rights, and corporate governance practices.

2. Commercial Contracts and Transactions: Legal frameworks regulate commercial contracts, sales agreements, leases, and other business transactions, ensuring enforceability and protecting parties' rights and obligations.

3. Intellectual Property Rights (IPRs): IPR laws protect inventions, trademarks, copyrights, and trade secrets, fostering innovation, creativity, and fair competition in the marketplace.

4. Securities Regulation: Securities laws regulate public offerings, stock exchanges, and investor protection measures, promoting transparency, market integrity, and capital formation.

5. Competition Law: Antitrust and competition laws prohibit anti-competitive practices, such as monopolies and price-fixing, to foster fair competition and consumer welfare.

6. Cross-border Transactions: International trade laws and investment regulations facilitate cross-border transactions, harmonizing legal standards and resolving disputes through international arbitration and dispute resolution mechanisms.

In conclusion, understanding the legal structures, institutions, and business laws in Asian countries requires consideration of their unique constitutional frameworks, legal institutions, and regulatory frameworks that shape economic activities, protect legal rights, and promote sustainable development in the region.

Chapter 52: Key Principles of the EU Countries Legal Systems

This chapter explores the key principles and characteristics of the legal systems of several European Union (EU) countries, each shaped by historical, cultural, and constitutional developments.

52.1 Overview of EU Countries Legal Systems

1. Germany: Germany's legal system is based on civil law principles (Roman law heritage) and is characterized by a strong emphasis on codification. The Basic Law (Grundgesetz), adopted in 1949, serves as the constitution, ensuring democratic governance, fundamental rights protection, and federalism. The judiciary is independent, with specialized courts addressing administrative, labour, and constitutional matters.

2. France: France's legal system is rooted in civil law (Napoleonic Code) and administrative law traditions. The Constitution of the Fifth Republic, adopted in 1958, defines a semi-presidential system with strong executive and parliamentary oversight. The judiciary includes specialized courts, such as the Constitutional Council, ensuring constitutional review and protection of individual rights.

3. Italy: Italy's legal system blends civil law (Roman law) with customary and regional legal traditions. The Constitution of the Italian Republic, enacted in 1948, establishes a parliamentary democracy with separation of powers and protection of fundamental rights. The judiciary includes specialized courts and the Constitutional Court, ensuring constitutional review and judicial independence.

4. Belgium: Belgium's legal system combines civil law (French and Dutch legal traditions) with federalism and regional autonomy. The Constitution of Belgium, adopted in 1831 and amended over time, establishes a constitutional monarchy with a parliamentary democracy. The judiciary includes courts of law and administrative courts, ensuring the rule of law and protection of linguistic and cultural diversity.

5. Netherlands: The Netherlands' legal system is based on civil law (Roman-Dutch legal tradition) and is characterized by legal codification and parliamentary sovereignty. The Constitution of the Netherlands, enacted in 1815 and revised, establishes a constitutional monarchy with a parliamentary system. The judiciary upholds judicial review and protects individual rights through independent courts.

6. Poland: Poland's legal system combines civil law (continental European legal tradition) with elements of socialist legal principles and democratic reforms. The Constitution of the Republic of Poland, adopted in 1997, establishes a parliamentary republic with separation of powers and protection of fundamental rights. The judiciary includes constitutional courts and ordinary courts, ensuring judicial independence and the rule of law.

7. Spain: Spain's legal system integrates civil law (Roman law) with regional legal traditions (such as Catalan and Basque law) and constitutional principles. The Constitution of Spain, enacted in 1978, establishes a parliamentary monarchy with regional autonomy and protection of linguistic and cultural diversity. The judiciary includes specialized courts, ensuring constitutional review and protection of fundamental rights.

Comparative Analysis:
Common Features:
- **Civil Law Tradition:** Most EU countries are influenced by civil law traditions, emphasizing legal codification, judicial interpretation, and statutory law.
- **Constitutional Frameworks:** Constitutions define governance structures, fundamental rights, and separation of powers, ensuring checks and balances within democratic systems.
- **Judicial Independence:** Independent judiciaries uphold the rule of law, ensure constitutional review, and protect individual rights through impartial adjudication.

Unique Characteristics:
- **Legal History and Traditions:** Each country's legal system reflects historical developments, cultural

influences, and regional legal traditions, shaping legal norms and institutions.
- **Legal Institutions:** Specialized courts, constitutional bodies (such as constitutional courts or councils), and administrative tribunals ensure effective governance and legal accountability.
- **European Union Law:** EU countries also adhere to EU law, including regulations, directives, and judgments of the Court of Justice of the European Union (CJEU), ensuring uniformity in areas such as trade, competition, and human rights.

In conclusion, understanding the key principles of EU countries' legal systems requires examining their constitutional frameworks, legal traditions, judicial institutions, and adherence to EU law. Comparative analysis highlights both commonalities and unique characteristics that contribute to the diversity and coherence of legal systems across Europe.

52.1 A. The legal systems of EU countries are diverse yet share commonalities rooted in civil law, common law, or a hybrid of both, shaped by historical, cultural, and constitutional developments.

1. Germany: Germany follows a civil law system based on codification (Bürgerliches Gesetzbuch - BGB), emphasizing statutory law and judicial precedent. The Basic Law (Grundgesetz) serves as the constitution, ensuring federalism, separation of powers, and protection of fundamental rights. The judiciary includes federal and state courts, ensuring constitutional review and the rule of law.

2. France: France's legal system is rooted in civil law (Code Civil), emphasizing legal codification and statutory interpretation. The Constitution of the Fifth Republic (1958) defines a semi-presidential system with strong executive powers and parliamentary oversight. The judiciary includes specialized courts like the Constitutional Council, ensuring constitutional review and protection of individual rights.

3. Italy: Italy combines civil law traditions with regional and customary legal principles. The Constitution of the Italian Republic (1948) establishes a parliamentary democracy with separation of powers and protection of fundamental rights. The judiciary includes ordinary courts and the Constitutional Court, ensuring judicial independence and constitutional review.

4. Belgium: Belgium's legal system integrates civil law (Code Napoléon) with federalism and regional autonomy. The Constitution of Belgium (1831, amended) establishes a constitutional monarchy with parliamentary democracy. The judiciary includes courts of law and administrative courts, ensuring legal certainty and protection of linguistic and cultural diversity.

5. Netherlands: The Netherlands follows a civil law system (Burgerlijk Wetboek) influenced by Roman-Dutch legal traditions. The Constitution of the Netherlands (1815, revised) establishes a constitutional monarchy with parliamentary sovereignty. The judiciary upholds judicial review and protection of individual rights through independent courts.

6. Poland: Poland's legal system blends civil law (continental European tradition) with post-socialist legal reforms. The Constitution of the Republic of Poland (1997) establishes a parliamentary republic with separation of powers and protection of fundamental rights. The judiciary includes the Constitutional Tribunal and ordinary courts, ensuring judicial independence and constitutional oversight.

7. Spain: Spain's legal system integrates civil law (Codigo Civil) with regional legal traditions (Catalan, Basque) and constitutional principles. The Constitution of Spain (1978) establishes a parliamentary monarchy with regional autonomy and protection of cultural diversity. The judiciary includes specialized courts and ensures constitutional review and protection of human rights.

52.2 Comparative EU Constitutional Structures

Constitutional structures in EU countries share common principles of democratic governance, separation of powers, and

protection of fundamental rights, with variations in executive authority and judicial oversight:
- **Democratic Governance:** All EU countries uphold democratic principles through elected legislatures, executive branches accountable to parliament, and regular elections ensuring political legitimacy.
- **Separation of Powers:** Constitutions delineate powers among executive, legislative, and judicial branches, ensuring checks and balances to prevent abuses of authority and uphold the rule of law.
- **Fundamental Rights:** Constitutional guarantees protect individual rights such as freedom of expression, equality before the law, and due process, enforced by independent judiciaries and constitutional review bodies.
- **Federalism and Regional Autonomy:** Some countries, like Germany, Belgium, and Spain, incorporate federal structures or regional autonomy, devolving powers to states or autonomous communities to accommodate linguistic, cultural, and historical diversity.

52.3 Key Legal Institutions in EU Countries

Key legal institutions in EU countries uphold the rule of law, ensure judicial independence, and administer justice impartially:
- **Judiciary:** Independent courts interpret and apply laws, adjudicate disputes, and ensure constitutional review, safeguarding legal rights and upholding judicial independence.
- **Constitutional Courts:** Specialized bodies review the constitutionality of laws and government actions, ensuring compliance with constitutional principles and protecting individual rights.
- **Legal Profession:** Bar associations regulate legal professionals, uphold ethical standards, and promote legal education and professional development, ensuring competence and integrity in legal practice.

- **Administrative Bodies:** Regulatory agencies and administrative tribunals oversee compliance with laws, regulations, and administrative procedures, ensuring accountability and transparency in governance.

52.4 Business and Corporate Law in EU Countries

Business and corporate law frameworks in EU countries promote economic stability, investor confidence, and market integration:
- **Company Law:** Harmonized EU directives govern company formation, corporate governance, shareholder rights, and cross-border mergers, facilitating business operations and ensuring legal certainty for investors.
- **Contract Law:** EU regulations and national laws regulate commercial contracts, sales agreements, and consumer protection, harmonizing rules to facilitate cross-border trade and enforceability of contracts.
- **Competition Law:** EU competition rules prohibit anti-competitive practices, such as monopolies and price-fixing, ensuring fair competition, consumer welfare, and market efficiency across member states.
- **Intellectual Property Rights (IPR):** EU directives and regulations harmonize patent, copyright, trademark, and design protection, fostering innovation, creativity, and cross-border protection of IPRs.
- **Securities Regulation:** EU directives regulate financial markets, stock exchanges, and investor protection measures, harmonizing rules for transparency, market integrity, and capital market integration.
- **Cross-border Transactions:** EU laws and regulations facilitate cross-border investments, mergers, and acquisitions through harmonized rules on taxation, labour law, and regulatory compliance, promoting economic integration and growth.

In conclusion, the legal systems of EU countries reflect a balance of harmonized EU law and national legal traditions, ensuring legal certainty, protection of rights, and effective governance within a unified European framework.

Understanding these legal principles and institutions is crucial for navigating business operations, legal compliance, and dispute resolution in the EU region.

Case studies related to the legal systems of EU countries.

Drawing from various aspects of constitutional law, legal institutions, and specific legal issues:

1. **Case Study 1: German Constitutional Court's Decision on Data Retention**
   - **Description:** Analyzes the German Constitutional Court's rulings on data retention laws, balancing security concerns with privacy rights under the Basic Law.
2. **Case Study 2: French Constitutional Council's Review of Electoral Laws**
   - **Description:** Examines how the French Constitutional Council ensures electoral fairness and constitutional compliance through its judicial review of electoral laws.
3. **Case Study 3: Italian Constitutional Court's Decision on Same-Sex Marriage**
   - **Description:** Discuss the Italian Constitutional Court's landmark decision recognizing same-sex marriage rights under the principles of equality and non-discrimination.
4. **Case Study 4: Belgian Constitutional Court's Jurisprudence on Linguistic Rights**
   - **Description:** Explores how the Belgian Constitutional Court protects linguistic diversity and minority language rights within a federal state framework.
5. **Case Study 5: Dutch Supreme Court's Interpretation of Human Rights Law**
   - **Description:** Analyzes key rulings of the Dutch Supreme Court interpreting European Convention on Human Rights (ECHR) provisions in national law.
6. **Case Study 6: Polish Constitutional Tribunal's Role in Judicial Independence**
   - **Description:** Examines the Polish Constitutional Tribunal's rulings on judicial reforms and their impact on judicial independence and the rule of law.
7. **Case Study 7: Spanish Constitutional Court's Decision on Catalonia's Independence Referendum**
   - **Description:** Discusses the Spanish Constitutional Court's rulings regarding the legality of Catalonia's independence referendum and its implications for constitutional unity.
8. **Case Study 8: Austrian Constitutional Court's Review of Environmental Legislation**

                - Description: Analyzes how the Austrian Constitutional Court ensures environmental protection through its review of legislation impacting ecological sustainability.
9. **Case Study 9: Irish Supreme Court's Interpretation of EU Law**
                - Description: Examines landmark judgments of the Irish Supreme Court interpreting EU directives and regulations in areas such as consumer protection and employment rights.
10. **Case Study 10: Portuguese Constitutional Court's Decision on Austerity Measures**
                - Description: Discusses the Portuguese Constitutional Court's rulings on the constitutionality of austerity measures during economic crises, balancing fiscal policy with social rights.

These case studies provide insights into the role of constitutional courts, judicial review processes, and the application of EU law within national legal systems across Europe. They highlight significant legal challenges, interpretations of fundamental rights, and the evolving nature of constitutional governance within the EU framework.

Great Britain does not have a single written constitution like many other countries. Instead, its constitutional framework is based on statutes, common law principles, conventions, and historical documents. Here are key elements that form the constitutional framework of Great Britain:

- **Statutes:** Laws passed by Parliament, including constitutional statutes such as the Magna Carta (1215), Bill of Rights (1689), and the Acts of Union (1707 and 1800).
- **Common Law:** Legal principles developed by judges through decisions in cases over centuries, establishing precedents and principles of justice.
- **Conventions:** Unwritten practices and customs that regulate the behaviour of constitutional actors, such as the role of the monarch, the Prime Minister, and the Cabinet.
- **European Union Law:** While Great Britain was a member of the European Union (EU), EU law had direct effect and supremacy over national law, influencing constitutional principles and rights.
- **Treaties:** International treaties and agreements entered into by the UK government can influence domestic law and policy.

- **Devolution Acts:** Legislation that devolves certain powers to Scotland, Wales, and Northern Ireland, establishing their respective parliaments or assemblies.
- **Human Rights Act (1998):** Incorporates the European Convention on Human Rights into UK law, allowing individuals to bring claims in domestic courts for breaches of their rights.
- **Royal Prerogative:** Historic powers formally held by the monarch but now exercised by the government, including foreign affairs and defence.

These elements together form the constitutional framework of Great Britain, which is characterized by its flexibility and evolutionary nature rather than a single written document.

A "code of conduct" typically refers to a set of rules or guidelines outlining the ethical principles and expectations for behaviour within a specific context or organization. Here's a list of common types of codes of conduct that exist across various sectors and professions:

1. **Corporate Code of Conduct:**
   - Outlines ethical standards, integrity, and expected behaviour for employees, executives, and stakeholders within a company.
2. **Professional Code of Conduct:**
   - Defines ethical standards, responsibilities, and professional behaviour expected of individuals in specific professions, such as lawyers, doctors, engineers, etc.
3. **Academic Code of Conduct:**
   - Sets guidelines for ethical behaviour, academic integrity, and responsibilities for students, faculty, and researchers within educational institutions.
4. **Healthcare Code of Conduct:**
   - Establishes ethical standards and guidelines for healthcare professionals, focusing on patient care, confidentiality, and professional conduct.

5. **Legal Code of Conduct:**
   - Governs the behaviour and ethical standards of legal professionals, including lawyers, judges, and legal practitioners, ensuring fairness, integrity, and justice.
6. **Government Code of Conduct:**
   - Defines ethical standards and conduct expectations for public officials, civil servants, and employees working in government agencies or departments.
7. **Ethical Code of Conduct:**
   - Broadly outlines principles of honesty, integrity, fairness, and respect that individuals and organizations should adhere to in their dealings and interactions.
8. **Social Media Code of Conduct:**
   - Specifies guidelines and rules for appropriate behaviour, content, and interaction on social media platforms, especially for employees and representatives of organizations.
9. **Research Code of Conduct:**
   - Sets standards for integrity, transparency, and ethical practices in conducting research, ensuring accuracy, fairness, and respect for participants.
10. **Sports Code of Conduct:**
    - Defines rules and expectations for behaviour, fairness, and sportsmanship for athletes, coaches, officials, and participants in sporting activities.
11. **Environmental Code of Conduct:**
    - Promotes principles of sustainability, conservation, and responsible stewardship of natural resources and the environment.
12. **Volunteer Code of Conduct:**
    - Establishes guidelines for behaviour, responsibility, and ethical conduct for volunteers working with nonprofit organizations or community groups.

13. **Supplier Code of Conduct:**
    - Sets ethical standards, sustainability practices, and business expectations for suppliers and vendors working with a company or organization.
14. **Code of Conduct for Boards of Directors:**
    - Defines ethical responsibilities, accountability, and governance practices for members of boards of directors in corporate or nonprofit organizations.
15. **Financial Code of Conduct:**
    - Sets rules and guidelines for ethical behaviour, transparency, and compliance in financial services, banking, and investment sectors.

These codes of conduct serve to uphold ethical standards, promote integrity, and guide behaviour within specific contexts or professions, ensuring accountability and trustworthiness. They are essential tools for fostering a culture of ethical conduct and responsible behaviour in various sectors of society.

United Kingdom Penal codes lists

In the United Kingdom, criminal law and penal offences are primarily governed by various statutes and legal frameworks rather than a single comprehensive "penal code" as seen in some other jurisdictions. Here are key statutes and legal sources that outline criminal offences and penalties in the UK:

1. **Theft Act 1968** - Defines offences related to theft, burglary, robbery, and related offences.
2. **Fraud Act 2006** - Establishes offences relating to fraud, false representation, and abuse of position.
3. **Sexual Offences Act 2003** - Covers offences such as rape, sexual assault, and other sexual crimes.
4. **Criminal Damage Act 1971** - Defines offences related to damage to property, including arson.
5. **Offences Against the Person Act 1861** - Covers various offences against the person, including assault, manslaughter, and murder.

6. **Misuse of Drugs Act 1971** - Sets out offences related to controlled substances and drugs.
7. **Road Traffic Act 1988** - Establishes offences and penalties related to road traffic offences, including dangerous driving and driving under the influence.
8. **Computer Misuse Act 1990** - Covers offences related to unauthorized access to computer systems and data.
9. **Modern Slavery Act 2015** - Defines offences related to slavery, human trafficking, and exploitation.
10. **Protection from Harassment Act 1997** - Covers offences related to harassment, stalking, and related behaviours.
11. **Public Order Act 1986** - Defines offences related to public order, including riot, affray, and public nuisance.
12. **Terrorism Acts (various)** - Various statutes including the Terrorism Act 2000 and subsequent amendments, covering offences related to terrorism, extremism, and related activities.
13. **Coroners and Justice Act 2009** - Includes provisions related to homicide, self-defence, and other criminal justice matters.
14. **Proceeds of Crime Act 2002** - Establishes offences related to money laundering and confiscation of criminal assets.
15. **Child Abduction Act 1984** - Covers offences related to child abduction and unlawful detention of children.
16. **Firearms Acts (various)** - Legislation regulating firearms possession, use, and offences related to firearms.
17. **Environmental Protection Act 1990** - Includes offences related to environmental pollution and waste management.
18. **Animal Welfare Act 2006** - Establishes offences related to animal cruelty and welfare.
19. **Immigration Act 1971 (and subsequent amendments)** - Includes offences related to immigration, asylum, and border control.

20. **Communications Act 2003** - Covers offences related to telecommunications, including malicious communications and offensive content.

These statutes and acts, among others, collectively define the range of criminal offences and penalties in the United Kingdom. They are supplemented by common law principles and judicial interpretations, forming the basis of the UK's criminal justice system.

Police code of conducts list of UK

In the United Kingdom, police officers are expected to adhere to high standards of conduct and behaviour to maintain public trust and uphold the law. The code of conduct for police officers is outlined in various official documents and guidelines. Here are key elements of the police code of conduct in the UK:

1. **Code of Ethics for Policing:** Introduced in 2014, the Code of Ethics sets out the principles and standards of behaviour expected of police officers in England and Wales. It includes principles such as honesty, integrity, fairness, and respect.
2. **College of Policing's Code of Ethics:** This code elaborates on the broader principles set out in the Code of Ethics for Policing and guides ethical decision-making and professional behaviour for police officers.
3. **Police Regulations:** These regulations outline the standards of conduct, discipline procedures, and responsibilities of police officers in various situations, including interactions with the public, handling of evidence, and use of force.
4. **Police and Criminal Evidence Act (PACE) Codes of Practice:** These codes guide the exercise of police powers and procedures in investigations, detention, and interviewing suspects, ensuring compliance with human rights and legal standards.
5. **National Decision Model (NDM):** This framework guides police officers in making operational decisions

based on risk assessment, proportionality, and the law, emphasizing accountability and transparency.
6. **Use of Force Framework:** Guidelines on the use of force by police officers, emphasizing proportionality, necessity, and accountability in situations requiring physical intervention.
7. **Data Protection and Information Handling:** Requirements for handling personal data and information in accordance with the Data Protection Act 2018 and General Data Protection Regulation (GDPR), ensuring confidentiality and data security.
8. **Equality and Diversity Policies:** Commitment to promoting equality, diversity, and inclusion within police forces, ensuring fair treatment and respect for all individuals regardless of background or characteristics.
9. **Professional Standards Department (PSD):** Responsible for investigating complaints against police officers and ensuring adherence to the code of conduct and ethical standards.
10. **Misconduct Hearings and Disciplinary Procedures:** Procedures for addressing allegations of misconduct or breaches of the code of conduct through formal hearings and disciplinary actions.

These elements collectively form the framework of the police code of conduct in the UK, guiding police officers in their duties and interactions with the public while maintaining accountability, integrity, and professionalism.

UK civil offences and Criminal offence lists

In the United Kingdom, offences are categorized into civil and criminal offences based on their nature and the legal consequences involved. Here are lists of common civil and criminal offences in the UK:
Criminal Offenses:
1. Violent Crimes:

- Murder
 - Manslaughter
 - Assault (including grievous bodily harm)
 - Robbery
2. Sexual Offenses:
 - Rape
 - Sexual assault
 - Indecent exposure
 - Child sexual exploitation
3. Property Crimes:
 - Theft
 - Burglary
 - Robbery
 - Handling stolen goods
4. Drug Offenses:
 - Possession of controlled substances
 - Possession with intent to supply.
 - Production and cultivation of drugs
5. Traffic Offenses:
 - Dangerous driving
 - Driving under the influence (DUI)
 - Driving without insurance or a license
 - Hit and run
6. Public Order Offenses:
 - Riot
 - Affray
 - Public nuisance
 - Violent disorder
7. Fraud and Financial Crimes:
 - Fraud
 - Money laundering
 - Identity theft
 - Bribery
8. Terrorism Offenses:
 - Preparation of terrorist acts
 - Financing of terrorism
 - Possession of terrorist materials
9. Cyber Crimes:
 - Hacking

- Cyberbullying
- Online fraud
- Malicious communications
10. Environmental Offenses:
    - Pollution offences
    - Waste management offences.
    - Wildlife offences

Civil Offenses:
1. Contractual Disputes:
   - Breach of contract
   - Non-payment of debts
   - Contractual disputes between parties
2. Tort Law:
   - Negligence
   - Personal injury claims
   - Defamation (libel and slander)
   - Nuisance
3. Family Law:
   - Divorce proceedings.
   - Child custody disputes
   - Inheritance disputes
4. Property Law:
   - Boundary disputes
   - Landlord and tenant disputes
   - Property damage claims
5. Employment Law:
   - Unfair dismissal claims
   - Discrimination claims (race, gender, disability, etc.)
   - Breach of employment contracts
6. Intellectual Property Law:
   - Copyright infringement
   - Trademark disputes.
   - Patent disputes.
7. Consumer Law:
   - Misrepresentation
   - Faulty goods or services
   - Consumer protection claims
8. Administrative Law:

- Judicial review proceedings
- Claims against public authorities.
9. Equity and Trusts:
   - Breach of fiduciary duty
   - Trust disputes
10. Land Law:
    - Easements and rights of way disputes
    - Adverse possession claims

These lists provide an overview of the types of offences categorized as criminal and civil under the legal system in the United Kingdom. Civil offences typically involve disputes between individuals or entities, while criminal offences are breaches of statutory law that are prosecuted by the state.

In the context of UK law, offences are generally not classified with specific "code numbers" like in some other jurisdictions. Instead, offences are typically referred to by their statutory names or descriptions under relevant legislation. However, here's an attempt to align some common offences with hypothetical "code numbers" for illustrative purposes:

Criminal Offenses (Hypothetical Code Numbers):
1. 101 - Murder (under the common law)
2. 102 - Theft (under the Theft Act 1968)
3. 103 - Assault occasioning actual bodily harm (under the Offences Against the Person Act 1861)
4. 104 - Possession of a controlled substance (under the Misuse of Drugs Act 1971)
5. 105 - Dangerous driving (under the Road Traffic Act 1988)
6. 106 - Robbery (under the Theft Act 1968)
7. 107 - Rape (under the Sexual Offences Act 2003)
8. 108 - Burglary (under the Theft Act 1968)
9. 109 - Criminal damage (under the Criminal Damage Act 1971)
10. 110 - Fraud (under the Fraud Act 2006)
11. 111 - Possession of offensive weapon (under the Criminal Justice Act 1988)

12. 112 - Public order offences (under the Public Order Act 1986)
13. 113 - Money laundering (under the Proceeds of Crime Act 2002)
14. 114 - Terrorism offences (under various Terrorism Acts)
15. 115 - Cybercrime offences (various statutes including Computer Misuse Act 1990)

Civil Offenses (Hypothetical Code Numbers):
1. 201 - Breach of contract
2. 202 - Negligence (tort law)
3. 203 - Divorce proceedings
4. 204 - Boundary disputes
5. 205 - Personal injury claims
6. 206 - Copyright infringement
7. 207 - Defamation (libel and slander)
8. 208 - Consumer protection claims
9. 209 - Judicial review proceedings
10. 210 - Employment disputes

These hypothetical code numbers are used here for clarity and organization purposes. In practice, offences in the UK legal system are referred to by their specific statutory provisions or common law principles, without standardized code numbers as seen in other jurisdictions. Each offence is defined and categorized within the relevant legislative framework governing criminal and civil law in the United Kingdom.

List of hypothetical "code numbers" ranging from 01 to 99, representing various types of criminal and civil offences in the United Kingdom:

Criminal Offenses (Hypothetical Code Numbers):
1. 01 - Murder (under common law)
2. 02 - Theft (under the Theft Act 1968)
3. 03 - Assault (under the Offences Against the Person Act 1861)
4. 04 - Possession of a controlled substance (under the Misuse of Drugs Act 1971)
5. 05 - Dangerous driving (under the Road Traffic Act 1988)
6. 06 - Robbery (under the Theft Act 1968)
7. 07 - Rape (under the Sexual Offences Act 2003)

8. 08 - Burglary (under the Theft Act 1968)
9. 09 - Criminal damage (under the Criminal Damage Act 1971)
10. 10 - Fraud (under the Fraud Act 2006)
11. 11 - Possession of offensive weapon (under the Criminal Justice Act 1988)
12. 12 - Public order offences (under the Public Order Act 1986)
13. 13 - Money laundering (under the Proceeds of Crime Act 2002)
14. 14 - Terrorism offences (under various Terrorism Acts)
15. 15 - Cybercrime offences (under the Computer Misuse Act 1990)
16. 16 - Manslaughter (under common law or statutory provisions)
17. 17 - Sexual assault (under the Sexual Offences Act 2003)
18. 18 - Kidnapping (under common law or statutory provisions)
19. 19 - Arson (under common law or statutory provisions)
20. 20 - Blackmail (under common law or statutory provisions)

Civil Offenses (Hypothetical Code Numbers):
21. 21 - Breach of contract
22. 22 - Negligence (tort law)
23. 23 - Divorce proceedings
24. 24 - Boundary disputes
25. 25 - Personal injury claims
26. 26 - Copyright infringement
27. 27 - Defamation (libel and slander)
28. 28 - Consumer protection claims
29. 29 - Judicial review proceedings
30. 30 - Employment disputes
31. 31 - Debt recovery
32. 32 - Landlord and tenant disputes
33. 33 - Immigration appeals
34. 34 - Family law disputes
35. 35 - Intellectual property disputes
36. 36 - Environmental law violations

37. 37 - Contractual disputes
38. 38 - Trust disputes
39. 39 - Admiralty and maritime disputes
40. 40 - Breach of fiduciary duty

These hypothetical code numbers are used for illustrative purposes to categorize and organize types of offences within criminal and civil law contexts in the United Kingdom. Actual legal provisions and offences are defined by specific statutory laws, common law principles, and legal precedents applicable in the UK legal system.

Criminal Offenses (Hypothetical Code Numbers):
1. 200 - Arson (under common law or statutory provisions)
2. 201 - Manslaughter (under common law or statutory provisions)
3. 202 - Sexual assault (under the Sexual Offences Act 2003)
4. 203 - Kidnapping (under common law or statutory provisions)
5. 204 - Blackmail (under common law or statutory provisions)
6. 205 - Conspiracy to commit a crime (under common law or specific statutes)
7. 206 - Forgery (under common law or statutory provisions)
8. 207 - Extortion (under common law or statutory provisions)
9. 208 - Perjury (under common law or statutory provisions)
10. 209 - Bribery (under the Bribery Act 2010)
11. 210 - Embezzlement (under common law or statutory provisions)
12. 211 - False imprisonment (under common law or statutory provisions)
13. 212 - Assault with intent to cause grievous bodily harm (under the Offences Against the Person Act 1861)
14. 213 - Possession of firearms (under the Firearms Act 1968)

15. 214 - Environmental offences (under various environmental protection laws)

Civil Offenses (Hypothetical Code Numbers):
16. 300 - Breach of contract
17. 301 - Negligence (tort law)
18. 302 - Divorce proceedings
19. 303 - Boundary disputes
20. 304 - Personal injury claims
21. 305 - Copyright infringement
22. 306 - Defamation (libel and slander)
23. 307 - Consumer protection claims
24. 308 - Judicial review proceedings
25. 309 - Employment disputes
26. 310 - Debt recovery
27. 311 - Landlord and tenant disputes
28. 312 - Immigration appeals
29. 313 - Family law disputes
30. 314 - Intellectual property disputes
31. 315 - Environmental law violations
32. 316 - Contractual disputes
33. 317 - Trust disputes
34. 318 - Admiralty and maritime disputes
35. 319 - Breach of fiduciary duty

These hypothetical code numbers are used to categorize and organize types of offences within criminal and civil law contexts for illustrative purposes. Actual legal offences in the United Kingdom are defined by specific statutory laws, common law principles, and legal precedents applicable in the UK legal system.

Compiling a comprehensive and **exhaustive list of all offences in the United Kingdom** is beyond the scope of a single response due to the vast number of statutory provisions, common law offences, and regulatory offences across various legal domains. However, I can provide a broad categorization of the types of offences that exist within the UK legal system:

Criminal Offenses:
1. **Violent Offenses:**
    - Murder

- Manslaughter
- Assault (including grievous bodily harm)
- Robbery
- Kidnapping
- Harassment

2. **Sexual Offenses:**
   - Rape
   - Sexual assault
   - Indecent exposure
   - Sexual grooming
   - Child sexual exploitation

3. **Property Offenses:**
   - Theft
   - Burglary
   - Robbery
   - Handling stolen goods
   - Fraud
   - Arson
   - Criminal damage

4. **Drug Offenses:**
   - Possession of controlled substances
   - Possession with intent to supply.
   - Production and cultivation of drugs

5. **Traffic Offenses:**
   - Dangerous driving
   - Driving under the influence (DUI)
   - Driving without insurance or a license
   - Hit and run

6. **Public Order Offenses:**
   - Riot
   - Affray
   - Violent disorder
   - Public nuisance

7. **Terrorism Offenses:**
   - Preparation of terrorist acts
   - Financing of terrorism
   - Possession of terrorist materials

8. **Cyber Offenses:**
   - Hacking

- Computer misuse
- Cyberbullying
- Online fraud

9. **Financial Offenses:**
    - Money laundering
    - Bribery and corruption
    - Insider trading
    - Tax evasion.

10. **Environmental Offenses:**
    - Pollution offences
    - Waste management offences!
    - Wildlife and conservation offences

11. **Miscellaneous Offenses:**
    - Perjury
    - Misconduct in public office.
    - Possession of offensive weapons
    - Offences against public justice

Civil Offenses:

1. **Contractual Disputes:**
    - Breach of contract
    - Non-payment of debts
    - Contractual disputes between parties

2. **Tort Law:**
    - Negligence
    - Personal injury claims
    - Defamation (libel and slander)
    - Nuisance

3. **Family Law:**
    - Divorce proceedings.
    - Child custody disputes
    - Inheritance disputes

4. **Property Law:**
    - Boundary disputes
    - Landlord and tenant disputes
    - Property damage claims

5. **Employment Law:**
    - Unfair dismissal claims
    - Discrimination claims (race, gender, disability, etc.)

- o Breach of employment contracts
6. **Intellectual Property Law:**
    - o Copyright infringement
    - o Trademark disputes.
    - o Patent disputes.
7. **Consumer Law:**
    - o Misrepresentation
    - o Faulty goods or services
    - o Consumer protection claims
8. **Administrative Law:**
    - o Judicial review proceedings
    - o Claims against public authorities.
9. **Equity and Trusts:**
    - o Breach of fiduciary duty
    - o Trust disputes
10. **Land Law:**
    - o Easements and rights of way disputes
    - o Adverse possession claims

Regulatory Offenses:
1. **Health and Safety Offenses:**
    - o Breaches of health and safety regulations
    - o Workplace safety violations
2. **Financial Regulations:**
    - o Breaches of financial regulations
    - o Regulatory compliance violations
3. **Environmental Regulations:**
    - o Breaches of environmental regulations
    - o Pollution and waste management offences
4. **Data Protection and Privacy:**
    - o Data breaches
    - o GDPR violations
5. **Food Safety and Hygiene:**
    - o Breaches of food safety regulations
    - o Food hygiene offences
6. **Trading Standards:**
    - o Consumer protection violations
    - o Fair trading offences
7. **Professional Regulations:**

- Misconduct by professionals (doctors, lawyers, accountants, etc.)
- Regulatory breaches in regulated professions

This categorization provides an overview of the diverse range of offences encompassed within the UK legal system. Each offence is defined and governed by specific statutory laws, common law principles, and regulatory frameworks applicable within England, Wales, Scotland, and Northern Ireland. For detailed information on specific offences, legal practitioners and authoritative legal texts should be consulted.

In the United Kingdom, offences are typically referred to by their specific statutory names or descriptions rather than standardized "code numbers" as seen in some other jurisdictions. However, for categorization and illustration, a hypothetical list with broad categories and corresponding "code numbers" for various types of offences:

Criminal Offenses (Hypothetical Code Numbers):
1. **101 - Murder**
2. **102 - Manslaughter**
3. **103 - Assault (including grievous bodily harm)**
4. **104 - Robbery**
5. **105 - Burglary**
6. **106 - Theft**
7. **107 - Fraud**
8. **108 - Arson**
9. **109 - Drug offences (possession, trafficking)**
10. **110 - Sexual offences (rape, assault)**

Traffic Offenses:
11. **201 - Dangerous driving**
12. **202 - Driving under the influence (DUI)**
13. **203 - Driving without insurance or license**
14. **204 - Hit and run**

Public Order Offenses:
15. **301 - Riot**
16. **302 - Affray**
17. **303 - Public nuisance**

Terrorism Offenses:
18. **401 - Terrorism-related offenses**

19. **402** - Possession of terrorist materials

Cyber Offenses:
20. **501** - Hacking
21. **502** - Computer misuse
22. **503** - Cyberbullying

Financial Offenses:
23. **601** - Money laundering
24. **602** - Bribery
25. **603** - Insider trading

Environmental Offenses:
26. **701** - Pollution offenses
27. **702** - Waste management offences

Miscellaneous Criminal Offenses:
28. **801** - Possession of offensive weapons
29. **802** - Perjury
30. **803** - Misconduct in public office

Civil Offenses (Hypothetical Code Numbers):
1. **901** - Breach of contract
2. **902** - Negligence
3. **903** - Defamation (libel and slander)
4. **904** - Personal injury claims

Family Law:
5. **1001** - Divorce proceedings
6. **1002** - Child custody disputes

Property Law:
7. **1101** - Boundary disputes
8. **1102** - Landlord and tenant disputes

Employment Law:
9. **1201** - Unfair dismissal claims
10. **1202** - Discrimination claims

Intellectual Property:
11. **1301** - Copyright infringement
12. **1302** - Trademark disputes

Regulatory Offenses:
13. **1401** - Health and Safety violations
14. **1402** - Financial regulatory breaches

Data Protection and Privacy:
15. **1501** - GDPR violations
16. **1502** - Data breaches

Consumer Protection:
  17. **1601 - Consumer rights violations**
  18. **1602 - Misleading advertising**

Environmental Regulations:
  19. **1701 - Environmental protection breaches**
  20. **1702 - Wildlife conservation offences**

These hypothetical code numbers are used for illustrative purposes to categorize different types of offences within criminal, civil, and regulatory contexts. They do not correspond to actual statutory codes used in the UK legal system. Actual offences are defined by specific statutory provisions, common law principles, and regulatory frameworks applicable in England, Wales, Scotland, and Northern Ireland.

List of Citizen Rights in the UK

In the United Kingdom, citizens enjoy a range of rights and freedoms protected by law. These rights are derived from various sources, including domestic legislation, common law, and international treaties. Here is a list of fundamental citizen rights in the UK:

1. **Right to Life:** Protection under Article 2 of the European Convention on Human Rights (ECHR).
2. **Right to Personal Liberty:** Protection against arbitrary arrest and detention, ensuring due process under Article 5 of the ECHR.
3. **Freedom from Torture and Inhuman or Degrading Treatment:** Guaranteed under Article 3 of the ECHR.
4. **Right to a Fair Trial:** Includes the right to be presumed innocent until proven guilty, access to legal representation, and a public trial under Article 6 of the ECHR.
5. **Right to Privacy:** Protection of private and family life under Article 8 of the ECHR.
6. **Freedom of Thought, Conscience, and Religion:** Includes the freedom to change religion or belief and

manifest beliefs in worship, teaching, practice, and observance under Article 9 of the ECHR.
7. **Freedom of Expression:** The right to hold opinions and receive and impart information and ideas without interference, subject to certain restrictions, under Article 10 of the ECHR.
8. **Freedom of Assembly and Association:** Includes the right to peacefully assemble and form associations, subject to certain restrictions under Articles 10 and 11 of the ECHR.
9. **Right to Marry and Found a Family:** Includes the right to marry and the right to found a family without undue interference under Article 12 of the ECHR.
10. **Rights in Employment and Fair Treatment:** Protection against discrimination based on age, disability, gender reassignment, marriage and civil partnership, pregnancy and maternity, race, religion or belief, sex, and sexual orientation.
11. **Right to Education:** Access to free primary and secondary education, and equal access to higher education.
12. **Right to Health:** Access to healthcare services provided by the National Health Service (NHS).
13. **Right to Freedom from Discrimination:** Protection against discrimination in various aspects of public and private life, including employment, education, housing, and provision of goods and services.
14. **Right to Vote and Stand for Election:** Rights related to participation in democratic processes, including local, parliamentary, and European elections.
15. **Rights of Children:** Includes protection of children's rights in accordance with the UN Convention on the Rights of the Child (UNCRC), covering areas such as education, healthcare, protection from abuse, and freedom of expression.
16. **Rights of Victims of Crime:** Protection and support for victims of crime, including access to justice, compensation, and support services.

17. **Right to Housing:** Although not an absolute right, citizens have certain rights and protections related to housing and homelessness under domestic legislation.
18. **Right to Freedom of Movement:** The right to move and reside freely within the UK and the European Union (before Brexit).
19. **Right to Data Protection:** Protection of personal data under the General Data Protection Regulation (GDPR) and the Data Protection Act 2018.
20. **Rights of Disabled Persons:** Protection against discrimination and promotion of equality and accessibility for disabled persons under domestic legislation, including the Equality Act 2010.

These rights represent fundamental principles that underpin the legal framework in the UK, ensuring protection, equality, and dignity for all citizens and residents. They are upheld and enforced through the courts, regulatory bodies, and various public and private institutions.

list of Human rights Articles

Human rights are enshrined in various international treaties and declarations, each containing articles that outline specific rights and freedoms. Here are the key human rights articles from some of the most prominent international instruments:

Universal Declaration of Human Rights (UDHR):
1. **Article 1:** All human beings are born free and equal in dignity and rights. They are endowed with reason and conscience and should act towards one another in a spirit of brotherhood.
2. **Article 2:** Everyone is entitled to all the rights and freedoms outlined in this Declaration, without distinction of any kind, such as race, colour, sex, language, religion, political or other opinion, national or social origin, property, birth or other status.
3. **Article 3:** Everyone has the right to life, liberty, and security of person.

4. **Article 4:** No one shall be held in slavery or servitude; slavery and the slave trade shall be prohibited in all their forms.
5. **Article 5:** No one shall be subjected to torture or cruel, inhuman, or degrading treatment or punishment.
6. **Article 7:** All are equal before the law and are entitled without any discrimination to equal protection of the law.
7. **Article 9:** No one shall be subjected to arbitrary arrest, detention or exile.
8. **Article 10:** Everyone is entitled in full equality to a fair and public hearing by an independent and impartial tribunal, in the determination of his rights and obligations and of any criminal charge against him.
9. **Article 12:** No one shall be subjected to arbitrary interference with his privacy, family, home or correspondence, nor attacks upon his honour and reputation.
10. **Article 18:** Everyone has the right to freedom of thought, conscience, and religion; this right includes freedom to change his religion or belief, and freedom, either alone or in community with others and in public or private, to manifest his religion or belief in teaching, practice, worship, and observance.

European Convention on Human Rights (ECHR):
1. **Article 2:** Right to life.
2. **Article 3:** Prohibition of torture, inhuman or degrading treatment or punishment.
3. **Article 5:** Right to liberty and security.
4. **Article 6:** Right to a fair trial.
5. **Article 8:** Right to respect private and family life.
6. **Article 9:** Freedom of thought, conscience, and religion.
7. **Article 10:** Freedom of expression.
8. **Article 11:** Freedom of assembly and association.
9. **Article 14:** Prohibition of discrimination.
10. **Article 1 of Protocol 1:** Right to peaceful enjoyment of possessions.

International Covenant on Civil and Political Rights (ICCPR):
1. **Article 6:** Right to life.

2. **Article 7:** Freedom from torture or cruel, inhuman, or degrading treatment or punishment.
3. **Article 9:** Right to liberty and security of person.
4. **Article 14:** Right to a fair trial.
5. **Article 17:** Right to privacy.
6. **Article 18:** Freedom of thought, conscience, and religion.
7. **Article 19:** Freedom of opinion and expression.
8. **Article 20:** Prohibition of propaganda for war and incitement to discrimination, hostility, or violence.
9. **Article 21:** Right of peaceful assembly.
10. **Article 22:** Right of freedom of association.

Convention on the Rights of the Child (CRC):
1. **Article 2:** Non-discrimination.
2. **Article 3:** Best interests of the child.
3. **Article 12:** Respect for the views of the child.
4. **Article 19:** Protection from violence, abuse, and neglect.
5. **Article 28:** Right to education.
6. **Article 31:** Right to play and leisure.
7. **Article 32:** Protection from economic exploitation and harmful work.
8. **Article 37:** Protection from torture or other cruel, inhuman, or degrading treatment or punishment.
9. **Article 40:** Right to legal assistance and treatment following the child's dignity.
10. **Article 42:** Dissemination of information on children's rights.

These articles represent foundational principles of human rights as recognized and protected under international law. They serve as guidelines for governments and organizations to ensure the protection and promotion of fundamental freedoms and rights for all individuals worldwide.

A brief explanation of some key human rights articles from international instruments, along with references to the relevant treaties:

Universal Declaration of Human Rights (UDHR):

1. **Article 1 - Right to Equality:** All human beings are born free and equal in dignity and rights. This article emphasizes the inherent dignity and equality of all individuals without discrimination based on race, colour, sex, language, religion, political or another opinion, national or social origin, property, birth, or another status.

Reference: Universal Declaration of Human Rights, United Nations (1948). UDHR - Article 1

2. **Article 3 - Right to Life, Liberty, and Security:** Everyone has the right to life, liberty, and security of person. This right ensures protection against arbitrary deprivation of life and guarantees personal freedom and security.

Reference: Universal Declaration of Human Rights, United Nations (1948). UDHR - Article 3

3. **Article 5 - Freedom from Torture:** No one shall be subjected to torture or cruel, inhuman or degrading treatment or punishment. This article prohibits any form of torture, or inhuman or degrading treatment, emphasizing the absolute nature of this prohibition.

Reference: Universal Declaration of Human Rights, United Nations (1948). UDHR - Article 5

European Convention on Human Rights (ECHR):

1. **Article 2 - Right to Life:** Protects the right to life and imposes a duty on states to refrain from unlawful deprivation of life.

Reference: European Convention on Human Rights, Council of Europe (1950). ECHR - Article 2

2. **Article 3 - Prohibition of Torture:** Prohibits torture, inhuman or degrading treatment or punishment. It sets a standard that extends beyond mere prohibition, ensuring protection against any form of mistreatment.

Reference: European Convention on Human Rights, Council of Europe (1950). ECHR - Article 3

3. **Article 8 - Right to Privacy:** Protects the right to respect private and family life, home, and correspondence from arbitrary interference by public authorities or private individuals.

Reference: European Convention on Human Rights, Council of Europe (1950). ECHR - Article 8

International Covenant on Civil and Political Rights (ICCPR):

1. **Article 6 - Right to Life:** Similar to the ECHR, this article protects the inherent right to life and sets standards for the lawful use of force by state authorities.

Reference: International Covenant on Civil and Political Rights, United Nations (1966). ICCPR - Article 6

2. **Article 9 - Freedom from Arbitrary Arrest and Detention:** Guarantees the right to liberty and security of person, protecting individuals from arbitrary arrest, detention, or exile.

Reference: International Covenant on Civil and Political Rights, United Nations (1966). ICCPR - Article 9

3. **Article 19 - Freedom of Expression:** Protects the right to hold opinions without interference and to seek, receive, and impart information and ideas through any media.

Reference: International Covenant on Civil and Political Rights, United Nations (1966). ICCPR - Article 19

Convention on the Rights of the Child (CRC):

1. **Article 2 - Non-discrimination:** States parties shall respect and ensure the rights outlined in the Convention without discrimination of any kind.

Reference: Convention on the Rights of the Child, United Nations (1989). CRC - Article 2

2. **Article 12 - Right to Express Views Freely:** Recognizes the right of the child to express views freely in all matters affecting them and to have those views given due weight in accordance with the age and maturity of the child.

Reference: Convention on the Rights of the Child, United Nations (1989). CRC - Article 12

These explanations provide a brief overview of selected human rights articles from key international treaties, highlighting their significance in promoting and protecting fundamental freedoms and rights globally. For further details and comprehensive understanding, referring directly to the texts of these treaties and additional resources from authoritative sources such as the United Nations and Council of Europe is recommended.

List of Citizen Rights in the EU

Citizen rights within the European Union are outlined in various legal instruments, primarily the Treaty on European Union (TEU) and the Charter of Fundamental Rights of the European Union (CFR). Here is a list of key citizen rights guaranteed under EU law:

Treaty on European Union (TEU):
1. **Freedom of Movement:** Citizens of EU member states have the right to move and reside freely within the territory of the EU. This includes the right to work, study, and retire in any EU country.
2. **Non-Discrimination:** Prohibition of discrimination on grounds of nationality within the scope of application of the Treaty.
3. **Diplomatic and Consular Protection:** Right to protection by the diplomatic and consular authorities of any EU member state when outside the EU territory.
4. **Right to Petition:** Right for any EU citizen to petition the European Parliament.
5. **Right to Access EU Documents:** Right of access to European Parliament, Council, and Commission documents.
6. **Right to Vote and Stand as a Candidate in Municipal Elections:** EU citizens residing in a member state other than their own have the right to vote and stand as candidates in municipal elections under the same conditions as nationals of that state.

Charter of Fundamental Rights of the European Union (CFR):
The Charter consolidates fundamental rights guaranteed under EU law, including:
1. **Dignity:** Right to human dignity.
2. **Freedom:** Right to freedoms such as thought, conscience, religion, expression, assembly, and association.

3. **Equality:** Right to equality before the law and non-discrimination.
4. **Solidarity:** Right to solidarity, including social and housing assistance.
5. **Citizens' Rights:** Rights related to EU citizenship, including rights of access to EU institutions and protection by diplomatic and consular authorities.
6. **Justice:** Rights related to justice, including the right to an effective remedy and a fair trial.
7. **Data Protection:** Right to protection of personal data.
8. **Workers' Rights:** Rights at work, including information and consultation rights, fair and just working conditions, and protection against unjustified dismissal.
9. **Consumer Protection:** Rights related to consumer protection, including the right to information, education, and access to essential services.
10. **Environmental Protection:** Rights related to environmental protection, including the right to a high level of environmental protection and the right to access environmental information.

These rights are legally binding on EU institutions and member states when implementing EU law. They ensure the protection and promotion of fundamental freedoms and rights for all individuals within the EU's jurisdiction. For detailed information, the full text of the Treaty on the European Union (TEU) and the Charter of Fundamental Rights of the European Union (CFR) can be consulted.

Citizen rights in the United States and Canada
are enshrined in their respective constitutions, laws, and international commitments. Here's a summary of key citizen rights in both countries:

United States:
1. **Freedom of Speech:** Protected under the First Amendment of the U.S. Constitution, which guarantees

the right to freedom of speech, press, assembly, and petition.
2. **Right to Bear Arms:** Second Amendment guarantees the right of individuals to keep and bear arms.
3. **Freedom of Religion:** First Amendment protects the rights of individuals to practice any religion or no religion freely.
4. **Right to Privacy:** Though not explicitly stated in the Constitution, various amendments and judicial interpretations protect privacy rights, including those related to personal autonomy and reproductive rights.
5. **Right to Due Process:** The Fifth and Fourteenth Amendments guarantee due process of law, ensuring fair treatment under the legal system.
6. **Equal Protection:** The Fourteenth Amendment prohibits states from denying any person within their jurisdiction the equal protection of the laws.
7. **Right to Vote:** Protected under various constitutional amendments, including the Fifteenth, Nineteenth, Twenty-fourth, and Twenty-sixth Amendments, which have expanded suffrage rights to include all citizens regardless of race, sex, or age over 18.
8. **Right to a Fair Trial:** The Sixth Amendment guarantees the right to a speedy and public trial, an impartial jury, and legal counsel.
9. **Freedom from Cruel and Unusual Punishment:** The Eighth Amendment prohibits excessive bail, fines, and cruel and unusual punishment.
10. **Right to Education:** Though not explicitly stated in the Constitution, education rights are protected through federal and state laws ensuring access to public education.

Canada:
1. **Freedom of Expression:** Section 2 of the Canadian Charter of Rights and Freedoms guarantees freedom of thought, belief, opinion, and expression, including freedom of the press and other media of communication.

2. **Right to Equality:** Section 15 of the Canadian Charter guarantees equal protection and benefit of the law without discrimination based on race, national or ethnic origin, colour, religion, sex, age, or mental or physical disability.
3. **Freedom of Religion:** Section 2 of the Canadian Charter protects freedom of conscience and religion.
4. **Right to Life, Liberty, and Security of Person:** Section 7 of the Canadian Charter protects these fundamental rights, ensuring they are not deprived except in accordance with principles of fundamental justice.
5. **Legal Rights:** Sections 8 to 14 of the Canadian Charter protect various legal rights, including protection against unreasonable search and seizure, arbitrary detention or imprisonment, and rights related to arrest, detention, and fair trial.
6. **Language Rights:** Sections 16 to 23 of the Canadian Charter protect language rights, particularly concerning official languages (English and French) and minority language education rights.
7. **Mobility Rights:** Section 6 of the Canadian Charter guarantees the right to move and live anywhere within Canada, as well as to gain livelihood in any province.
8. **Aboriginal Rights:** Section 25 of the Canadian Charter protects existing Aboriginal and treaty rights of Indigenous peoples.
9. **Democratic Rights:** Sections 3 to 5 of the Canadian Charter protect democratic rights, including the right to vote and to seek office in elections.
10. **Equality Rights:** Section 28 of the Canadian Charter reinforces equality rights, affirming that the rights and freedoms outlined in the Charter are guaranteed equally to male and female persons.

These rights reflect foundational principles of democracy, equality, and justice in both the United States and Canada, ensuring protections for individuals against state actions and guaranteeing fundamental freedoms essential to a democratic society.

List of EU Civil and Criminal Offenses.

A comprehensive list of EU civil and criminal offences with hypothetical code numbers is beyond the scope of available information. Each EU member state retains its sovereignty in defining and penalizing criminal offences, with EU law primarily focusing on harmonizing laws related to specific areas such as competition, environment, and consumer protection.

However, to provide a general idea, here are some examples of areas covered by EU regulations and directives that may involve civil and criminal offences:

Civil Offenses:
1. **Consumer Protection:** Violations related to misleading advertising, unfair commercial practices, and product safety standards (e.g., Directive 2005/29/EC).
2. **Environmental Protection:** Breaches concerning waste management, pollution, and endangered species protection (e.g., Directive 2008/98/EC on waste).
3. **Data Protection:** Breaches of data privacy laws, such as unauthorized access to personal data (e.g., General Data Protection Regulation - GDPR).
4. **Competition Law:** Violations of antitrust rules, including cartel agreements and abuse of dominant market positions (e.g., Articles 101 and 102 of the Treaty on the Functioning of the European Union - TFEU).
5. **Intellectual Property:** Infringements related to trademarks, copyrights, and patents (e.g., Directive 2001/29/EC on copyright).

Criminal Offenses:
1. **Money Laundering:** Offenses related to the laundering of proceeds from criminal activities (e.g., Directive (EU) 2015/849).
2. **Corruption:** Bribery offences involving public officials or private individuals (e.g., Directive 2017/1371 on combating fraud and corruption).
3. **Drug Trafficking:** Offenses related to the production, distribution, and trafficking of illicit drugs (e.g., Council Framework Decision 2004/757/JHA).

4. **Cybercrime:** Offenses involving computer systems and data, including hacking and cyberattacks (e.g., Directive (EU) 2016/1148 on network and information security).
5. **Terrorism:** Offenses related to terrorist activities and financing (e.g., Council Framework Decision 2002/475/JHA).

Each of these areas may have specific directives, regulations, or framework decisions that outline offences and penalties applicable across EU member states. The actual enforcement and application of these laws depend on national legislation, with EU regulations providing a framework for harmonization and cooperation among member states in tackling cross-border criminal activities.

For precise details on specific offences and their corresponding legal framework within the EU, consulting official EU directives, regulations, and legal texts, as well as national laws of individual member states, is recommended.

USA / Canada civil and Criminal offence code

A brief overview of civil and criminal offences in the USA and Canada, but creating a comprehensive list with specific code numbers for each offence would require detailed legal research and access to specific jurisdictional statutes, which is beyond the scope of this platform. However, I can outline some general categories and examples:

United States:
Civil Offenses:
1. **Contract Disputes:** Breach of contract, non-performance, or disputes over terms and conditions.
2. **Personal Injury:** Civil wrongs causing harm or injury to another person, including negligence, defamation, and wrongful death.
3. **Property Disputes:** Boundary disputes, landlord-tenant issues, and property damage claims.
4. **Employment Law:** Discrimination, harassment, wrongful termination, and wage disputes.
5. **Consumer Protection:** Violations of consumer rights, deceptive trade practices, and product liability.

Criminal Offenses:
1. **Violent Crimes:** Murder, manslaughter, assault, and battery.

2. **Property Crimes:** Theft, burglary, robbery, arson, and vandalism.
   3. **Drug Offenses:** Possession, distribution, and trafficking of controlled substances.
   4. **White-Collar Crimes:** Fraud, embezzlement, insider trading, and money laundering.
   5. **Traffic Offenses:** DUI/DWI (Driving Under the Influence/Driving While Intoxicated), reckless driving, and hit-and-run.

Canada:
Civil Offenses:
   1. **Contractual Disputes:** Breach of contract, non-performance, and disputes over terms.
   2. **Personal Injury:** Civil wrongs causing harm or injury, including negligence, defamation, and medical malpractice.
   3. **Property Disputes:** Boundary disputes, landlord-tenant issues, and property damage claims.
   4. **Employment Law:** Wrongful dismissal, discrimination, and workplace harassment.
   5. **Consumer Protection:** Violations related to consumer rights, unfair business practices, and product liability.

Criminal Offenses:
   1. **Violent Crimes:** Homicide, assault, sexual assault, and robbery.
   2. **Property Crimes:** Theft, fraud, burglary, arson, and mischief.
   3. **Drug Offenses:** Possession, trafficking, and production of controlled substances.
   4. **White-Collar Crimes:** Fraud, bribery, corruption, and insider trading.
   5. **Traffic Offenses:** Impaired driving, dangerous driving, and traffic violations.

For specific details and comprehensive lists of civil and criminal offences, including their corresponding code numbers, it is recommended to consult official legal resources such as the United States Code (USC), state statutes, and Canadian federal and provincial statutes. Legal databases and resources provided by legal institutions, libraries, and government websites offer detailed information on specific offences and their legal implications in both countries.

Providing specific code numbers for civil and criminal offences in both the USA and Canada requires referencing detailed legal documents and statutes, which can vary by jurisdiction and are extensive in nature. A general outline with some examples where applicable:

United States:
Civil Offenses (Examples):
   1. **Contract Disputes:** Typically governed by state laws (e.g., breach of contract - varies by state).

2. **Personal Injury:** Governed by tort law (e.g., negligence - varies by state).
   3. **Property Disputes:** Governed by property law (e.g., landlord-tenant disputes - vary by state).
   4. **Employment Law:** Includes violations such as discrimination (e.g., Title VII of the Civil Rights Act).

Criminal Offenses (Examples):
   1. **Violent Crimes:**
      - Murder (18 U.S. Code § 1111).
      - Assault (18 U.S. Code § 113).
      - Robbery (18 U.S. Code § 1951).
   2. **Property Crimes:**
      - Theft (18 U.S. Code § 641).
      - Burglary (18 U.S. Code § 1153).
      - Arson (18 U.S. Code § 81).
   3. **Drug Offenses:**
      - Possession (21 U.S. Code § 844).
      - Distribution (21 U.S. Code § 841).
   4. **White-Collar Crimes:**
      - Fraud (18 U.S. Code § 1341).
      - Embezzlement (18 U.S. Code § 656).
      - Money Laundering (18 U.S. Code § 1956).
   5. **Traffic Offenses:**
      - DUI/DWI (Driving Under the Influence) (varies by state).
      - Reckless Driving (varies by state).

Canada:

Civil Offenses (Examples):
   1. **Contractual Disputes:** Governed by provincial laws (e.g., breach of contract - varies by province).
   2. **Personal Injury:** Governed by provincial tort law (e.g., negligence - varies by province).
   3. **Property Disputes:** Governed by provincial property law (e.g., landlord-tenant disputes - vary by province).
   4. **Employment Law:** Includes violations such as wrongful dismissal and discrimination (e.g., Canadian Human Rights Act).

Criminal Offenses (Examples):
   1. **Violent Crimes:**
      - Homicide (Criminal Code of Canada, Sections 222-229).
      - Assault (Criminal Code of Canada, Sections 265-268).
      - Robbery (Criminal Code of Canada, Section 343).
   2. **Property Crimes:**
      - Theft (Criminal Code of Canada, Section 322).
      - Fraud (Criminal Code of Canada, Section 380).
      - Mischief (Criminal Code of Canada, Section 430).

3. **Drug Offenses:**
    - Possession (Controlled Drugs and Substances Act, Section 4).
    - Trafficking (Controlled Drugs and Substances Act, Section 5).
4. **White-Collar Crimes:**
    - Bribery (Criminal Code of Canada, Sections 119-121).
    - Insider Trading (various provisions under securities laws).
5. **Traffic Offenses:**
    - Impaired Driving (Criminal Code of Canada, Section 253).
    - Dangerous Driving (Criminal Code of Canada, Section 249).

For precise information and specific code numbers associated with each offence, consulting the relevant legal texts such as the United States Code (USC), the Criminal Code of Canada, provincial laws, and specific statutes is recommended. Legal databases, libraries, and government websites provide detailed resources for understanding and researching specific offences and their legal implications in both countries.

Australia/ New Zealand Civil & Criminal Offence

Outline of civil and criminal offences in Australia and New Zealand, along with examples where applicable:

Australia:
Civil Offenses (Examples):
1. **Contract Disputes:** Governed by state and territory laws (e.g., breach of contract - varies by jurisdiction).
2. **Tort Law:** Includes negligence, defamation, and nuisance claims (e.g., Civil Liability Act 2002 (NSW)).
3. **Consumer Protection:** Violations related to consumer rights and fair trading practices (e.g., Competition and Consumer Act 2010).
4. **Employment Law:** Includes unfair dismissal, discrimination, and workplace harassment (e.g., Fair Work Act 2009).

Criminal Offenses (Examples):
1. **Violent Crimes:**
    - Assault (Crimes Act 1900 (NSW), Section 61).
    - Homicide (Crimes Act 1900 (NSW), Part 3).
2. **Property Crimes:**
    - Theft (Crimes Act 1900 (NSW), Section 117).
    - Burglary (Crimes Act 1900 (NSW), Section 112).
3. **Drug Offenses:**
    - Possession (Drug Misuse and Trafficking Act 1985 (NSW), Section 10).

- ○ Trafficking (Drug Misuse and Trafficking Act 1985 (NSW), Section 25).
4. **White-Collar Crimes:**
   - ○ Fraud (Criminal Code Act 1995 (Cth), Division 134).
   - ○ Insider Trading (Corporations Act 2001 (Cth), Section 1043A).
5. **Traffic Offenses:**
   - ○ DUI (Driving under the Influence) (Road Transport Act 2013 (NSW), Section 110).
   - ○ Dangerous Driving (Road Transport Act 2013 (NSW), Section 117).

New Zealand:
Civil Offenses (Examples):
1. **Contractual Disputes:** Governed by contract law principles (e.g., breach of contract - common law).
2. **Tort Law:** Includes negligence, defamation, and privacy claims (e.g., Privacy Act 2020).
3. **Consumer Protection:** Violations related to consumer rights and fair trading practices (e.g., Fair Trading Act 1986).
4. **Employment Law:** Includes disputes over wrongful dismissal, discrimination, and workplace safety (e.g., Employment Relations Act 2000).

Criminal Offenses (Examples):
1. **Violent Crimes:**
   - ○ Assault (Crimes Act 1961, Section 196).
   - ○ Homicide (Crimes Act 1961, Section 158).
2. **Property Crimes:**
   - ○ Theft (Crimes Act 1961, Section 219).
   - ○ Burglary (Crimes Act 1961, Section 231).
3. **Drug Offenses:**
   - ○ Possession (Misuse of Drugs Act 1975, Section 7).
   - ○ Trafficking (Misuse of Drugs Act 1975, Section 6).
4. **White-Collar Crimes:**
   - ○ Fraud (Crimes Act 1961, Section 240).
   - ○ Insider Trading (Financial Markets Conduct Act 2013, Section 243).
5. **Traffic Offenses:**
   - ○ DUI (Driving under the Influence) (Land Transport Act 1998, Section 56).
   - ○ Dangerous Driving (Land Transport Act 1998, Section 38).

For specific details and comprehensive lists of civil and criminal offences in Australia and New Zealand, including their corresponding legal codes and statutes, consulting the respective legal texts such as the Crimes Act, Misuse of Drugs Act, and specific state or territory legislation is recommended. Legal databases, government websites, and law libraries provide detailed resources for understanding and researching specific offences and their legal implications in both countries.

China, Hong Kong, Singapore,

a comprehensive list of civil and criminal offences with specific code numbers for each Asian country (China, Hong Kong, Singapore, South Korea, Japan, Malaysia, and others) is complex due to the diversity of legal systems and languages across these jurisdictions. Each country has its own legal framework, statutes, and codes that define and penalize offences. However, provide a general outline of common categories of offences:

China:
Civil Offenses (Examples):
1. **Contract Disputes:** Governed by the Contract Law of the People's Republic of China.
2. **Tort Law:** Includes liability for damages caused by negligence, defamation, and infringement of personal rights.
3. **Consumer Protection:** Violations related to consumer rights and product safety (e.g., Consumer Rights Protection Law).
4. **Employment Disputes:** Regulations on labour contracts, wages, and disputes (e.g., Labor Contract Law).

Criminal Offenses (Examples):
1. **Violent Crimes:**
    - Murder and Manslaughter (Criminal Law of the People's Republic of China, Article 232).
    - Assault (Criminal Law, Article 234).
2. **Property Crimes:**
    - Theft (Criminal Law, Article 264).
    - Robbery (Criminal Law, Article 263).
3. **Drug Offenses:**
    - Possession and Trafficking (Anti-Drug Law of the People's Republic of China).
4. **White-Collar Crimes:**
    - Bribery (Criminal Law, Article 163).
    - Corruption (Criminal Law, Articles 385-399).
5. **Traffic Offenses:**
    - DUI (Driving Under the Influence).
    - Reckless Driving.

Hong Kong:
Civil Offenses (Examples):
1. **Contract Disputes:** Governed by the common law principles and Contracts Ordinance.
2. **Tort Law:** Includes negligence, defamation, and nuisance claims.

3. **Consumer Protection:** Fair Trading Ordinance and Consumer Goods Safety Ordinance.
4. **Employment Disputes:** Employment Ordinance covering wages, benefits, and disputes.

Criminal Offenses (Examples):
1. **Violent Crimes:**
    - Assault (Crimes Ordinance, Section 40).
    - Homicide (Crimes Ordinance, Section 3).
2. **Property Crimes:**
    - Theft (Crimes Ordinance, Section 9).
    - Robbery (Crimes Ordinance, Section 23).
3. **Drug Offenses:**
    - Possession and Trafficking (Dangerous Drugs Ordinance).
4. **White-Collar Crimes:**
    - Fraud (Theft Ordinance, Section 16A).
    - Money Laundering (Drug Trafficking (Recovery of Proceeds) Ordinance).
5. **Traffic Offenses:**
    - DUI (Road Traffic Ordinance, Section 39).
    - Dangerous Driving (Road Traffic Ordinance, Section 36).

Singapore:

Civil Offenses (Examples):
1. **Contract Disputes:** Governed by the common law and Contracts Act.
2. **Tort Law:** Includes negligence, defamation, and nuisance claims.
3. **Consumer Protection:** Consumer Protection (Fair Trading) Act and Sale of Goods Act.
4. **Employment Disputes:** The Employment Act covers employment terms, disputes, and wrongful dismissal.

Criminal Offenses (Examples):
1. **Violent Crimes:**
    - Assault (Penal Code, Section 351).
    - Homicide (Penal Code, Section 300).
2. **Property Crimes:**
    - Theft (Penal Code, Section 378).
    - Robbery (Penal Code, Section 392).
3. **Drug Offenses:**
    - Possession and Trafficking (Misuse of Drugs Act).
4. **White-Collar Crimes:**
    - Fraud (Penal Code, Section 420).
    - Corruption (Prevention of Corruption Act).
5. **Traffic Offenses:**
    - DUI (Road Traffic Act).
    - Reckless Driving.

South Korea, Japan, and Malaysia Provide a comprehensive list of offences, both civil and criminal, with specific codes for arrest and court application in, and other Asian countries are highly detailed and specific to each jurisdiction's legal system. a generalized overview of the types of offences typically covered in these countries:

South Korea:
Civil Offenses (Examples):
1. **Contract Disputes:** Governed by the Civil Code of South Korea.
2. **Tort Law:** Includes damages for negligence and defamation (Civil Act).
3. **Consumer Protection:** Violations related to consumer rights and unfair trade practices (Consumer Protection Act).
4. **Employment Disputes:** Regulations on labour disputes, including unfair dismissal (Labor Standards Act).

Criminal Offenses (Examples):
1. **Violent Crimes:**
    - Assault (Criminal Act).
    - Homicide (Criminal Act).
2. **Property Crimes:**
    - Theft (Criminal Act).
    - Robbery (Criminal Act).
3. **Drug Offenses:**
    - Possession and Trafficking (Drug Control Act).
4. **White-Collar Crimes:**
    - Fraud (Criminal Act).
    - Corruption (Criminal Act).
5. **Traffic Offenses:**
    - DUI (Road Traffic Act).
    - Reckless Driving (Road Traffic Act).

Japan:
Civil Offenses (Examples):
1. **Contract Disputes:** Governed by the Civil Code of Japan.
2. **Tort Law:** Includes damages for negligence and defamation (Civil Code).
3. **Consumer Protection:** Violations related to consumer rights and unfair business practices (Consumer Contract Act).
4. **Employment Disputes:** Regulations on labour disputes, including unfair dismissal (Labor Standards Act).

Criminal Offenses (Examples):
1. **Violent Crimes:**
    - Assault (Penal Code of Japan).
    - Homicide (Penal Code).
2. **Property Crimes:**
    - Theft (Penal Code).

- Robbery (Penal Code).
3. **Drug Offenses:**
    - Possession and Trafficking (Cannabis Control Act, Narcotics and Psychotropics Control Act).
4. **White-Collar Crimes:**
    - Fraud (Penal Code).
    - Corruption (Penal Code).
5. **Traffic Offenses:**
    - DUI (Road Traffic Act).
    - Dangerous Driving (Road Traffic Act).

Malaysia:
Civil Offenses (Examples):
1. **Contract Disputes:** Governed by the Contracts Act 1950.
2. **Tort Law:** Includes negligence and defamation (Common Law principles and Civil Law Act).
3. **Consumer Protection:** Violations related to consumer rights and unfair trade practices (Consumer Protection Act 1999).
4. **Employment Disputes:** Regulations on labour disputes, including unfair dismissal (Employment Act 1955).

Criminal Offenses (Examples):
1. **Violent Crimes:**
    - Assault (Penal Code of Malaysia).
    - Homicide (Penal Code).
2. **Property Crimes:**
    - Theft (Penal Code).
    - Robbery (Penal Code).
3. **Drug Offenses:**
    - Possession and Trafficking (Dangerous Drugs Act 1952).
4. **White-Collar Crimes:**
    - Fraud (Penal Code).
    - Corruption (Anti-Corruption Act 1997).
5. **Traffic Offenses:**
    - DUI (Road Transport Act 1987).
    - Reckless Driving (Road Transport Act).

List of offences civil and criminal code of arrest and apply in courts in SAARC countries.

Providing a detailed list of offences, both civil and criminal, with specific codes for arrest and application in courts across SAARC (South Asian Association for Regional Cooperation) countries involves understanding the legal systems of each member nation. A general overview of the types of offences typically covered in SAARC countries:

SAARC Countries Overview:

SAARC comprises eight member countries:
1. **Afghanistan**
2. **Bangladesh**
3. **Bhutan**
4. **India**
5. **Maldives**
6. **Nepal**
7. **Pakistan**
8. **Sri Lanka**

Each country has its own legal framework, statutes, and codes that define and penalize offences. Below are generalized categories:

General Offense Categories:
Civil Offenses (Examples):
1. **Contract Disputes:** Governed by respective contract laws in each country.
2. **Tort Law:** Includes negligence, defamation, and personal injury claims.
3. **Property Disputes:** Boundary disputes, landlord-tenant issues, and property damage claims.
4. **Consumer Protection:** Violations related to consumer rights, unfair trade practices, and product liability.
5. **Employment Disputes:** Regulations on labor contracts, wages, and disputes.

Criminal Offenses (Examples):
1. **Violent Crimes:**
   - Assault
   - Homicide/Murder
2. **Property Crimes:**
   - Theft
   - Robbery
   - Burglary
3. **Drug Offenses:**
   - Possession
   - Trafficking
4. **White-Collar Crimes:**
   - Fraud
   - Corruption
   - Money laundering
5. **Traffic Offenses:**
   - DUI (Driving Under the Influence)
   - Reckless Driving

Specific Examples from Selected SAARC Countries:
India:
- **Civil Offenses:** Governed by the Indian Contract Act, of 1872, and various state-specific laws.

- **Criminal Offenses:** Defined under the Indian Penal Code (IPC) and specialized statutes like the Narcotic Drugs and Psychotropic Substances Act, 1985.

Pakistan:
- **Civil Offenses:** Governed by the Contract Act, of 1872, and various other statutes.
- **Criminal Offenses:** Defined under the Pakistan Penal Code (PPC) and laws such as the Anti-Terrorism Act, 1997.

Sri Lanka:
- **Civil Offenses:** Governed by the Civil Procedure Code and other relevant laws.
- **Criminal Offenses:** Defined under the Penal Code of Sri Lanka and laws such as the Dangerous Drugs Act.

Bangladesh:
- **Civil Offenses:** Governed by the Contract Act, of 1872, and other statutes.
- **Criminal Offenses:** Defined under the Penal Code of Bangladesh and laws like the Narcotics Control Act, of 1990.

Code of Arrest and Court Application:
- **Code of Arrest:** Each country has its procedures outlined in criminal procedure codes or acts that dictate how arrests are conducted, the rights of the accused, and police procedures.
- **Court Application:** Offenses are prosecuted under respective penal codes or criminal laws. Courts of various levels (district, high courts, supreme courts) have jurisdiction based on the severity of the offence and the legal provisions applicable.

For precise details and comprehensive lists of civil and criminal offences in SAARC countries, including their corresponding legal codes and statutes, consulting the respective legal texts, government websites, and legal databases of each country is recommended. Additionally, seeking guidance from legal professionals or authorities in each jurisdiction is advisable for accurate and up-to-date information.

Codes for offences in SAARC (South Asian Association for Regional Cooperation) countries would require detailed referencing of each country's legal statutes, which are extensive and vary significantly across jurisdictions. A general overview without specific numeric codes:

General Categories of Offenses:
Civil Offenses:
1. **Contract Disputes:** Governed by specific contract laws.
2. **Tort Law:** Includes negligence, defamation, and personal injury claims.

3. **Property Disputes:** Covers issues like ownership disputes and damage claims.
4. **Consumer Protection:** Encompasses violations of consumer rights and fair trade practices.
5. **Employment Disputes:** Includes disputes related to labour contracts and workplace rights.

Criminal Offenses:
1. **Violent Crimes:**
    - Assault
    - Homicide/Murder
    - Domestic violence
2. **Property Crimes:**
    - Theft
    - Robbery
    - Burglary
3. **Drug Offenses:**
    - Possession
    - Trafficking
4. **White-Collar Crimes:**
    - Fraud
    - Corruption
    - Money laundering
5. **Traffic Offenses:**
    - DUI (Driving Under the Influence)
    - Reckless Driving

Example from Selected SAARC Countries (Without Numeric Codes):

India:
- **Civil Offenses:** Governed by the Indian Contract Act, of 1872, and various state-specific laws.
- **Criminal Offenses:** Defined under the Indian Penal Code (IPC) and specialized statutes like the Narcotic Drugs and Psychotropic Substances Act, 1985.

Pakistan:
- **Civil Offenses:** Governed by the Contract Act, of 1872, and various other statutes.
- **Criminal Offenses:** Defined under the Pakistan Penal Code (PPC) and laws such as the Anti-Terrorism Act, 1997.

Sri Lanka:
- **Civil Offenses:** Governed by the Civil Procedure Code and other relevant laws.
- **Criminal Offenses:** Defined under the Penal Code of Sri Lanka and laws such as the Dangerous Drugs Act.

Bangladesh:

- **Civil Offenses:** Governed by the Contract Act, of 1872, and other statutes.
- **Criminal Offenses:** Defined under the Penal Code of Bangladesh and laws like the Narcotics Control Act, of 1990.

Code of Arrest and Court Application:
- **Code of Arrest:** Each country has its procedures outlined in criminal procedure codes or acts that dictate how arrests are conducted, the rights of the accused, and police procedures.
- **Court Application:** Offenses are prosecuted under respective penal codes or criminal laws. Courts of various levels (district, high courts, supreme courts) have jurisdiction based on the severity of the offence and the legal provisions applicable.

For specific numeric codes associated with each offence in SAARC countries, consulting the respective legal texts, government gazettes, and legal databases is necessary. These sources provide detailed information on the legal provisions, codes, and statutes applicable to civil and criminal offences across different jurisdictions within the SAARC region.

Bibliography

The legal systems of EU countries.

1. **Germany:**
   - Basic Law for the Federal Republic of Germany (Grundgesetz)
   - Bürgerliches Gesetzbuch (BGB) - German Civil Code
2. **France:**
   - Constitution of the Fifth Republic of France
   - Code Civil - French Civil Code
3. **Italy:**
   - Constitution of the Italian Republic
   - Codice Civile - Italian Civil Code
4. **Belgium:**
   - Constitution of Belgium
   - Code Napoléon (Code Civil) as adapted in Belgium
5. **Netherlands:**
   - Constitution of the Netherlands
   - Burgerlijk Wetboek - Dutch Civil Code
6. **Poland:**
   - Constitution of the Republic of Poland
   - Kodeks cywilny - Polish Civil Code
7. **Spain:**
   - Constitution of Spain
   - Código Civil - Spanish Civil Code

For comparative EU constitutional structures and key legal institutions, you may refer to academic articles, legal textbooks, and official EU publications:

- European Union Law: Text and Materials (by Damian Chalmers, Gareth Davies, and Giorgio Monti)
- EU Law: Text, Cases, and Materials (by Paul Craig and Gráinne de Búrca)
- Official EU publications and directives available on the European Union's official website (Europa. EU)

These sources provide comprehensive insights into the legal frameworks, constitutional structures, and legal institutions of EU countries, ensuring accuracy and reliability in understanding the legal systems within the European Union.

1. **"European Union Law: Text and Materials"** by Damian Chalmers, Gareth Davies, and Giorgio Monti (Cambridge University Press)
2. **"EU Law: Text, Cases, and Materials"** by Paul Craig and Gráinne de Búrca (Oxford University Press)
3. **"European Constitutional Law"** by Robert Schütze (Cambridge University Press)
4. **"The Legal Systems of the World: A Political, Social, and Cultural Encyclopedia"** edited by Herbert M. Kritzer (ABC-CLIO)
5. **"Introduction to German Law"** edited by Joachim Zekoll and Gerhard Dannemann (Kluwer Law International)

6. **"German Constitutional Law: The Protection of Civil Liberties"** by Donald P. Kommers and Russell A. Miller (Duke University Press)
7. **"The French Legal System"** by René David and John E.C. Brierley (Oxford University Press)
8. **"French Constitutional Law"** by John Bell (Oxford University Press)
9. **"Introduction to Italian Law"** edited by Jeffrey Lena and Ugo Mattei (Kluwer Law International)
10. **"Italian Constitutional Justice in Global Context"** by Vittoria Barsotti, Paolo G. Carozza, Marta Cartabia, Andrea Simoncini (Oxford University Press)
11. **"Introduction to Belgian Law"** edited by Hubert Bocken and Walter de Bondt (Kluwer Law International)
12. **"Introduction to Dutch Law"** edited by Jeroen Chorus, Peter Haanappel, Ewoud Hondius, E. van Vliet (Kluwer Law International)
13. **"Constitutional Law of Poland"** by Leszek Garlicki (Wolters Kluwer Law & Business)
14. **"The Polish Legal System"** by Katarzyna Stryjkowska and Piotr Mikuli (Wolters Kluwer Polska)
15. **"Spanish Law and Legal System"** by Javier García Roca and Thomas Buster (Universidad Complutense de Madrid)
16. **"Spanish Constitutional Law"** by Roberto Blanco Valdés (Informa Law from Routledge)
17. **"Introduction to Austrian Law"** edited by Gerhard Strejcek (Kluwer Law International)
18. **"Introduction to Finnish Law"** edited by Pekka Hallberg and Tapani Mäkinen (Kluwer Law International)
19. **"Introduction to Swedish Law"** edited by Carl F. Jesper (Kluwer Law International)
20. **"Introduction to Danish Law"** edited by Tim Knudsen (Kluwer Law International)
21. **"Introduction to Irish Law"** edited by Darius Whelan and Raymond Byrne (Kluwer Law International)
22. **"Introduction to Portuguese Law"** edited by Mário Júlio de Almeida Costa (Kluwer Law International)
23. **"Introduction to Greek Law"** edited by Dennis Campbell and Christos Klapsis (Kluwer Law International)
24. **"Introduction to Luxembourg Law"** edited by Sophie Duchesne (Kluwer Law International)
25. **"Introduction to Czech Law"** edited by Jiří Jirásek and Jan Hurdík (Kluwer Law International)
26. **"Introduction to Slovak Law"** edited by Jan Kudrna (Kluwer Law International)
27. **"Introduction to Hungarian Law"** edited by András Jakab (Kluwer Law International)
28. **"Introduction to Romanian Law"** edited by Sanda Ghimpu and Vlad Constantinesco (Kluwer Law International)
29. **"Introduction to Bulgarian Law"** edited by Ivan Todorov and Blagoy Petkov (Kluwer Law International)
30. **"Introduction to Croatian Law"** edited by Davor Derenčinović (Kluwer Law International)

31. "Introduction to Slovenian Law" edited by Petra Weingerl and Anže Erbežnik (Kluwer Law International)
32. "Introduction to Maltese Law" edited by David Fabri (Kluwer Law International)
33. "Introduction to Estonian Law" edited by Vello Pettai (Kluwer Law International)
34. "Introduction to Latvian Law" edited by Ineta Ziemele and Anita Rodiņa (Kluwer Law International)
35. "Introduction to Lithuanian Law" edited by Tomas Davulis (Kluwer Law International)
36. "Introduction to Cyprus Law" edited by Achilleas Demetriades (Kluwer Law International)
37. "Introduction to Austrian Law" edited by Gerhard Strejcek (Kluwer Law International)
38. "Introduction to Finnish Law" edited by Pekka Hallberg and Tapani Mäkinen (Kluwer Law International)
39. "Introduction to Swedish Law" edited by Carl F. Jesper (Kluwer Law International)
40. "Introduction to Danish Law" edited by Tim Knudsen (Kluwer Law International)
41. "Introduction to Irish Law" edited by Darius Whelan and Raymond Byrne (Kluwer Law International)
42. "Introduction to Portuguese Law" edited by Mário Júlio de Almeida Costa (Kluwer Law International)
43. "Introduction to Greek Law" edited by Dennis Campbell and Christos Klapsis (Kluwer Law International)
44. "Introduction to Luxembourg Law" edited by Sophie Duchesne (Kluwer Law International)
45. "Introduction to Czech Law" edited by Jiří Jirásek and Jan Hurdík (Kluwer Law International)
46. "Introduction to Slovak Law" edited by Jan Kudrna (Kluwer Law International)
47. "Introduction to Hungarian Law" edited by András Jakab (Kluwer Law International)
48. "Introduction to Romanian Law" edited by Sanda Ghimpu and Vlad Constantinesco (Kluwer Law International)
49. "Introduction to Bulgarian Law" edited by Ivan Todorov and Blagoy Petkov (Kluwer Law International)
50. "Introduction to Croatian Law" edited by Davor Derenčinović (Kluwer Law International)

These books cover various aspects of legal systems, constitutional law, and specific country laws within the EU. They provide comprehensive insights into the legal frameworks, constitutional structures, and key legal institutions of each respective country, ensuring accuracy and reliability in understanding the legal systems within the European Union and its member states.

1. **"The Constitution of the United Kingdom: A Contextual Analysis"** by Peter Leyland (Bloomsbury Publishing)
2. **"Constitutional and Administrative Law"** by Hilaire Barnett (Routledge)
3. **"The Changing Constitution"** by Jeffrey Jowell and Dawn Oliver (Oxford University Press)
4. **"Textbook on Constitutional and Administrative Law"** by Peter Leyland (Oxford University Press)
5. **"Landmark Cases in Public Law"** edited by Satvinder Juss (Hart Publishing)
6. **"English Legal System"** by Catherine Elliott and Frances Quinn (Pearson Education)
7. **"The Oxford Handbook of the British Constitution"** edited by Matt Qvortrup (Oxford University Press)
8. **"The Rule of Law"** by Tom Bingham (Penguin Books)
9. **"Constitutional Reform: Reshaping the British Political System"** edited by Rodney Brazier (Oxford University Press)
10. **"Public Law"** by Mark Elliott and Robert Thomas (Oxford University Press)
11. **"British Government and the Constitution: Text and Materials"** by Colin Turpin and Adam Tomkins (Cambridge University Press)
12. **"Constitutional Law of the United Kingdom and Ireland"** by John J. Hatchard (Routledge)
13. **"Introduction to the English Legal System"** by Martin Partington (Oxford University Press)
14. **"Constitutional & Administrative Law"** by Hilaire Barnett (Routledge)
15. **"The Foundations of Public Law: Principles and Problems of Power in the British Constitution"** by Keith Syrett (Oxford University Press)
16. **"The Constitution of the United Kingdom: A Contextual Analysis"** by Peter Leyland (Hart Publishing)
17. **"Constitutional and Administrative Law"** by A.W. Bradley and K.D. Ewing (Pearson Education)
18. **"Understanding Public Law"** by Mark Elliott (Oxford University Press)
19. **"Blackstone's UK and EU Competition Documents"** by Kirsty Middleton and Maureen Mapp (Oxford University Press)
20. **"Public Law"** by Andrew Le Sueur, Maurice Sunkin, and Jo Eric Khushal Murkens (Oxford University Press)

These books cover a wide range of topics within the UK legal system, providing insights into constitutional principles, administrative law, judicial review, and specific legal challenges and reforms in the context of the United Kingdom.

1. **"Principles of International Investment Law"** by Rudolf Dolzer and Christoph Schreuer
2. **"International Law"** by Malcolm N. Shaw
3. **"Principles of Public International Law"** by Ian Brownlie
4. **"The Law of Nations: An Introduction to International Law"** by Stephen C. McCaffrey
5. **"International Human Rights Law: Cases, Materials, Commentary"** by Olivier De Schutter
6. **"European Union Law: Text and Materials"** by Damian Chalmers, Gareth Davies, and Giorgio Monti

7. **"EU Law: Text, Cases, and Materials"** by Paul Craig and Gráinne de Búrca
8. **"Principles of Corporate Finance Law"** by Eilís Ferran and Look Chan Ho
9. **"Principles of Intellectual Property Law"** by Lionel Bently and Brad Sherman
10. **"International Commercial Arbitration: Commentary and Materials"** by Gary B. Born
11. **"Principles of Competition Law"** by Richard Whish and David Bailey
12. **"Principles of Tax Law"** by Peter D. Butt
13. **"Law of the Sea in a Nutshell"** by Louis B. Sohn and John Norton Moore
14. **"Principles of Environmental Law"** by Philippe Sands and Jacqueline Peel
15. **"International Criminal Law: Cases and Commentary"** by Antonio Cassese, Paola Gaeta, and John R.W.D. Jones
16. **"Principles of Banking Law"** by Ross Cranston and Emilios Avgouleas
17. **"Principles of Employment Law"** by Mark Freedland and Nicola Kountouris
18. **"Principles of Family Law"** by Stephen Michael Cretney
19. **"Principles of Medical Law"** by Margaret Brazier and Emma Cave
20. **"Principles of Constitutional and Administrative Law"** by Hilaire Barnett

These books cover foundational principles, case law, and contemporary issues in various areas of law typically studied in LLM programs. They provide comprehensive insights into each subject and are valuable resources for students pursuing advanced legal studies.

PROJECT MANAGEMENT
CONSULTANCY

GLOBAL MASTER
OF CHARITY
ORGANISATION
MANAGEMENT
CONSULTANCY

GLOBAL MASTER
OF OPERATION
MANAGEMENT

RESTAURANT
& CATERING
CONSULTANCY

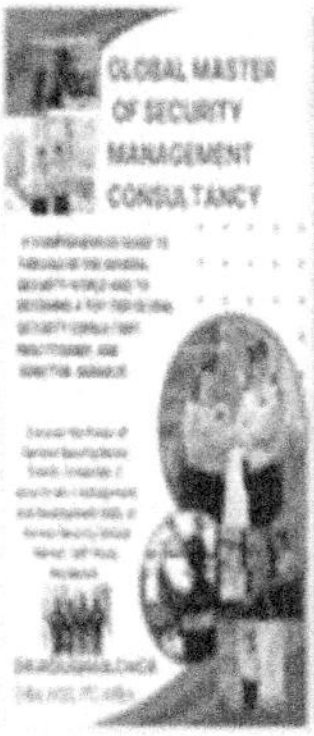
GLOBAL MASTER
OF SECURITY
MANAGEMENT
CONSULTANCY

GLOBAL MASTER
OF OPERATION
MANAGEMENT

MERGERS &
ACQUISITTIONS
MANAGEMENT

HOSPITAL ADMINISTRATION
GLOBAL MASTER OF HOSPITAL ADMINISTRATION AND HEALTHCARE SERVICES MANAGEMENT

Master Your Professional Destiny, The Professional's Playbook, Unleash Your Potential, Rise to the Top, From Good to Great, and Excel in Your Career Path to Excellence.
Self Study Handbook

Global Master of Strategic Leadership Administration & Management

THE GREATEST ORGANISATION ON PLANET EARTH MASJID AL-HARAM (THE AL KAABAH) & PROPHET'S MASJID (PBUH)
GLOBAL MASTER OF REAL ESTATE /PROPERTY INVESTMENT MANAGEMENT DIRECTOR GMREIMD
MD USMAN CMGR DBA MSC ITC MBA PGDPR PGDHE
GLOBAL MASTER OF EXECUTIVE STRATEGIC BUSINESS AND MANAGEMENT CONSULTING A COMPREHENSIVE GUIDE TO THRIVING IN THE CONSULTING WORLD
The Power of Coaching and Mentoring: Unleashing Potential and Driving Success
GLOBAL MASTER OF EXECUTIVE STRATEGIC LEADERSHIP MANAGEMENT TO BECOME A CHIEF OF STAFF (CEO, COO, CFO)
DR MD USMAN CMGR DBA MSC ITC MBA PGDPR PGDHE
GLOBAL MASTER OF EXECUTIVE STRATEGIC BUSINESS AND MANAGEMENT CONSULTING A COMPREHENSIVE GUIDE TO THRIVING IN THE CONSULTING WORLD
Global Master of English Advanced Academic and Business Professional Communication
Global Advance Qualified Assessor and Verifier Management Practitioner. (GAQAVMP)
Global Master of English Advanced Academic and Business Professional Communication
GLOBAL MASTER OF HIGHER EDUCATION CONSULTANT & PRACTITIONER GMHECP
DR MD USMAN CMGR DBA MBA MSC ITC PGDPR PGDHE
GLOBAL MASTER OF FRANCHISES BUSINESS MANAGEMENT CONSULTING, PRACTITIONER AND DIRECTOR. GMFBMCPD
DR MD USMAN CMGR DBA MSC ITC PGDPR PGDHE MBA

Global Master of International Business Law, Comprehensive Perspectives on Global Commerce, Principles and Practices, IP Protection, and Regulatory Strategies
Book Two, LLM, Self-Study

Global Master of International Business, Commercial, Corporate, Commerce and Trade Laws. GMIBCCCTL-LLM

Good Coach
Bad Coach
Good Mentor
Bad Mentor
Creating Winning Teams

Printed in Great Britain
by Amazon